THE DIPLOMITE

DIANA CARR

THE DIPLOMITE

Print ISBN: 978-1-09839-5-476
eBook ISBN: 978-1-09839-5-483

For my sister Patterson

who is the other side of my heart.

CONTENTS

PROLOGUE

SAY "FOREIGN SERVICE," AND MY HEART SWELLS WITH MEMories and pride. Malign the Foreign Service and I bristle. As a child, I witnessed the discipline, integrity, education, and training demanded of its officers.

My father joined the Foreign Service in 1946, and along with him, my mother, sister, and I became a part of it. The world was in turmoil as it settled into the aftermath of World War II. British colonialism was ebbing, communism was rising, nuclear war had become a possibility, and the cold war had begun. People wondered how they would survive the times.

Our first post was New Delhi. We were there when Mahatma Gandhi was assassinated. Next came Paris. Its residents were war worn and weary but determined to recover. Vienna was our third post. The Viennese, defeated, shuffled through the British, French, Russian, and American sectors of their city. Next was Tehran. With the Shah and Mosaddegh at odds and the Tudeh party on the rise, there were heated demonstrations in the streets. Last for me was Cairo. We arrived just after General Naguib and Colonel Nasser took over from King Farouk. Egypt was in a state of flux between monarchy and republic, and I was about to leave my family for college.

My story is about the adventures I experienced growing up in these places so far from home. It is about how I learned what it is like to be the "other." It is about what I needed to know as a young representative of the United States, and how I learned that I could not expect my country's culture, perfect though it was in my eyes, to be right for everyone. It is about learning the importance of staying calm in the face of danger. It is about how my parents kept my sister and me happy and safe. It is about the strength and importance of family.

PART I.

WASHINGTON D.C.

1946

"HE'S COMING! I SEE HIM!" MY LITTLE SISTER STRETCHED her arm out pointing to the end of our small residential street in Washington D.C. A dim figure was barely visible. "I'm going to get Mother."

She raced up the porch steps and into the house. I squinted, watching the figure grow as it approached. Patty was right! Father was on his way home from work.

Within a minute she rejoined me. We held hands jumping up and down on our lawn. Now only half a block away, the gray suit, the white shirt, and the dark tie looked crisp and business like. So did the leather briefcase. Father walked with his head slightly down like he was tired but when he looked up and saw us, he covered the rest of the distance from his bus stop in record time. We squealed and flung ourselves at him.

"Tricks or treats?" we demanded.

The screen door behind us opened with a creek, and Mother stepped out onto our front porch. She fussed with her apron ruffles and patted her hairdo, making sure all the hairpins and combs held her pompadour upsweep in place, as she always did just before greeting Father.

"Today it's tricks!" he announced.

Patty and I immediately bent over with our backsides facing him and arms stretched behind us as far as we could reach between our legs. He grabbed Patty's hands first and in one swift motion, he lifted her up in the air and flipped her over. Then it was my turn. Up and over I tumbled. Mother watched with one hand over her heart, eyes nearly closed while shaking her head slowly from side to side.

"More! More!" we begged. "Airplane rides. We want the airplane rides!"

"Just one airplane each. Your mother is waiting."

"Me first! Me first!" Patty pushed past me. She held her left arm out for Father to grab and lifted her left leg for him to take in his other hand. Holding her just inches above the grass, he leaned back into a spin. Around she flew, swooping up and down as he raised and lowered his arms. After three revolutions he "landed" her gently on the grass. I stepped up for my turn.

"Bob. No!" The surprise of Mother raising her voice and the sharp urgency of her tone froze us all on the spot. "It isn't safe." Looking down from the porch at me, she said," Deedee, you're getting taller every day. One fraction of an inch … I'm afraid your father might not be able to swing you high enough, you could be hurt badly. No airplane rides. It scares me too much."

I jabbed the lawn with my toe and said, "But Patty got to…"

"I know, Honey." Now Mother's voice was a soft purr. "Being four years older is hard sometimes. But just think of all the things you can do that Patty can't because she is too little." She turned to face Father who was busy retrieving his briefcase.

He nodded in agreement. He turned to me, ruffled my hair and said, "Your mother's right. We'll find something else for a big eight-year-old to do. Like maybe stay up a little later for a game of checkers?"

"Big" sounded good. Most grownups called Patty and me tiny, and kids at school teased me for being the smallest in class. I nodded. *Checkers isn't as exciting as the airplane ride, but I'll get to stay up later than Patty.*

Father climbed the porch steps and hugged our mother. She tilted her head back and looked up at him she asked, "Do you know yet, Bob?"

"No," he answered. "The State Department will have our answer soon. Don't worry. I know it will come through."

Mother sighed one of her longer worried sighs. She moved to the edge of the porch and looked out at my sister and me standing on the lawn. Over her shoulder she said, "They're happy here. They're a part of the neighborhood. They play hide and seek and roller-skate up and down the block with all the other kids. Is it fair to them, even though you and I want it so much?"

"Don't worry, Betty. We'll keep them happy and safe no matter where we are. Don't listen to anyone who says otherwise."

I didn't know what they were talking about, but I guessed it was something big.

I was right because, four days later, Father called Patty and me into the kitchen before breakfast for an important announcement. "Girls, I have a new job. I have transferred from the State Department to the Foreign Service. This summer we are moving to New Delhi, India. Your mother and I are excited and happy about it. I'm sure you will be too, although it means a lot of changes in our lives."

Soon evenings became crowded with my parents' friends and acquaintances. *Is this what Father meant by changes?* When parties were held at our house, Patty and I hunched down at the top of our stairs to spy on the gathering below. When we accompanied our parents to friends' homes, we wore starched white pinafores over matching dresses and remembered to be quiet and to smile. Guests clicked glasses filled with frothy bubbles. Some laughed while hugging Mother or clapping Father on the back and congratulating them. Other friends seemed teary eyed and murmured that it would be all right while patting Mother's arm or nodding wisely at Father.

Two months after Father's announcement about his new job, packers arrived carrying large cardboard cartons and stacks of paper that they crumbled and stuffed into the cartons along with our things. The men whisked everything into containers like they were having a contest to see who could fill the most boxes. I wondered if I would ever see my toys and books again. I crossed my fingers. Patty asked me, "Will our things stay on the truck forever?"

When the front door closed behind the packers, Mother sank into a borrowed folding chair. "Oh Bob, it's too wonderful! But should we go through with it?"

"This is our dream come true, Betty. And we'll be serving our country. Remember that part. Besides, it's too late to change our minds; we're on our way now."

"Can you believe those packers told me we didn't have anything worth insuring and that we were only a three-barrel family?" Mother's indignant snort followed this question.

Father laughed. "Knowing you, my dear, I am sure that won't be the case next time."

Next time? Our parents had explained to us that we were going to make a big move, but I didn't know another one was coming after that or why did I have to get so many shots? *I hate shots, and so does Patty!*

Patty followed me into the kitchen where Mother was reheating a casserole that friends had dropped off for our dinner. Although Patty only came up to my waist, I felt brave and strong when she was beside me. My loyal sidekick. I tapped Mother's arm to get her attention and said, "We want to know everything. Where are they taking our things? What does Father mean by next time? Are we going to move two times? Does that mean more shots?"

Mother sighed. "Oh dear. We told you we're moving to New Delhi, but maybe we didn't explain how far away that is, and that there will be other posts after India."

"Why can't we stay here? Don't you like our home anymore?" I asked.

"Of course we do, but your father has a very important new job."

I reminded her, "You said the State Department was important. Just as important as being a soldier in the war."

Patty nodded in agreement, "Important."

Mother stopped fixing dinner and called, "Bob. Bob, we need you in here. The girls want to know about your new job."

When Father joined us in the kitchen, he crossed his arms and leaned against the counter. "I am in the Foreign Service now, Girls. It's just as important as the State Department. Your mother and I will be representing the United States in different places around the world. You two will be little diplomates too. It's a way of serving our country, just like people in the Army and Navy and State Department do."

Mother interrupted with a short laugh. "Diplomites! They'll be wonderful little diplomites!"

Father smiled at her and said, "Yes! Exactly."

He turned back to us. "To start with, we are going by train to California. It will take four nights and five days. We'll have our own compartment and bunks to sleep in. We'll have a month in California to visit family and friends, and then we'll board a ship to India. You will be big girls with your own room on the ship, but your mother and I will be on the other side of the door that connects our rooms. We'll be on the ship a long time. Seven weeks. There's a pool on the ship, you'll like that."

Mother walked around the table to cup my chin in one hand and Patty's in the other. She looked deep into our eyes and said slowly, "We will see and do so many new and wonderful things!" Then she kissed us each on our foreheads.

Patty and I hugged each other while we hopped in circles. *Bunk beds on a train! A room of our own on a ship! A swimming pool! Maybe we would see whales! And many new and wonderful things! Boy oh boy!* Moving wasn't scary anymore.

We were running late the morning we rushed to the station to catch the train to California. Hurrying down the platform alongside the giant snake of hissing pullman cars, Mother fussed with her handbag and us. "Patty, don't let go of my hand! Deedee, don't go so far ahead!"

Father shuffled behind us rechecking tickets and luggage. When a voice called out, "All Aboard!" he looked startled. Mother grabbed his arm and asked in a worried voice, "Which way Bob?" My parents weren't feeling well. We had been out late at last night's farewell party. I asked a nearby Redcap to help us. He quickly loaded us into our Pullman compartment, luggage and all, lifted his hat in thank you for the tip my father gave him, and hopped off the train as it began to chug forward in slow soft spurts.

Patty looked up and patted Mother's moist cheek. I asked, "Are you sad we're going to India?"

"No, Darling, I'm not sad, a little unsettled maybe, but mostly I'm happy and excited. My heart is so full it is spilling over."

"Well, Little Red Cap" Father said to me, "Thanks to you we are on our way to see the world. Say goodbye to Washington D.C." Mother nodded. She gathered us into a long hug.

Father read *Black Beauty* aloud to us all the way across the country.

My parents called California "home." It is where they grew up and went to school all the way through to Father's PHD and Mother's almost PHD.

We bounced as house guests from one set of hosts to the next. Patty and I shared couches or mattress pads on the floor. California seemed stuffed with aunts, uncles, grandparents, two cousins, and dear old friends. Everyone was delighted to meet us, but I grew tired of being a guest. I felt frustrated when Mother put an arm around each of us and said, "Well Girls, now you see that California is your second home." *Sort of,* I thought, *but where's my first home and why can't we leave here and have our own place not to be guests in?* But it wasn't up to me. We continued our rounds as house guests until the day came when it was time to board the ship.

Aboard Ship

OUR VISIT ENDED IN SAN FRANCISCO WHERE WE BOARDED the SS President Polk. The gang plank swayed upward, and the ship bellowed in long low roars as it inched away from its berth. The four of us squeezed into the passenger line-up at the deck railing which loomed far above the well-wishers looking up at us from the dock below. I glanced at buildings nearby and realized we were as high as some of the rooftops. We blew paper horns and waved. The crowd waved back. Mother blew kisses while a few tears rolled off her cheeks.

"Why are you crying, Mother?" Patty asked, wide-eyed and frightened.

"Because that is what you do, Darling, when you are sailing halfway around the world to start a new life far away from all that you call family, home, and country. Because it's exciting and sad all at once, that is what you do." She waved her handkerchief up and down, back and forth, and swirled it in circles. I guessed her heart was too full again.

Father shook his head at the handkerchief circles, but I could tell his heart was full too. His eyes were extra misty. They were almost silver instead of their usual soft brown.

He led the way down a flight of steps to our rooms. Two single beds, a narrow bedside table between them, and a small dresser filled Patty's and my room. I hopped up on the bed that had a small circle window above it. "Mine! I dibbies it!"

Patty didn't pay any attention because she was practicing opening and closing the connecting door.

"Why are you doing that?" I asked.

"I want to see the big room." Our parent's room had one big bed, a wide bedside table, a bigger dresser, and a table with two chairs.

The Polk was home territory to a dozen or so children of American businessmen, military attaches, and diplomats, all sailing to posts in the Far East. As a group we swarmed onto the shuffleboard and deck tennis courts until shooed away by whichever purser was assigned to watch us. We cannon-balled en masse into the swimming pool. At Children's Mess which was served two hours before the adult dining hour, we plotted the next day's activities. George, who was twelve, was our leader, and he came up with most of our plans. Spaghetti dinners were our favorite. We measured the strands. It was George who led our ceremony of tossing the longest strand of spaghetti overboard while chanting, "May you rest in peace and not be eaten by a fish."

Life with the gang settled into a comfortable neighborhood-like routine. It was a congenial group except for Marty, the boy from Montreal, who refused to agree with me that Canada was a part of the United States. After two days of arguing with him, when our family was together in my parents' stateroom one morning before breakfast, I complained about Marty. "He is the dumbest, stupidest boy I ever met. He doesn't even know anything. He makes me so mad! The Foreign Service should kick him out because everyone who meets him will think all American children are stupid."

"And why is that?" Father asked.

"Because he doesn't even know Canada is a state, and he won't believe me when I tell him."

My parents exchanged a look, the kind that had no words but said things that Patty and I were left out of. Father raised both eyebrows. Mother wrinkled her brow with her head tilted to the side like she was trying to solve a puzzle. Then her face cleared, and she said, "Bob, the ship has a library. I'll bet there's an Atlas."

Father snapped his fingers. "Of course!" That afternoon he took me to the library and pointed out parts of the world, including North and South America. I was flabbergasted that the U.S. wasn't the only country in North America. Father also explained why our voyage was so long by using his finger to trace the Polk's route to India and ports of call along the way. Then he put a finger on San Francisco and zipped it across the map, straight to New Delhi. He smiled, shaking his head side to side, and said, "I hear that someday we will fly across the world in only a few days!"

I learned that no matter how sure you are, you can be wrong, Canada was not a part of the United States, and that the future would probably be full of surprises.

There were stops along the way. First among them was Hawaii where my mother fell in love with the sound of Queen Liliuokalani's name and repeated it over and over for days. Father explained that was because Mother was a poet and that poets fall in love with words and ideas. In the Queen's Palace, Mother explained that Liliuokalani's kingdom was taken from her by people who wanted it for themselves. Patty and I stamped our feet and chanted "Not fair. Not fair."

The day before we docked in Shanghai, as the ship's engines changed to a quieter hum in a steady glide toward port, Father talked through breakfast and lunch about his good friend Ching Lee. He and Ching Lee formed a lasting friendship while majoring in economics as undergraduates at Stanford. Ching Lee lived in Shanghai now and had invited us all out to dinner. The sparkle in Father's eyes and the way he smoothed his mustache showed how much he looked forward to seeing his old college friend. Mother added "It will be nice meet his wife, too."

Father continued to talk about his friend the next day, but it was boring stuff about their time at Stanford together, so I didn't pay attention until Patty opened the door between our parents' stateroom and ours to show them we were dressed for our outing. Father stopped talking mid-sentence. He held a letter in one hand that he had been reading to Mother when we burst into the room. He lowered his eyebrows into a frown and asked, "What are you two doing in here?"

Patty darted behind me and held onto my waist, leaving me to be spokesperson, as usual. "We just wanted to show you we put on the things Mother left on our beds. We're ready except for our hair."

Mother nodded. "You both look very nice. I have blue ribbons to match the flowers in your dresses and I'll fix your hair in a minute, but first your father and I have something we need to discuss. Wait in your room, Sweetie Pies. Hurry, scoot, scoot." She made little scooping movements with her hands to urge us along.

Father closed the door behind us. Patty climbed up on her bed and sat with her legs dangling over the edge and her gathered skirt spread out on each side. She folded her hands in her lap and waited. But I knelt by the door with my ear pressed against it.

"Deedee, what …."

"Shh!" I put a finger to my lips and shushed her. Mother and Father were talking in hushed voices. "War," and "danger," were words I caught in Mother's voice. Father's low rumble gave me, "turbulence, American, safe." I raced to sit on my bed as Father's voice came closer to the door.

He opened it and said, "Okay, Girls, hair time."

I tried not to blurt out what I overheard, but every part of me itched with questions. Patty and I had the same hairdo as well as matching dresses. We sat still in a chair while Mother stood behind, weaving French braids from our temples to the nape of our necks. Then she divided our long hair into two braids that hung below our shoulders.

While she fussed with our hair, Father paced back and forth in front of our "beauty shop." He cleared his throat and said, "Girls, I want to warn you that tonight will be a little different." He held up the letter I had seen earlier. "Ching Lee was able to get a note to the ship to … warn, um, um… to let us know … Well, that he is having some trouble with his government so there might be extra people standing around our table at dinner. Some of them might look like policemen or soldiers. Don't pay any attention to them. Your mother and I are sure the evening will be lovely, and there will be more food for you to try than you can imagine. Do **not** make a face if you think something on your plate looks strange. Show what good manners Americans have. Smile and don't kick each other under the table. Remember you represent your country."

Mother hugged us in turn and said, "My sweet little diplomites! I know you will make us proud."

Although what I heard through the door sounded scary, I felt safe. It was twilight when we walked down the gangplank into our waiting taxi. Patty and I were sandwiched between our parents in the backseat. I could only see the silhouettes of fancy roof tops, but I could feel the taxi make quick darts and turns during the fifteen-minute drive to the restaurant. The driver stopped in front of the entrance and Father hurried us in because we were five minutes late.

The restaurant's walls were shiny red silk laced with wooden swirls of gold. I wanted to touch them, to make sure they were silk, but Father was urging us forward. I noticed three men wearing matching muddy green jackets, sitting at a table near the one we were led to. Mr. Ching Lee rose to greet us. He was wearing a black suit and tie. He looked skinny and small to me. We were seated in a row across the table from him.

Two waiters, each wearing a white cloth wrapped around his waist, presented platter after platter of food, including one with a fish, complete with its head and shiny black eyes that stared at me. I recognized shrimp, rice and noodles.

When we first sat down, Mother said to our host, "I am sorry not to meet your wife. I hope she is well."

He glanced around the room, then said quietly, "She is well, thank you, Betty."

Mother reached across the table and patted his arm. She said, "Please give her our best. We are so sorry she couldn't come tonight."

One of the green men stood up. Father cleared his throat and Mother withdrew her hand. Father and Ching Lee talked about their days at Stanford while Mother whispered reminders to Patty and me, "Taste it dears. Just taste it. You don't have to eat it all. Just a taste."

In the back seat of the taxi on the way back to our ship, Patty curled up on Mother's lap and fell asleep. I leaned into Father's shoulder and asked, "Why didn't Mrs. Lee come too?"

The taxi driver shifted in his seat to lean his head slightly toward us. Father patted my knee and said softly, "We'll talk about it when we're in our rooms."

"You promise?"

"Yes, I promise." He looked at Mother and she nodded in agreement. He carried my sleeping sister up the gangplank all the way to her bed. Mother took over getting Patty into her night gown without waking her.

Father motioned for me to follow him. He said, "Now let's see if we can tackle some of your questions." We sat at the table in my parent's room.

My questions tumbled out. "Why wasn't your friend's wife there? Were those green guys policemen at the restaurant? Why were you and Mother whispering about the letter?"

"Well, Deedee girl, we didn't want to upset you. China is going through a rough time right now. They just finished a big war with Japan, and now there are two sides that want to be in charge, and they are starting to fight each other. A civil war. The side that is in charge where Ching Lee lives are Nationalists. They think he was giving information to the other side, so they arrested him."

"He came to dinner from jail?"

"No, Honey, but he and his wife are under house arrest. That means they can't leave their house without permission and guards. Tonight, they kept Mrs. Lee at home so her husband wouldn't try to run away. Maybe your "green guys" were tonight's guards.

"That's awful! It isn't fair! Will they keep him in his house forever?" I wiggled all over to chase away the creepy feeling in my back.

"I don't think so. It was all a mistake. Ching met an old friend for tea last week. He didn't know his friend was an important part of the communist side. I will do what I can to help him. Write letters, make some calls. I knew we would be safe tonight. The Nationalists like American diplomats. I'm not too worried because we have General Marshall there to work out a compromise." He patted my head. "My word! It's only been a little over a month since we left the States, and you already have seen the big wide world at work."

"What do you mean?"

"Oh, I mean learning about things unfair, and how leaders in power can control lives… Never mind. You did very well tonight. Time for bed."

I thought about how the world worked before I fell asleep. *Leaders make things happen, like George, our gang's leader, but sometimes they are mean and*

do things that aren't fair like stealing Hawaii from the Queen and keeping Mrs.
Lee locked up in her house in China.

When our ship left port, we stood on the deck, waving goodbye to
China.. Father leaned toward me and put his hand on my shoulder. He said,
"You look very serious today, Honey, and so you should be. You have just
witnessed a country in transition." He took a deep breath. "We certainly hope
it is to our side."

Turbulence

WITHIN TWO DAYS OUR ROUTINES WERE IN PLACE AGAIN
and the ship resumed its rhythmic rocking. Patty and I snuggled with Mother
on the big couch in the ship's lounge as she read to us.

The rocking grew more pronounced. We cuddled closer, happy and
relaxed.

Suddenly the ship's horns boomed through the air in loud short blasts.
Bells clanged in piercing discord. The loudspeaker bellowed, "All passengers
return to your cabins at once! All passengers return to your cabins at once!
This is an emergency!"

"Come, Girls." Mother held out a hand to each of us as we all stood up
together, but the couch slipped forward to bang against our legs, knocking
us back onto it. We landed in a squealing heap. Mother tucked Patty under
her left arm and me under her right. She squeezed us close and looked across
the room. Chairs and tables began moving toward us on their own. The ship's
rocking gained force and speed. Mother took a deep breath, nodded once, and
said, "I don't think we would make it across the room, much less than down
the hallways and stairs. We'll be safer here on the couch. It is the biggest and
heaviest thing in the room. It's like a raft, a lifeboat."

Patty began to whimper. I clutched Mother's waist and asked, "What's the matter with the ship?"

Patty's whimper turned into a wail. "Is the ship broken?"

Mother pulled us even closer. "No, Patty dear, it's not broken. I think we are in a bad storm. It happens sometimes, and ships know how to get through them."

I looked at the closed doorway across the lounge, the one that opened to the hallways that led to our rooms below. "I wish Father was here. Maybe he's waiting for us in the room. Are you sure we shouldn't go?" I took a deep breath and swallowed to keep from crying,

"Sweetie, I'm doing the best I can to keep us safe. The most important thing is for us to stay calm. Patty, take a deep breath. Deedee, your father will find us as soon as he can. He'll be fine. We'll all be fine. Now, let's watch what this silly furniture is doing. It's like a cartoon show, isn't it?"

Small tables whipped around the room. Chairs smacked into each other. Our couch rose following the motion of the ship, hesitated a second, then slid forward downhill. Like a seesaw, we rose up again, and then slid backward. Mother joined in "oohing" with each slide. She pointed out how a chair just missed a lamp and we cheered for the lamp. She made up a game of guessing which table would slide to the other side fastest, and we cheered for the winner. But neither Patty nor I let go of Mother for an instant.

"What if our couch turns over, Mother? Are we going to get killed?" Patty buried her head so deeply into the crook of Mother's arm that it was hard to hear her over the horns, bells, smashing furniture, and roar of wind.

Mother took a deep breath and tossed her head back. Then she bent to kiss us each on the top of our heads. "Of course not! We will just cuddle underneath it like little bunnies. Don't let go of me. Stay calm. We'll be fine."

Just as I was ready to scream that I didn't want any more seesaw rides and the sliding furniture wasn't funny anymore, the ship won its battle. The room rocked gently. Mother stood. "Come, my dears, it's time to freshen up."

Father was pacing in front of our door. He rushed to meet us. He hugged us all and said, "Thank Goodness! Thank Goodness! They wouldn't let me look for you. I figured you would come here as soon as you could." He put his arm around Mother. She sniffed three deep shaky breaths and rested her head on his chest. He kissed her forehead and said, "I was worried, but all the time I knew your Mother would keep you safe."

"Yes!" Patty grabbed Mother's hand. "She made a life raft."

Father raised an eyebrow and looked down at the top of Mother's head. "Made a life raft?"

I thought I'd better clear things up. "She said the couch was the biggest thing and so it was like a lifeboat, and she made us stay calm. She said that was the most important thing of all."

Father smiled. "It is. It certainly is. Girls, you have just weathered a typhoon! A seriously strong one according to the crew." He hugged Mother closer to him. "And your mother… your mother kept you safe through it all. She is the bravest person I know!"

We stood there, clasped in a four person hug, feeling safe and grateful. But we knew we had over two more weeks on board and India ahead. Anything could happen.

The ship docked at Manilla next. A couple my parents had known in Washington waited for us at the bottom of the gangplank. They were stationed in Manilla with U.S. Navy. The man wore a white uniform and stood still with his hat tucked under his arm. The woman rushed right up to Mother and hugged her and started talking without stopping. "Oh Betty! How wonderful to see you again! And the girls are so big now." She stooped to hug me. "Diana, you were just four and very angry about having a baby sister the last time I saw you."

I stared straight ahead at the embroidered flowers running down a wide strip on the front of her blouse. *The blue ones are prettier than the yellow ones.* I muttered, "I'm Deedee."

She didn't hear me because she had already knelt and grabbed Patty. "So, this is little Patterson!"

Patterson? Little Patterson? Why does Mrs. Navy have to hug everybody when we don't even know her? There she goes, hugging Father now.

"Well, we have a special treat for you. We're going to have lunch at the Officer's club where there's a big pool for you to swim in. Much better than that tiny thing on your ship." She turned to Mother, "Betty, I have bathing suits and caps for them. We keep spares for guests of all sizes!"

The borrowed suit flopped off my shoulders and the rubber cap came to the middle of my eyebrows. The skirt on Patty's suit sagged past her knees. Her cap almost covered her eyes.

The grownups were sitting at a table by the pool when we joined them after changing. Mother said, "Oh my!" Then she added quickly, "You look ready, Girls! Don't worry, when wet everything will fit much better and you can swim like little eels."

My sister and I stood on the edge of the pool staring into its mottled brown depths. Patty took my hand and moved close to my side. We didn't say a word. Mrs. Navy chirped behind us. "Well, Children. Hop in. Don't mind the color of the water. It's something about chlorine and the filter. It's fresh, just filled this morning. Nothing like a nice little dip on such a hot day." She and Mother were both fanning themselves with handkerchiefs and I noticed that Father and Mr. Navy had taken their jackets off.

Patty and I didn't move. "Go on, Dears, take a quick dip and then we can all go inside to eat where it's cooler." Mother's voice sounded squeezed to me.

I turned to face her. "I don't want to. It's uggy muddy dirty green!"

Patty clutched my hand with both of hers. Her voice sounded ready to cry. "I don't want to swim."

Father frowned at me. I frowned back and said, "I can't see the bottom. I can always see the bottom on the ship. And it has pretty water."

Mother took a deep breath. Mrs. Navy put a hand over her heart and gasped. She looked away from us and then she turned to Mother and said, "Oh my! Oh my! Betty, you poor thing. You certainly have your hands full getting them ready for diplomatic life. I wish you luck."

Father glared at us. Mother muttered something about recovering from a typhoon and that I must be coming down with something. She motioned me to come to her and felt my forehead, then she looked up at Father. "Bob, she has a fever. We need to get her back to the ship to see the doctor before she gets worse." I tried to tell her I felt fine, but she interrupted by telling us to go change back into our clothes.

Mr. Navy gathered up his jacket and said, "I'll drive you back right away."

The minute we reached our rooms, Father gestured for Patty and me to sit at the table in the Big Room. He stood in front of us and started the scolding I had guessed was coming. "I expected much better behavior from the two of you. You were rude to our hosts. Your mother and I were embarrassed."

I didn't look up from staring at my hands in my lap. I asked, "Is that why Mother pretended I was sick?" Patty's head stayed down too.

Mother stood beside Father. "You really hurt their feelings. Sally planned a special time for you, and you were awful about it."

"But the pool was ugly." I tried not to sound whiny.

Patty chimed in. "Dirty."

"Like baby vomit." That popped out of my mouth without thinking. Mother made a little noise that sounded almost like a cough. Father covered his mustache and looked away.

Mother turned to us. "It did look pretty awful. But! But! But there was a better way to handle it. Just like the food in China, you try it to be polite. Wade a bit and then say you were cold, or hungry."

"We weren't cold. That would be telling a lie. But I guess we were hungry, weren't we Patty?"

Patty nodded.

Father took a deep breath and sat on his bed to face us. "This will be Rule Number One for you as part of the diplomatic service; When someone is telling you about something that is important in their life, don't brag that you have the same thing but yours is better."

I sat up straight. "You mean like saying our pool had prettier water because the dirty pool was important to the Navy people?"

Father stood. "Exactly. You got it! You're a smart cookie. Smart enough to always remember Rule Number One." His compliment and sandwiches from the snack bar helped me feel better, even though we were grounded from the pool for two days so we would have plenty of time to think about Rule Number One. *It must be the most important rule of all because it is Number One. I'll try to remember, but it's awful hard not to think about my own things when someone is being braggy about theirs.*

Our days at sea started to follow each other at a faster pace. Only two stops left before Bombay! It seemed just a few days after Manilla that our family stood on the on the deck waiting to disembark as the ship eased into the next port of call, Penang. Father patted my back and said, "Just wait until you see the Temple of the Snakes. You will never forget it."

I hope they don't have pointy faces. Grandpa taught me that snakes with pointy faces are poisonous. As we climbed steps to get to the temple, snakes flowed past us. Inside the temple they oozed in out of statues and urns. They were everywhere and they had pointy faces. I lasted fifteen minutes before I tugged at Father's hand and said, "Let's go! I don't like it here!"

He laughed and assured me that we were safe because the snakes were guests of the monk who had invited them to share his space, and therefore very polite, but we left. Mother and Patty seemed as relieved as I was.

Then came Columbo with an enormous Buddha that I guessed was bigger than an elephant. We had to take our shoes off in his temple.. Mother explained that was the polite thing to do in a Buddhist place of worship. I had time to think while my parents walked slowly around the giant. *It's more peaceful here than the snake place, and I don't think there ever could possibly be a bigger Buddha anywhere, but I am tired of sightseeing. I want to go home. But I guess home's in the new place I don't know yet.*

Mother enjoyed the stops. She found small shops where she bought all kinds of things that Father called "the Littles". She found a family of pottery ducks she loved in Penang, and an ivory Buddha as big as a loaf of bread in Columbo. Father wasn't impressed with the Buddha. He said he thought it might be made of dog bones, not ivory.

After Columbo, I knew our next stop would be the last one for us. The ship was nearing India. I had trouble sleeping. When I closed my eyes, I saw snakes crawling over Buddhas and people chasing dogs to steal their bones. *The ship is like my old neighborhood. Maybe India is full of big Buddhas and snakes with pointy faces and I won't have any friends. I wish we could just stay on the ship and go back halfway around the world to my real home and stay there. It's hard learning how the world works.*

PART II.

NEW DELHI

1946

The Taj

ONCE AGAIN THE CHANGE IN THE RHYTHM OF THE SHIP'S
engines signaled our approach to a port. Disembarking passengers gathered
at the railing to catch their first glimpse of India.

The crowd began flowing down the gangplank murmuring, "At last.
Bombay at last." Patty and I squeezed together as we followed close behind
Mother and Father. At the top of the gangplank, we could finally see over the
herd of grownups in front of us. I stopped, frozen in shock. Scarlet! Yellow!
Lime Green! Orange! Peacock blue! Colors darted and whirled across the
landing below bombarding my eyes. High pitched, urgent, loud. command-
ing, unintelligible shouts slapped my ears. The teeming dock sent a stench
racing upwards: sour, sweaty, earthy, peppery. My arms felt sticky. The foreign
smells crawled across my face and burrowed deep into my wrinkled-up nose.

Patty and I grabbed the railing and refused to budge. "We don't want
to leave!" I wailed. Patty shook her head back and forth, over and over, and
clutched the railing tighter.

Patty yelped, "We want to stay on the ship."

Our mother gently pried our hands from the railing. "Come, come my dears. Everything we do from now on will be how other people see our country. Let's go make America proud of us."

The embassy sent a car and driver to fetch us from Bombay. Our road trip ended in front of a pair of tall metal gates and a group of uniformed guards. Patty and I poked our heads out of the back windows, straining to see beyond the ornate wrought iron while our driver gained permission to enter. The gates rolled open and we drove into the compound that had recently been barracks for British Army Officers. The driver deposited us and our suitcases on a veranda lining the entire length of our assigned "private wing." A series of doors opened onto the veranda.

It was Mother's turn to be stunned. She stood looking at the pile of suitcases, the line of doors, the barren ground between our wing and the next. After a short silence and a prolonged sigh, she said. "Oh." And soon, "Oh" again. Then "Oh, Bob, I somehow expected more from a place called The Taj Mahal Hotel."

Father bit his lip, inhaled, making a swishing sound. "Me too. British humor, I guess. But it's only temporary, just until the new Indian government and our embassy work out a better solution."

"And how long do you think that will be?" Mother asked.

Father shrugged.

We referred to our new home simply as "The Taj."

There were no interior doors between rooms at The Taj. Instead, each room had a heavy wooden door backed by a substantial screen door opening onto the veranda. When I wanted to ask Mother a question, I had to open the doors of the room I shared with my sister, walk out, close our doors, walk down the veranda to my parent's room, open their door, walk in, and close their doors behind me. The doors were harder for Patty to handle because she was smaller. We had to be very sure the doors were closed behind us because of the monsoon season which began soon after our arrival. Everything had to be closed to keep the rain out.

"Must you be so dramatic?" Mother asked more than once when Patty and I expressed our annoyance with the doors by slamming them shut with all our might.

One night I answered, "Well, what else can we do? It's muddy and rainy outside and all chopped up inside." *I wish we never came. I miss our house in Washington. I miss Sunday morning most because Patty and I could crawl up into your bed without any stupid doors in our way and Father read the funnies to us.*

Our new life included a staff of servants. I soon discovered the staff had a hierarchy.

At the very top was Daniel, the head bearer, who ran all affairs of the household and attended personally to my father. Kulwant Singh, our driver, "a beautiful, dignified and gentle soul" according to Mother, hovered high in a close second. Lawrence, the second bearer, was next. Although his job was to do what Daniel told him to do and to attend to my mother, the latter part of his duties was shifted to the ayah. She ranked next to the bottom. Patty and I took offense at having a nursemaid, so we never did get her name straight and were happy that it was Lawrence who had to keep track of us instead. Equal to Lawrence was John, the cook. He ruled the kitchen. Patty and I did not like John. He insisted that we were not allowed in the kitchen, even when he was off duty. He served us eggs so often that we staged protests by marching in and out of the rooms chanting,

> "Eggs, eggs, eggs
> That's all we get to eat.
> Eggs, eggs, eggs
> We never get any meat."

At the bottom of the hierarchy was the sweeper whose name was never mentioned, but his ten -year- old son's name was Sonja. Patty and I, the only children housed in the compound at that time, sought Sonya out as a playmate when it wasn't raining.

Sonja never came in the house or on the veranda, although his job was to keep the kooskoos wet. During the hottest months, these thick mats of tightly embedded coconut fiber walled the outer side of the veranda, turning it into a deeply shaded and almost chilly hallway. Sonja and his father doused the mats with buckets of water all day. If the mats dried out, evaporation would not take place; there would be no "air conditioning" for the rooms when we opened the wood doors and the cooled air flowed in through the screens. The doors were not a problem when it was hot and not raining. They stayed open night and day.

When Sonja could sneak away, we played with him on the sun baked ground between wings of the barracks. I got used to the pale-yellow ringworm scars that splotched his brown face, his baggy cotton shorts and lack of shirt. Patty and I wore freshly ironed seersucker shorts and matching midriff tops. We laughed with him, repeating words in his language and in ours, but mostly we communicated by pantomiming. We pantomimed our way through days of building toy airplanes of sticks and paper. We held them out at arm's length and swooped them through the air in acrobatic flights as we ran across the barren space between the wings of The Taj. But at any hint of someone approaching us, Sonja disappeared.

One day everything went wrong when Sonja's father appeared without warning and found him playing with us. I raced down our veranda and into my mother's room screaming, "Make him stop! Make him stop!"

Mother put down the stack of calling cards she was sorting and put her hands on my shoulders. "What are you going on about? Make who stop?"

"Sonja's father. He's hitting Sonja all over his head! Make him stop!"

My mother followed me through the veranda, and out onto the heat-cracked ground. She quickened her pace when she heard the steady "Whack!" Smack! Whack!" and a child moaning. My playmate huddled in a low crouch while his father stood over him shouting and slapping the boy's head from side to side with alternate backhand and open palm blows. When Sonja's father saw my mother, he bowed, mumbled a few words, shuffled backward, and then, looking sternly at his son, he pointed to the servants' compound set a distance behind our building. Sonja ran. His father continued backing away from us, eyes lowered, head down until he spun around to face the direction Sonja had taken. With his head held high, he followed his son. Mother stared at his retreat. Her mouth seemed frozen in a straight line.

As we walked back down the veranda together, I pushed Mother's arm off my shoulder. I scrunched my face into a ferocious pout. "Why did Sonja have to go? We were having fun."

Mother stopped. She put a hand on each of my shoulders and turned me to face her. "Hmm. I know you are upset. It is lonely for you here. I'll talk to Daniel about it, but I think you had better leave Sonja out of your games unless you want to get him in trouble."

I stamped my foot. "But why?"

"Because his father is a Sweeper."

"Sonja helps him sweep, and he pours water on the kooskoos all day. Why can't he play with me sometimes? Patty's too little. I'd rather play with a ten year old than a four year old. There isn't anyone else."

"I know it doesn't make sense to you, Honey. Sweepers are Untouchables. Sonja can't play with you because he is untouchable because his father is a Sweeper."

"What's untouchable?"

"Oh Honey." Mother drew in a deep breath. "It is so hard to explain. I don't understand it myself. It is an old rule in India. It means Sonja's people can't do anything with other people. They must sit away from all the others. They eat in separate places and can only use their separate things. They're supposed to just work hard and be as invisible as possible."

I jumped up and down in the loudest two-foot stamp I could make. "That isn't fair. It isn't fair."

"It certainly isn't, not at all fair, anywhere." Mother took my chin in her hand and tilted my head upward so she could look straight into my eyes. "Remember, this is not our country. It's not for us to say what is right or wrong here. But things are changing. India is changing. The world is changing. We will figure out something." Her hug was warm and reassuring.

We did not play with Sonja again. I tried to understand but trying made me angry. *I suppose this how the world works. But it still isn't fair. I'm glad my country doesn't have untouchables.*

July 23rd came, and I was nine. Three months later, I came down with yellow jaundice in the middle of a family picnic. Sunday picnics were our family tradition. In Washington we picnicked in Rock Creek Park, or the zoo. In India, this outing was at the Red Fort. Our favorite picnic menu was Mother's fried chicken, but since John wouldn't allow her to use the kitchen, Vienna Sausages in tiny cans replaced the fried chicken.

"They taste a lot better than John's old mutton and eggs," I declared. I hogged a whole can and then felt sick to my stomach. The next day I turned yellow and threw up almost nonstop.

The family bathroom was between our parents' room and the one Patty and I shared. I was there, throwing up as usual, when I overheard my parents talking. I pressed my ear against against the wall.

"Sending her to our army hospital in Beirut is a reasonable option, Betty."

"Being alone, without her family, sick... that's more dangerous to her health than jaundice. You know it is!"

Send me away! No! No! I'll be good. I'll try not to throw up anymore. Don't send me away. Please. I pressed my ear harder against the wall and squeezed my eyes shut, willing myself not to throw up and miss hearing everything.

I could hear Father's footsteps as he paced their room. "Yes, that's true, but Jaundice is a serious illness. It could destroy her liver. Maybe you could set up camp near the hospital."

"I can't imagine her there alone for the several months it might take. But splitting our family apart, Bob! I would be away from you. In another strange country to manage on my own, alone with a five-year-old and a child in the hospital. That isn't reasonable, if you ask me."

"I know. I know. Maybe somehow we could manage to visit her often. I could get a few long weekends off."

"Not often enough." Mother's voice had a sharper tone than usual. I pictured her chin stuck up in the air. Sometimes her eyes seemed to flash blue sparks. I could almost see those sparks aimed at Father.

I swallowed hard to keep the sick feeling from rising from my stomach into my throat. *Please, please, please don't make me go away. I'll stop throwing up. Please…*

Father continued. "If she stays here we would have to have special food for her. No fats. None. And she must stay in bed for maybe four months or more. And I'm not sure the local doctor is up to standard…"

Mother interrupted. "Now you're sounding like some of those stuffy British colonials here that think anything Indian is beneath them. I'm sure Dr. Jarwali is as well-educated as the army doctors. He studied in the States, you know."

"Sorry. Point taken. But almost everyone assures me she would get the best care available in Beirut."

That did it! I burst in their room shouting, "I'm not going to any stinky army hospital! I won't go away. I won't. I won't." I stamped my foot, and threw up, right there in front of them between sobs.

I got to stay. John cooked a lot of omelets and made tomato and lettuce (no bacon) sandwiches for me. I read in bed for four months. Books poured in from friends and family. Among them: Kipling" s *Jungle Books* and *Just So Stories, Nancy Drew* books, and a *Child's Guide to Greek Mythology*. I was proud that my parents named me after Diana, Goddess of the Hunt, The Moon, and Young Maidens and they were proud I had become such a good reader. Although everyone told her I was not contagious, Patty sat in a chair far enough away from my bed not to catch throwing up from me, while I read some of the Nancy Drew stories out loud to her.

Reading, rest, no fats, and six glasses of glucose water daily were my cure. *Dr. Jawali is the best doctor in the world even though he won't agree that I caught infectious hepatitis from a can of Vienna Sausages. I'm okay because of him and I didn't have to go away. He's my hero along with Mowgli and Nancy Drew, and, of course, Diana.*

Jail

As a reward for following the Doctor's orders so faithfully, Mother arranged a trip to The Alps, New Delhi's only air conditioned ice cream parlor. Patty and I flopped over each other in the back seat of our car, hot and impatient to reach our destination. Our dresses bunched damply around us. Our legs stung from the layer of salty sweat between them and the leather seat. The air entering through the open car windows pressed the smells of curry spices and warm donkey dung and the sounds of jangling bells and honking horns against our damp faces.

When our car stopped in the middle of the road and stayed there, frustration spilled out of me in a whine. "When are we getting to the ice cream place? You promised! You said it would be in just a minute. Why are we stopped? What is the policeman saying, Mother?"

"I don't know, my dear. Sit up. Please stop whining." She gently dabbed her face with her lace trimmed handkerchief to stop driblets of sweat and leaned forward to speak to our driver.

"Kulwant Singh, what is the problem? Why is the policeman holding us here?"

Kulwant Singh turned from his conversation with the policeman. "He crazy, Memsahib. He say we hit boy." He pointed to several women huddled over a small boy who held his leg and looked like he was groaning. "They want baksheesh."

"You tell him that is ridiculous. We didn't hit anyone. This is an old con game. Just drive on, ignore them." Kulwant Singh shrugged and inched the car forward. The policeman blew his whistle. Spit sprayed out of the sides of his mouth. Another policeman arrived on a bicycle. Both men began shouting and gesturing at us.

Kulwant Singh turned back to my mother. "Memsahib, they are very angry. We must follow them to jail. Maybe if you give them baksheesh?"

"I will do no such thing. We will call the American Embassy and they will be very sorry for the trouble they have caused us. Tell them that!"

Kulwant Singh yelled his way into the fray, but the police were louder, angrier, and growing in number. They streamed in from all directions, surrounding our car on bicycles, on motorcycles, and a few on foot. They yelled directions at Kulwant Sing and herded our car down several streets.

My frustration turned to creeping fear. "Mother, why are they all around us? Where are we going? Are they taking us to the ice cream place?"

"Hush, hush. Be as quiet as you can. We'll just see about this!" She began fishing in her large handbag until she found her fan. She loved the filigreed sandal wood fans of India and always had one within reach. She snapped it open.

Kulwant Singh stopped the car. The uniformed wall around us stepped back. We were parked in front of a mud-yellow building. Kulwant Singh, with his usual graceful bow, opened the back door for my mother. Patty and I followed her over a worn doorsill into a room dominated by a desk, a uniformed mustached man behind the desk, and floor to ceiling bars that turned half the room into a jail.

Mother marched straight in and rapped on the desk with her fan. "Call the American Embassy. Now!"

She was ignored. The desk policeman spoke in Hindi to the members of our escort. Patty and I watched in horror as this man slid the bars aside to make an opening to the caged area of the room, ushered our mother inside, and slid the bars back again to shut with a loud click.

"Mother! Mother!" we cried. We stuck our arms through the bars, sobbing, trying to pull her out.

"You must be brave. Deedee, don't let go of Patty! Hold on tight to each other! Everything will be fine as soon as the embassy is reached." We cried louder because her face was white, and her voice shook. She kissed our hands through the bars as she said, "Shh! Shh! Kulwant Singh just needs to explain to the police that we are with the American Embassy, and the embassy will scold them, and everything will be fine." Then she looked around for our driver. "Where is he?" Her voice rose. "Where is Kulwant Singh?"

"Kulwant Singh! Kulwant Singh!" Patty and I ran about the waiting room, calling him. Panic crept in, climbing up our backs, changing our wailing into screams. Police yelled in Hindi while chasing after the five- and nine -year- old banshees invading their station.

I clamped Patty's hand in mine and screeched, "They are trying to put us in jail too. Run! Run! We have to find Kulwant Singh!" We raced around the room.

"There he is!" I spotted the familiar turban coming through the entry towards us. Patty and I ran to him. "Kulwant Singh! Help! Help! Call our father! The bad men put Mother in jail and they are trying to catch us too. Call our father!"

Kulwant Singh smiled. "Yes Missy. I call."

The station's phone rang. During a quiet conversation, the desk guard glanced towards my mother and nodded. Forty- five minutes later, after paper shuffling, consultations with the men who led us to the station, and conversations with Kulwant Singh, none of which we understood, the door to my mother's cage was unlocked, and we were free to go.

As soon as we were in the car, Patty and I wrapped ourselves around Mother. We kissed her cheeks, patted her arms, hugged her, and cried. With an arm around each of us, she said, "Shh. Shh, my dears. We are safe now."

"But why were the policemen so mean?" I asked.

Patty burrowed into Mother's chest and whispered, "They were scary and bad."

I pushed my way onto Mother's chest and added, "I don't like India anymore."

Mother nudged us to sit up straight and said, "Nonsense! We are lucky to be in this wonderful land. It was just a bad misunderstanding, and your father will straighten everything out, I'm sure. And now, we are on our way to The Alps."

However, that evening, when my father joined us in the living room before dinner, he did not sit. He swept his hand towards us and said, "You had quite a time today! I'm glad that you're are all safe, and apparently unscathed."

Then he turned to Mother with his serious face. His raised eyebrow meant business.

"Betty, the reason we have a staff here is to help us navigate in a world we don't understand. Next time Kulwant Singh makes a suggestion in a circumstance like today, follow it. He knows how these situations work and what to do to get past them. Trust him. A little baksheesh in the beginning would have sufficed. You came close to causing an international incident."

Uh oh. Father's upset with Mother. I left my chair and moved to stand beside hers. Patty followed.

Mother took a deep breath. "Hmph! I just felt so set up. The idea of baksheesh goes against the grain. And I was worried … the children…" She reached out and patted each of us. "But you're right. Kulwant Singh saved the day. Finding a telephone outside the station was brilliant. And heroic." She looked up at Father and grinned, "Lesson learned. I will listen next time, I promise. Even if it involves baksheesh."

Father smiled back and said softly, "I was worried sick. Sorry I couldn't leave the office to be there. We were busy dealing with it at our end. It must have been really frightening!"

Patty and I left Mother's side and headed back to our chairs. However, Father wasn't finished.

"And Girls… "He crossed his arms and looked first at me, then Patty.

Uh Oh. Our turn.

"Kulwant Singh told me you two were making quite a scene in the Police Station. What happened to "Stay calm in an emergency?""

Patty grabbed my hand. She looked down at the floor, and mumbled, "Forgot."

"We had to run so they wouldn't catch us and put us in jail too and it wasn't Patty's fault because I wouldn't let go of her because Mother told me to hold on to her no matter what, and I did." I looked at Father, but he said nothing, just kept looking back at me.

Then he chuckled and said, "I see. Well, not so much yelling next time, okay? Try to stay calm. It takes practice."

Next time? Would we really go to jail again? The police didn't speak English and they were scary. But we know about baksheesh so I guess we'll get along better, and Kulwant Singh will keep us safe, too. Next time I'd better remember to stay calm.

Flood of Sorrow

BY LATE SPRING, AFTER ALMOST A YEAR AT THE TAJ, I longed for more open space, more color, more excitement, something beyond the small dirt area between wings, slam-the-door-tag. and school which was only Mother and the books The Calvert System sent her. I found a wonderful spot at the entrance of The Taj.

The old army compound was enclosed by a high earthen wall. Its wide iron gate, manned by Indian army guards, opened onto Queen's Way. Imposing gateposts flanked the entrance. To me they seemed to rise at least three feet above the wall to their squared off tops. The guards allowed me to scramble up the wall and onto the pillar top where I sat to watch life on Queen's Way, New Delhi's principal thoroughfare.

Cars whizzed past with drivers that never seemed to stop honking. Bicyclists pedaled by ringing their bells without pause. Donkeys brayed. I pinched my nose shut when the damp smell of their poo wafted up to my perch. Vendors carried food or trinkets in baskets on their heads. They sang out about their goods as they passed our gates. When I took long deep breaths, I could smell if they were selling a hot curry stew or sweet stickie jalebis. Passengers spilled out of buses in swaths of color, wearing dhotis, saris, droopy shorts, faded shirts, or Punjabi tunics.

July came again and I was ten. In early October, right in front of our gate, a bus smashed into a man on a bicycle. I heard the commotion and scampered up my pillar to see what the noise was all about. The cyclist lay on his back with his head split open. His brain poured out. A crowd gathered. Dark liquid oozed toward the circling fringe of onlookers.

Tiny spears of ice pierced my skin from within spreading cold horror throughout my body, yet a tingle of excitement warmed the small of my back. I could not look away.

Police came. They circled the man. They talked to each other, the bus driver, and the onlookers. Then they went away. No one checked the man, or covered him, or tried to move him. I could see him and his broken head, his lost brain, and the dried pool of blood from my perch. His bicycle stayed heaped in a mangled mess nearby. People stepped around him. Life carried on as before.

Daniel materialized beneath me. "Missy, this is not for you to see. Come away."

I pretended not to hear him. He stretched up to tap my leg. "Missy, come down now."

"No. I won't!" It took courage to defy Daniel. He left, but I knew I would not be able to stay much longer.

"Deedee, you get down from there this instant!" My mother stood beside Daniel. Her fists were clenched on her hips. I climbed down.

"You are not to look at this again, or even think about it," she added, leading me by a firm grip on my shoulder back to our rooms. *Ha! I can't help thinking about what dead looks like.*

I managed to sneak in peeks in the days that followed. The bus disappeared, but the man remained exactly as he had fallen.

"Daniel, why don't they take him away?" I asked when Daniel found me yet again on my forbidden perch.

"He is not Hindu. We cannot touch one who is unclean. His family will come from the north soon and take him away."

He was not there the fourth morning after the accident.

I asked my father why no one touched the man. Father explained that he probably was Pakistani and Muslim, and India and Pakistan were almost at war with each other. Each religion thought the other unclean.

"Don't they take baths?" I asked.

Father patted my head. "That's not the point, Honey. Being different is the point. People tend to think that only their way is the right way, and those not the same are less."

I went to bed with my head stuffed with thinking. *I guess saying people not like you aren't as good as you is another way the world works, but it doesn't fit in with Father's Number One rule of not bragging, and does it mean everyone here thinks I'm not clean because I'm different?*

That fear was displaced with excitement when in November the embassy informed us a house would be ready for us shortly after Christmas! We had been making do in the Taj for almost a year and a half.

1947 turned into 1948. Late in January, Mother called my sister and me into her room for a talk. Our parents' room had become the quiet heart of our home. Patty and I knocked before entering and hushed our voices once inside, so we did not clash with the serenity of the room. The ivory buddha had a place of honor on the dresser top between two large vases of flowers. Mother was sitting in her preferred chair, fidgeting with the pottery ducks and small brass boxes crowding the table by her chair. She looked up at us and motioned for us to sit. We were careful not to bounce as we settled on the edge of the white linen bed and waited to hear what was so important. I noticed how organized the table by Father's chair (also slipcovered in white linen, like Mother's) seemed with only a silver cigarette box and ashtray.

Mother took a deep breath and said, "Tomorrow a reporter is coming to interview me. He wants to tell people about how we, as representatives of the American government, are coping in this new India. I want you on your very best behavior. That means polite 'hellos,' and then to your room to play quietly. I do not want any interruptions during the interview." She looked us both, one by one, in the eye.

I said, "Sure."

Patty piped in with "No interruptions!" and finished with a salute, like the men on the ship did when the Captain spoke to them.

Mother folded her hands across her stomach and smiled. We turned to leave, but a sudden intake of breath warned us the talk was not over.

"Oh! I almost forgot. He thinks his readers may be interested in how we manage since the British closed their school before leaving. So, tomorrow morning we will make our worktable very neat, and spread out some of the books we're using. Deedee, make sure your mythology book is there, and the Atlas. And the times tables we're working on. We'll do our schoolwork after the reporter leaves. Your job will be to see that your room stays neat until then." She looked straight at me.

I said "Sure" again and followed Patty's example with a salute.

"Good girl. He will be so impressed with you both." She stood and put her arms out for a hug.

On our way out the door, she called after us, "But during the interview, no barging in for any reason. You may join us for tea afterwards. Promise me."

We crossed our hearts and said together, "We promise!"

The reporter arrived the next day. He carried a brief case like Father's. Patty and I shook hands with him and dutifully vanished. Our mother's voice trailed behind us down the veranda.

"Remember, dears, no interruptions."

We would have kept our promise if we had not heard the murmur of wailing. It came from the streets. Shouts and screams from the servants' quarters behind the barracks began to punctuate the moaning from the streets. I ran to the kitchen to find out what was going on because our household staff always knew what was happening anywhere, and the kitchen was the place to find them. Patty followed me.

They were all there, except for Kulwant Singh who was waiting at the embassy for my father. Daniel, Lawrence and John huddled together with their heads bowed. The ayah sat in a chair, bent over with her head in her arms. The sweeper was in a corner by himself, squatting in a dingy grey ball, rocking back and forth. They were all crying. Even Daniel. And John did not shout us out of his kitchen as usual. He only glanced at us. The words "Baba, Baba" muffled through his sobs while his hands clutched his shirt, twisting it and untwisting it.

"Daniel! What is it, Daniel? What is wrong?" I started crying out of fear.

Daniel looked straight at me, his soft brown eyes brimming over. "The Mahatma. His voice broke and came out in small high chunks. "Someone shot the Mahatma. He is dead."

"Mahatma Gandhi? Mahatma Gandhi?"

Daniel lowered his head. "Yes, Baba. Our father. Killed."

After living in India for over a year, I knew about Mahatma Gandhi. From what I overheard the grown-ups say, it seemed Mr. Gandhi wouldn't eat, and he was the most important thing in India. He was discussed at our dinner table. His name floated across our living room when it was filled with cocktail party guests. When Patty and I sneaked in to snitch hors d'ouvres, I heard the guests click their tongues against the roofs of their mouths when he was mentioned, sometimes in disapproval, most often in sympathy. I remembered some of the words they muttered: "troublemaker, powerful, peaceful, heart of India, instigator, saint."

I didn't understand the talk about Gandhi. After one of their cocktail parties, when just our family sat down to dinner, I had asked Father, "Doesn't everyone love Mahatma Gandhi? Daniel and Lawrence do. They call him 'Baba.' That means father."

Father coughed and put his fork down. He looked around the room. Daniel had finished serving and had already left. "It depends, Honey. In general, I think most people do, but there are Hindus who don't like his tolerance for Muslims. And the British don't like him much at all."

"Why?"

"One reason is because he helped send the British away from India."

"But you like him, don't you? Mother does."

Father was slow to answer. He patted his mustache. Then he said, "I think he is the beginning of a new page in history." Mother nodded and smiled at Father.

And now everyone in the kitchen was crying because someone just killed Mahatma Gandhi! As I raced out of the kitchen and down the veranda, I yelled over my shoulder to Patty, "We have to tell Mother. We have to, no matter what!" When I burst into the living room, she was gently fanning herself with her sandalwood fan. She leaned forward in her chair, smiled at me, and made tiny dismissal waves with the fan.

"Mother! I have to tell you something."

She snapped her fan shut, a signal of serious displeasure.

"I hope you remember we are not to be interrupted." She nodded to the reporter and then turned back to me. "I think we are almost done."

He looked up from his note pad at me and said,. "Yes. Just a few more questions. And I would like to see that schoolwork you mentioned."

"But Mother…"

She stood and took a step toward me making little flicks with her fan to shoo me out. "Now, now, Dear, please let us finish. I'll call you in just a few minutes." She glowered at me. Her eyes looked like blue ice when she did that. I shivered. She said over her shoulder to the reporter who was tapping his pencil on his notepad., "I am so sorry for the disturbance."

He shook his head from side to side with his mouth turned down. He said, "Children! I have two of my own. I understand. But I do have a deadline."

I began to cry in big loud gulps. I didn't care what the reporter thought. This was more important. I started again, "I have to tell you…" just as Patty ran into the room and clung to my leg, sobbing.

Mother took a loud breath and said, "Oh!" She turned to the reporter. "Excuse me! They are not being just children! They are genuinely upset." Then she turned to us. "What is it, my dears?" She put her hand gently under my chin. "Why are you crying? What is wrong?"

"Everyone is crying! Daniel is crying. And John. And Lawrence. Sonja's father. All over the compound. Everyone! Even Daniel! Can't you hear them? All over? Everywhere? Mahatma Gandhi is dead! Someone killed him!"

Her eyes popped wide open. She gasped and put her hand over her heart. She bowed her head and said, "Oh my God!" then rushed from the room, calling for Daniel. The reporter jumped up and grabbed his briefcase. He said, "Oh my God!" too and ran from the room.

Shouts and sobs were coming from Queen's Way. I ran to my gatepost. One of the guards noticed my tears. He nodded, and then offered me footholds with his cupped hands. His face was wet too. I didn't know soldiers ever cried.

The sidewalks were filling, and the wailing grew. I noticed the crowd on both sides of the highway drifting in the same direction, to my left, down the sidewalks of Queen's Way. I looked to the right. I could see no end of the lines as they passed by our gates.

I watched until I heard Daniel say, "Come down now, Missy. Dinner."

Mother told us Father was working and wouldn't be home in time to eat with us. Dinner was quiet. Daniel wore his white coat for serving as always. His face was frozen. Mother tapped the table with her fingers, picked her fan up, put it down, picked it up again and put it down again, all through dinner. Sometimes she sniffled like she was about to cry.

At bedtime Mother gently squeezed our hands and patted us often as she sat between our beds, reading to us until we fell asleep.

The next morning during breakfast when Father finally got home from work, Mother ran to him and put her arms around him the second he walked in the door. She talked into his neck, but I could still hear her. "I was frantic, Bob. I didn't see how you could get home with the roads blocked, or how Kulwant Singh could ever come for us if we needed to leave."

Father held her close. "It's alright, Betty. India did not fall apart. There is no need to worry about evacuation. Besides, Kulwant Singh knows the back ways through Delhi, and so does Daniel. We'll keep you all safe, always."

She sighed and said, "That's good news about things being stable." Then, she slowly shook her head and said softly, "But the sadness will linger forever."

For three days I watched a river of people flood down Queen's Way, completely filling the avenue from one side to the other. They were a flow of wailing, moaning, and sobbing mass of humanity surging to where Gandhi lay in state.

The first day the sidewalks on both sides of the busy thoroughfare filled. Men milled about calling to each other. Some beat their foreheads with the heels of their hands. Some howled, heads thrown back and mouths opened wide to the heavens. Some ripped at the buttons on their faded shirts. White dhotis sprinkled among darker slacks. On the second day I noticed that sari's added pattern and color to the dull slacks and faded plaid shirts. Women's voices pierced the air in with screeches and cries. The throng spread from the sidewalks past the gutters, jostling with occasional donkeys. I could see the donkeys jerk their heads and bray, but I could not tell which sounds were theirs in all the noises coming from the street. Soon the mourners overflowed into the traffic. Cars, honking in continual protest, stopped and started every few feet. Buses inched forward. Passengers exchanged shouted laments with the walking river. By the third day neither the street nor sidewalks were visible through the current of humanity.

Then, for three more days they flowed back again, a thick grey tide of heads lowered and weeping. My mother sometimes stood at the gate and watched too.

"Do I have to come down?" I asked the first time I saw her there.

"No, Honey. You may stay up there as long as you like. Watch, and remember. Remember this flood of people grieving the death of one small man. Remember how one person can change the world. Remember Mahatma Gandhi."

The Bungalow

I had to abandon my gatepost when the US State Department completed its dealings with the government of India concerning the purchase of several residences for American diplomats. We moved to the outskirts of New Delhi in early February.

My first glimpse of our new quarters was through a massive iron gate. It reminded me of our arrival at The Taj. Kulwant Singh stopped the car in front of it and we waited. Nothing happened. Kulwant Singh got out of the car and twisted the latch to open the gate. It didn't budge. He came back and said to Father, "It is locked, Sahib."

Father frowned. "No one mentioned that we needed keys to get in."

"Should I use the horn, Sahib?" Kulwant Singh stood outside beside the driver's seat, turning his head to see in all directions.

Father nodded "Yes."

Kulwant Singh got back in the car and honked the horn three times A man in a khaki uniform came running to the gate. His shirt wasn't tucked in and he was putting a turban on top of his head as he ran. Kulwant Singh got out of the car again and met the man at the gate. They talked through the bars. The man backed away bowing, and the gate opened.

"What was the hold up?" Father asked.

"Chocadoor say he is sorry. Very sorry. The government told him you coming tomorrow."

Mother squeezed Father's arm. "Oh well, this difference in the meaning of time will always be a puzzle. But we're here, the gate is open, complete with chocadoor which I assume means guard, and we are ready to start a new chapter!" We drove through the gate down a circular driveway to park in front of a wide curve of concrete steps leading up to our new home.

Patty and I raced up the bank of steps to the entrance. We gasped after blasting through the large double doors into a living room that seemed bigger and longer than our whole living space in The Taj.

"It's a palace!" Patty whispered. We held hands tightly as we explored our new home, room after room, veranda after veranda, even the kitchen where John stood, hands on hips, and scowled us out of his space..

We returned to the grand living room jumping up and down and squealing "It's a palace! It's a palace.

My mother had tears in her eyes. "Yes, it is." She turned to my father crying and laughing at the same time "Bob, it's so much more than I expected when the embassy said we were moving into a "rather nice bungalow."

Our family quarters and guest room took up one entire wing. Each bedroom had its own veranda. The dining room, kitchen, and other service areas occupied the other wing. The living room was a spacious bridge between the two wings. Our mother proclaimed it was "perfect in spite of the embassy issued furniture."

The bungalow nestled within its own compound surrounded by tall earthen walls. A day guard and a night guard were posted at its outer gate. Mango trees, banana trees, flower beds, roses, and a lush green lawn filled the half acre garden. Behind the garden, servants' quarters—a semi-circle of attached huts with a central water well—were also part of the enclosure.

Our staff grew with the move. Daniel, Lawrence, John, Kulwant Singh, Sonja and his father, and the ayah were still with us. A man called a dobie pounded our laundry on rocks in the garden. He squatted on the kitchen floor to iron our clothes on a thick pad of old blankets. A gardener and his helper, and other fleeting shadows that came and went.

Though seldom seen, the night guard became a vital part of our new staff. On nights when I couldn't sleep right away, I climbed a mango tree that grew beside my veranda. The front gate was visible from my perch. I spied on the guard and his son who came to work with his father every night. Daniel told Father the chocadoor had asked to bring his son because the boy's singing helped him stay alert all night. The boy, maybe about twelve, reminded me of Sonja. He wore baggy shorts and a too small tee shirt. In a sing song voice, he read aloud from a large worn book.

One night the chocadoor's shouts at the front gate woke me up. I climbed my tree for a serious spy mission. More voices joined his shouting. A crowd formed outside our gate. I climbed higher for a better view when a hand touched my leg. I yelped!

"Shh! Missy. You go back now." It was Daniel. I was going to argue but Father appeared in his robe.

"Deedee, go to your mother immediately!"

"It is best you go too, Sahib." Daniel's face looked pale. His eyes seemed to get larger each second.

Father pointed to the gate. "What's going on, Daniel? Can you tell what they are saying?"

"Yes Sahib. Men come to kill you. Best you go in the house now. Many guards are coming to help from next houses. Police coming."

Father took my hand and we hurried towards my parent's bedroom to join Mother and Patty who huddled together near the door. Sirens screeched louder and louder as they approached our compound. Abruptly they stopped. The noise at the gate dropped to almost inaudible conversations. Father tightened his arms around our huddle. He glanced in the direction of the garden and whispered, "Stay very quiet. It sounds like everything's already settled. But if I say 'Run!' you all go as fast as you can and hide."

Before I could even ask a question, Daniel appeared. "Everything is good now, Sahib. Best you come with me to talk to police."

"Don't go, Bob, it could be a trick." Mother did not trust the police after her time in jail.

"No, no. It's fine. We're safe now. The police probably need a statement from me." Father followed Daniel out.

Mother crossed her hands just below her neck and took deep breaths. "Girls, let's be nice and calm. Run like bunnies and get your favorite stories. I'll read to you until everyone is ready to go back to bed."

Patty and I headed towards our rooms. Patty reached her room first because it was right next to our parents. When she disappeared into her room, I hurried to slip outside and up my tree. I saw Father talking to one of the policemen. Daniel stood beside him. A group of policemen hovered over three men crouched on the ground. Another policeman held a bunch of long curved knives, Neighbors edged out of their gates to look. Chocadoors gathered in a group near the policemen.

"Deedee, where are you? Mother had noticed I hadn't returned with a book right away. I dashed back to my room and picked up the first book I could find.

Half an hour later, Father joined us. He told us what Daniel heard from the guard, the neighbors, and the police. Angry zealots mistook our compound for that of one of the judges for Gandhi's assassination trial. They planned to murder this judge along with his family, with the very long sharp knives they carried. When our chocadoor saw them sneaking toward the front gate, he called the police and yelled as loudly as he could for help. Chocadoors from nearby compounds came running and shouting, and then police cars came with sirens screaming and took the would- be assassins and their knives away.

Father gave the guard a present. It was an envelope full of money.

Before sending everyone to bed, Father led a family discussion. He pointed out we were living in a land we did not understand, and that yes, we faced unknown dangers. "But", he added, "We are so lucky to have Daniel and the rest of his staff looking out for us. They go far beyond attending to our material needs. Don't worry. We will be safe in our beautiful new home."

I did worry. *I didn't know people tried to kill judges. I was really scared when Father said we might have to run and hide. This time the police helped us. But the chocadoor helped most of all. Our new house is like a palace, but it's not home because home is the States where it's always safe. But I don't know what house that means because we don't have a house of our own I'm glad we are safe now because I really like this house and having my own room and veranda.*

Snakes

SOON AFTER OUR MOVE, MOTHER SET UP A SMALL SCHOOL of about nine English speaking children ranging from kindergarten through fifth grade. It had been a year and a half of homeschooling for me up to now, and although I was the only fifth grader, I was thrilled to be learning with other children again. Mother gathered the students around a long picnic table on our lawn and explained to us, "My dears, the British have left India for good and the English School System in New Delhi vanished with them. That is why our garden, and sometimes the dining room, will be your school now." Mother paused and smiled at the woman standing beside her. "Mrs. Neel and I will be your teachers." Mrs. Neel nodded her head to say "Hello" to the group of children assembled. I liked her smile and the way she wore her blond hair in a bun at the back of her neck. I also liked the blue and red flowered apron, almost like a pinafore, that she wore over her tan skirt and blouse.

At dinner that night Patty and I listened while our parents talked about the school and Mrs. Neel. As soon as Daniel finished serving our dinner, Father dismissed him with the one short nod that meant "Thank you, you are free until tomorrow morning, Lawrence can finish up." After Daniel left, Father raised his glass of wine towards Mother

"Well Betty, here's to your school. You are amazing! How did everything go on the first day?"

Mother put her fork down and smoothed the napkin on her lap several times before smiling at Father across the table. "Very well. I know it's going to be a lot of work on top of planning entertaining here and going out, keeping calling cards straight and making calls in the right order, showing visiting dignitaries' wives around... my 'diplomatic duties', but it'll be worth it. Ten times over. All the children showed up, despite the worry about Mrs. Neel." They both swished their glass upward and took a drink. But when Mother lowered her glass, she looked sad. She poked at her food. "It just isn't right,

Bob. The way people shun her. It's horrid. Katherine is a well-educated, well brought up English lady. Just because she married a nice Indian gentleman… She told me she knew what she was in for, but she is lonely. I want to have them to dinner."

"Of course, Darling. It's nice that you're good friends with her. Just be careful who else you put on the guest list. Some would take the company as an insult to their standing."

"Because something's wrong with her?" I asked.

Mother put her fork down again and looked at me. "No, Dear. There is absolutely nothing wrong with Katherine Neel. Something is wrong with the people who are acting ridiculous. and this conversation is closed. No repeating what we said. Promise?" She looked back and forth between me and my sister.

Patty and I crossed our hearts.

A week later, in the middle of math lessons one afternoon, William, one of the younger boys, screamed. He pointed to the edge of the lawn where the mango trees began.

"There's a cobra under the tree! See it? A cobra!" he screeched.

We all stared at the spot. Sunlight and shadows chased each other under the trees. I squinted. Maybe I saw it. Yes! That had to be a cobra right where William was pointing! One shadow stayed straight and still. Yes! A cobra with hood spread, standing up almost as tall as my sister. Everyone screamed and ran into the house. School was over for the day.

When Father got home from work a few hours later and sank onto living room couch, Patty and I spilled over him, interrupting each other as we blurted out the news.

"Guess what?"

"No, I'll tell him."

"No. I want to. Deedee, you always do."

"OK, together. One, two three."

"William saw a cobra in our garden!"

"A real big cobra. Deedee said it was a big as me. I saw it too."

Father looked at Mother. She shrugged. "It could be the children's imagination running wild, but maybe... Actually, Bob, I think I saw something that looked a lot like a cobra. And just the mere possibility is too much."

Father called for Daniel. Of course. Daniel had a solution for each problem we stumbled upon as foreigners in his India.

When Daniel entered with his usual small bow and "Yes Sahib?" Father said, "Daniel, we have a snake problem. It seems there is a cobra in the garden. I can't have cobras in the compound with children running about. What can we do? Before you answer, though, we'll have our drinks now."

This was my favorite time of the day; when my parents weren't rushing off to some country's embassy party and the four of us had a drink together before dinner. My parents called this time "The Children's Hour."

Daniel returned with a tray with two martinis and two orange squashes on it. Orange or lemon squashes were served every time we went to play with children of British diplomats. If I drank too quickly, or had more than one squash, a syrupy glob formed in the back of my throat. I longed for a good old coco cola.

"So, Daniel," my father persisted, "what do we do about the snakes?"

"Sahib." Daniel looked earnestly at my father. "Sahib, we will have to find a snake charmer to come and take them away."

Mother's eyes widened. Father's eyebrow went up.

A snake charmer! I took a deep breath and wondered if it could be true. I had only seen them with their magic flutes and dancing cobras when there was a big crowd watching with me in front of The Taj. *A snake charmer! A snake charmer at our house? All our own!*

Patty and I held hands and swung each other in circles back and forth across the living room. We came close to knocking into the coffee table that held the tray of drinks. I wouldn't have minded tipping over the orange squashes. Patty and I twirled our way away from the table, but Father frowned at us anyway. We let go hands and returned to our chairs.

Father stood. He looked at Daniel and shrugged. "How do we go about that?"

It turned out Lawrence knew where to find one, and for a price, the man would come and take our cobra away.

I didn't see the snake charmer arrive but the sound of a flute in our garden told me he had come at last. I rushed through the house towards the music.

Lawrence blocked my way. He stood in the doorway with his arms stretched to each side. My nose almost bumped into the knit vest he wore over his shirt even though India's summer was in full swing. "No, Missy, you no go."

"Mother!" I wailed across the dining room, the living room and all the way into her room. "Mother!"

Mother was at her desk writing letters When I entered, she put her pen down and turned in her chair. "My goodness, what **is** the matter? Are you alright?"

"No! Lawrence is being bossy and horrid. I hate him! He won't let me in the garden. The snake charmer is here! I want to watch the cobra come."

"Oh dear!" Mother stood up and started toward her door. Then she stopped, turned around, and went back to her desk. "Come here, Deedee Bug." I went and leaned against her knee. She put her arm around my waist and said, "Lawrence is right. Snakes are dangerous."

"But I want to watch!" I stamped my foot. The heat and disappointment mixed into a hot, sticky mess inside me. I stamped my foot two more times. "I want to see our cobra. And our snake charmer. It isn't fair!"

I pushed her arm away and headed for the dining room where I sat cross legged on the floor, next to the wide doors that opened onto our garden. I could hear the flute call from somewhere under the mango trees but no matter how hard I squinted, I could see nothing but shadows across the lawn and beneath the trees.

The kitchen was next to the dining room. Just outside the kitchen door John, Lawrence, and Daniel talked quietly. The flute song floated across our compound. Mother came into the dining room and stood behind me. She took a deep breath and said, "It is so plaintive, that sound. A sad song, luring creatures from their homes into a wicker basket." Two times the calling stopped, then continued. After about ten minutes, Mother clasped her hands and leaned down to whisper to me, "I heard the car. Your Father's home. He mustn't miss this." She left, then returned a few minutes later with Father and Patty. We listened together for another ten minutes or so.

The music stopped for the third time. Silence hung in the air.

A small dark man emerged from the trees and walked to the kitchen door where Daniel, Lawrence, and John waited. In one hand he held a flute. In the other, he held a muddy colored sack with a draw string top. It hung down almost to his feet. The bottom of the sack was rounded and moving. His faded brown shirt and baggy grey slacks blended into the evening. He did not look at all like the snake charmers I had seen performing on Queen's Way with their jewel embedded turbans and stark white dhotis. But the man held his bare head up high, like it had the fanciest of all turbans on it and looked straight at Daniel. He lifted the sack up, then lowered it and gave one sharp nod. Daniel spoke with him, then peered into the sack. Daniel motioned for the man to follow him to the dining door where we waited. The snake charmer made a small bow to us.

Daniel stepped into the room and said to Father, "He called three cobras, Sahib, "

`"Three!" Mother grabbed Father's arm.

"Let us see! Let us see!" Patty and I pleaded.

`Both parents shook their heads. "No!"

"Is that all of them, Daniel? Is he sure he got all?" Father asked.

Daniel and the snake charmer carried on an animated conversation with Daniel questioning and the charmer nodding vigorously.

"Yes, Sahib. He is sure"

"Very well, then." Father handed Daniel a stack of rupees. Daniel counted them, one by one, into the snake charmer's hand. Then, with another quick bow, the snake charmer left. Away went the sack of snakes. We were free to play in the garden once again. A new chore was added to Lawrence's list; he and the gardener were to carefully check for snakes each morning and again in the afternoon.

After dinner, Patty and I followed our parents to their room because we wanted to talk about the snakes some more before going to bed. Just like at The Taj, their room served as our private family meeting place. But unlike The Taj, the bungalow provided them with what they called a "retreat." It included a room with their bed, dresser, closet, bathroom, veranda, a sitting room complete with a couch and several upholstered armchairs, a coffee table, Mother's desk and a swivel desk chair. Fresh flowers from the garden and items from Mother's collection of "the littles" decorated most surfaces.

Our parents were in the middle of a conversation when we joined them. Mother was seated but Father was pacing. She asked him, "Do you suppose that whole thing was a set up? You know, I'm not positive I saw anything. It all could have been a case of contagious imagination."

Father answered slowly. "You mean the snakes planted? Lawrence and Daniel taking a cut?" He walked across the room and back, tapping his mustache which meant he was thinking. There was a long pause. He shook his head. "Could be, but I don't think so." He paused again, then shrugged and said, "Perhaps Lawrence?"

Mother sighed. "Is this the price we pay for being so green and so 'other?'"

"No, really, Betty, Daniel would never do a thing like that! Do you know he was nineteen when he first came to us? He had only a little experience with a British Colonel. Now he is the respected head bearer for an American Diplomat and in charge of a large staff. His future is guaranteed. He's grateful, and his loyalty is solid. I have no doubts about him."

"But maybe, if you remember the bet we had with him about there being no such thing as a two headed snake…He won that one, and suspiciously so. I swear the dormant head was sewn on." She shrugged. "But it did hiss."

Father cleared his throat and stopped pacing. "I looked it up. There are reports of two headed snake sightings."

Mother shrugged. "Who knows? India is a mysterious and unfathomable place. Especially to outsiders."

I thought about what their conversation when I climbed my mango tree that night. *Father really trusts Daniel, but I'm not sure Mother does. I wish I could have looked at our snakes. If I were bigger and had baksheesh, maybe I could have peeked in the sack without everyone bossing me around. Even Lawrence bosses me. The only person I get to boss is Patty.*

Intruders

LIZARDS CLIMBED UP AND DOWN OUR WALLS AND CEILINGS at will. All over the house. Daniel did not seem interested in my dismay the while I brushed my teeth, a lizard circled above.

"They will not hurt you, Missy, and they good to have. They eat flies."

When I complained to Mother about how much I hated sharing my room with lizards, she reminded me that "Making do with the way things are is an important part of getting along in a place that is not ours."

Stepping on a lizard's tail when it didn't move out of my path fast enough brought some satisfaction. Off it scuttled, leaving the tail behind. But still, they were everywhere.

My intolerance of lizards came to a head one Saturday when Mother called Patty and me into her room early that morning. She was sitting at her desk working on a seating chart when we entered and motioned for us to sit as she swiveled her chair around to face us. She folded her hands on her lap and leaned towards us. *Uh oh. Something important is coming.* I sat up straight and alert.

"Darlings," she began. *Oh no! When she starts that way with "Darlings" it means she is going to ask us to do something we don't like.* Mother continued, "Today we are having an important formal luncheon here for ladies only and I would like you two to attend. And I want "proper appearance and behavior" from you both. I know I will be proud of my daughters and all of the guests will admire your manners."

Nuts! Nuts! Nuts! Darn it! I have to sit with a bunch of boring grownups instead of going to the park. This is going to be a horrid day. Saturday was the day that Patty and I got to ride our bikes in the nearby park. Lawrence, whose job it was to accompany us, usually didn't spoil our fun except when he said it was time to go back. The highlight of our rides was braking in front of a group of peacocks, the pretty ones, not the dull brown ones. They danced for us, strutting in circles, waving their beautiful tails.

By noon the table was complete with starched linen tablecloth and napkins, collections of sparkling glassware at each place, several forks and spoons lined up beside plates, and elaborate table decorations of colored rice designs circling candles and flowers. An hour later, honored guests sat to the right and left of Mother. The luncheon was served in courses by both Daniel and Lawrence dressed in white serving jackets and orange cummerbunds.

Mother leaned back to whisper to me behind the two guests between us, "Deedee, sit up straight and don't play with your soup like that."

I answered in a loud voice. "I hate consommé. It tastes like rainwater and it jiggles." The guests laughed politely.

With a thin smile and slight nod, Mother said, "Try it again. It will cool you off. There is another course coming, I'm sure you will like it better." She turned back to her guests, intent on finishing her grownup conversation and maintaining the impression of a picture-perfect family coping in a foreign land.

"What is it? What's the next course?" I demanded. She faced me again. Her eyelids lowered just enough to warn me. *"Uh oh, even if I'm trapped in here and didn't get to go to the park, I'd better be careful not to go too far. But that guest of honor makes me cross when she fake smiles at me. And I'll scream if she says, "Oh My Goodness!" one more time.*

My arms prickled when they brushed against my starched dress. The big punka fan overhead only cooled my damp forehead. I looked up at it in hopes that by offering my whole face to the fanning, I would be less sticky and cross. But no! My annoyance only grew because I spotted lizards marching across the ceiling, laughing at me. I saw the grins on their smug little faces.

"Some lovely lamb and rice that John has cooked especially for today." Mother answered in her best hostess tones and then nodded to Daniel to clear away the jellied soup course, including my barely touched bowl.

Not mutton again! I hate mutton! Before Daniel could clear my consommé, I banged my fist down close to the bowl. I wanted it to jiggle right out of its bowl. Instead, the resounding thump caused one of the lizards above me to lose its footing.

Kerplop!

It landed right in my trembling soup.

The guest of honor said, "Oh my goodness!"

"That does it!" I stormed away from the table shouting over my shoulder, "I'm never going to eat another thing, ever, until all the lizards are gone."

I slammed the dining room door on my way out.

I was served dinner in my room for the next two nights. I could rejoin the family at the table when I had figured out how to behave in front of guests. I pouted through my first solitary dinner. *I already know how to behave in front of guests. I was just so hot I forgot. It isn't fair!* But by the second night of dinner alone, I realized a few things. *Even though I miss hide and seek with the kids on our block in Washington and how great it is to understand what people are saying because they speak real English. But I have my own veranda and mango tree here. Peacocks dance for me and Mother and Father take care of me and love me no matter where we are, even when I'm a brat. Living with lizards is part of living in India, and no matter how much I don't like it, it isn't going to change.*

Daniel was right, the lizards weren't that important after all.

February was hot so we slept on charpoys under the mango trees. The charpoys were not as high or as comfortable as my real bed. They were cots with a woven rope bottom instead of a mattress. Daniel explained that the sharp cornered wooden legs were made to keep snakes from climbing up and into our beds. Elaborate designs of flowers, swirls, paisley, and diamonds ran up those legs in reds, yellows, greens and oranges. I decided the painted decorations made snakes too dizzy to climb. It certainly was cooler outside and late in the night, along with my father's snoring, I could hear the chocadoor's son reading aloud in his sing song voice.

One night I heard Daniel whispering excitedly to Lawrence. In the moonlight, I could see them standing very still at the foot of my father's bed. I did not understand the few words I could make out, but I strained to hear, chilled by the crisp urgency of their whispers.

Lawrence slowly backed away from the bed and then spun around and rushed away. Daniel remained a statue, staring at my father's head.

My heart thumped. It became the only sound I could hear. Thump! Thump! Thump! Then through the loud thumping thoughts started whispering in my head. *Why are they here? Why are they whispering and sneaking around Father's bed? Where's Lawrence going? Why's Daniel staring at Father? Oh No! Are they like the men who were going to kill Father? Or kill all of us because we don't belong? Do they have those big knives? Maybe Lawrence went to get a knife.*

Why am I holding my breath? Why can't I move? I have to get up and scream and run to Father while it's only Daniel there! Father said he trusted Daniel. But if Daniel is bad after all and knows I see him, he might decide to kill Father quickly and then come for me. And Mother and Patty. How can I save everyone?

Oh no! Lawrence is back!

Lawrence had returned with the night guard. Daniel pointed at my father's head. My arms, legs, throat, voice, and heart froze into a silent scream. *The chocadoor is on their side!*

Then I realized Daniel wasn't pointing at Father's head. He pointed a few feet above. I moved my eyes upward and stared at the spot. *Nothing. Maybe… Maybe a leaf swaying there? Why are Daniel and Lawrence and the guard looking at it? Why is it important? Maybe it's not a leaf. Maybe it's a lizard hanging by its tail. Maybe it's something worse. Maybe that's where they hid a knife!*

Daniel slowly moved towards the head of the bed. He lowered himself into a squat right by my father's ear. Now I was trembling, too scared to talk, but I had to warn my father. Lawrence noticed me starting to move. He put his finger to his lips and crept toward me. I tried to scream as Lawrence clamped his hand over my mouth. He pointed above my father's head and whispered, "Snake, Missy. Bad, bad snake. No noise."

Daniel placed one hand on my father's chest. He was talking softly, but I could hear him. "Sahib. Sahib. Wake up slowly. Don't move, Sahib. Krait. Krait above you."

Father opened his eyes. Daniel looked up into the tree. Father followed his glance. "My God!" he whispered. "Daniel, for God's sake, what do I do now?"

"Sahib, move very slowly off the bed. I help you, Sahib. Very slowly over side to me."

My father inched off the charpoy. As soon as Father's feet were on the ground, Daniel jerked him away from the tree. The krait curled back up onto its branch and disappeared.

I stood up and looked at Patty asleep nearby, and then toward Mother. Her charpoy was two trees away where the ground was more even. Father motioned to me to wake Patty while he circled around to Mother.

Daniel, Lawrence, and the night guard helped us move our charpoys to the verandas skirting our bedrooms. It was too hot and sticky to sleep inside even beneath the whirring punkas hanging from the ceilings throughout the house.

The next morning as Daniel served breakfast, my father discussed with him what do about kraits in the garden. "Do we order in a snake charmer? The one you got us for the cobras worked well. Is there a specialist snake charmer for kraits? I know they're worse than cobras."

"Worse than cobras?" I asked. I couldn't believe it. "They are just tiny little things. Like my finger." I held up my index finger." How could they be worse than a big old cobra?"

"Most poisonous of all, Missy." Daniel nodded at me. "Too small to see most time. But they kill you fast. Come only at night. Garden safe in day." He smiled and snapped his chin downward to punctuate how certain he was of his facts.

Now I have to make-do with kraits as well as lizards. Can't sleep under the trees at night anymore. Check the branches above when I go near a tree even in the day, just to be sure. Really nothing could be done about kraits. This explained why Daniel had acted worried when we insisted on moving our charpoys under the mango trees two weeks ago. It turned out that he, Lawrence, and the guard had taken turns checking on our safety several times each night.

There were only two positive things that came out of the discussion about kraits. One was when Daniel mentioned off hand, "Monkeys don't like snakes. Sometimes monkeys are good. Most they are not." He showed us how monkeys grab a snake by its neck and rub its nose on a branch or in the dirt until it is dead. The other was knowing how safe we were in his hands.

I hated the idea of kraits. But I had been wanting a monkey ever since our first bike ride in the park shortly after Mother had arranged for Patty and me to inherit bikes from a family leaving for the States. My bike was medium sized, blue, with balloon tires.. Patty wobbled behind on a smaller pink bike with tires as big as mine, and Lawrence trailed us on his big black bike with skinny tires. Ten minutes into the ride, we had passed a man squatting alongside the road. He held the ends of several ropes in his hand. Each rope led to a monkey on the other end. The monkeys huddled together, picking bugs out of each other's hair. I stopped and pointed at him. "Look, Patty! I bet those monkeys are for sale! Right Lawrence? Isn't he selling monkeys?"

Lawrence scowled. "Yes. Monkeys no good. We go now." He started down the road. Patty looked back and forth from Lawrence moving away, and me standing beside my bike in front of the monkeys. She made up her mind and said, "We can't ride without Lawrence. Mother said." She started pedaling hard to catchup with Lawrence. I followed with my stomach roiling in anger and envy. It was hot. I hated my bike. I wanted a big black one with skinny tires. And I wanted a monkey. *No one lets me have anything!*

The day after the krait, the beginning of March, I whizzed along on my bike headed toward the spot where I had seen the man with monkeys. Maybe now that Daniel said monkeys killed snakes I could talk my parents into a monkey because it would protect us from cobras and kraits. My braids flapped in the currents of air by my ears as I sped down the path. With sun on my face, dust swirling around my ankles, pedaling as fast as I could, I was as free as the wind, as long as I pretended Lawrence wasn't poking along ten feet behind. I knew just where I was going.

The man in his well-worn dhoti squatted on the ground as he waited for customers. He held the end of only one rope this time. On the other end of the rope was what I had come for. A monkey, camel brown, the size of a small dog, with a cute little nose and ears. She sat on her haunches as far from the man as the rope allowed. She gathered up silt in her little monkey hand, and tossed it aside, gathered more, and let it loose in all directions. I wanted her. I had to have that monkey! I would save her and love her forever. I braked in front of the man and asked him how much for the monkey. Lawrence interrupted.

"What are you doing, Missy?"

"I'm going to buy this monkey from him," I answered pointing to the man. I didn't have any money, but I could send Lawrence back to the house to get some.

"No Missy. We must ask Sahib. Daniel will ask him." Lawrence spoke with the man. The monkey man nodded a lot but did not get up. Lawrence led the way home.

As we started for home, I came up with a new plan. "Lawrence, I'll ask Mother as soon as we get back, and then you can go get the monkey right away."

"No, Missy. Sahib must say."

That made me cross. *Why isn't Mother's word good enough?* I didn't argue because I wanted to stay on Lawrence's good side so he would convince Daniel to convince Father. Besides, I was working on another idea of how to go about this whole thing.

Lawrence talked to Daniel. Daniel agreed to talk to my father about the monkey. My plan was to beat him to it. When it was close to the time Father usually got home from work, I sat on the front steps and waited for him. As soon as Kulwant Singh opened the back door and bowed and Father got out of the car, I ran down the steps and hugged him. With my arms still around his waist and the side of my face against his chest, I began, "Guess what? I found the perfect monkey for us today. She will guard us from snakes, and I'll do all the jobs to take care of her so it won't bother Lawrence or anyone, and I will be good all year, and I love her. Please, please, please."

Father stepped back and lifted my chin. He moved his head side to side like he was trying to figure something out. He said, "Well, well. This is quite the greeting. You're full of surprises. I need to go in and freshen up for from work. And talk to your Mother to see what she thinks about this. I'll meet you in the living room for Children's Hour." He walked up the steps ahead of me, still shaking his head.

Oh, I wanted that monkey! I waited in the living room for Children's Hour to begin. When Mother and Father joined me, I hugged and patted them and piled up promises of how I would care for the monkey, how good and happy I would be, and how much I already loved her. Patty backed me up by nodding her head and interjecting things like "Yes, yes." or "Me too", and "Please, pretty please," whenever she could fit them in.

When Daniel entered with our drinks, I said, "Oh, Daniel, please tell us about monkeys and snakes again."

Daniel smiled at me, then turned to my parents. "Yes, Monkeys around, snakes go away." He acted out a monkey rubbing a snake's face in the dirt. Then let his arm go limp to represent a dead snake. "Lawrence say there is a man who has pretty good monkey. Lawrence say he can get a pretty good price for you. Monkey good for the garden." Daniel turned to leave but stopped and faced us again. He added. "Not good for the house," and looked straight at me before leaving.

When Daniel was out of the room, Mother and Father looked at each other and started laughing. Father raised his martini and moved the glass so the olive in it rolled around the bottom. He said, "I'm all for a good price."

Mother lifted her glass. "I wonder what percentage the finder's fee is?"

"Does this mean we can get the monkey?" I asked. Whatever Mother was talking about I didn't understand but it didn't matter. Only the monkey was important.

"Yes" Father answered. "But I will have Lawrence make certain we can return it if things don't work out. First, I will have someone check that it is not rabid or a health risk. And we need to set up a place to keep it. And figure out food, and…"

Patty and I held hands and did our happy twirls around the room. We were much too excited to hear the list of preparations.

Lady

LAWRENCE BROUGHT THE MONKEY HOME IN A SACK WHICH he held in one hand while his other hand clenched the rope coming out of the top of the sack. He called me outside, under the mango trees where he could introduce me to the monkey. He placed the sack on the ground with its top open and bottom side facing up and then carefully lifted it off its prisoner. The monkey cringed on all fours, shaking and making little squeaking sounds.

I loved that monkey to pieces already. I told Lawrence, "I am going to call her Lady because she is so sweet and pretty." I bent to pick her up.

Lawrence warned me, "No hold monkey, Missy, until she trained." But I scooped my new pet right up into my arms. Lawrence still held the end of her rope.

She bit me. I jumped backward, dropped her, and yelled "ouch" all at the same time. The bite left deep rosy pink teeth marks on my arm. It stung and ached at the same time. It didn't bleed although it throbbed like it wanted to. I took a deep breath and scolded myself. *Don't cry, no matter what. If I cry, I won't get to keep her. I probably just hugged her too hard and lots people have told me to move slowly around animals. The bite was my fault, I moved too fast..*

I still wanted to cuddle that monkey! I tried again. Carefully this time.

She bit again. Not as hard as the first time, but it left a print.

Lawrence pulled the rope to reel Lady in close to him. He put his hand out, palm towards me and said, "Not until she trained, Missy."

Trained? What did that mean? I asked, "Can't I train her? How do you train a monkey?"

Lawrence showed me. He grabbed Lady by the back of her neck while thrusting his other hand up to her mouth. He smacked her head and slapped her face when she bit him. He put his hand by her mouth again. She bit him again. SLAP! SMACK.

Part of me wanted to run away into the house, part of me wanted to stop him, part of me wanted to hit Lawrence, and part of me wanted to stay and see what happened. Lady wasn't crying or cringing in pain. She seemed angry and ready to bite. But Lawrence didn't seem to mind the bites because he kept putting his hand out. I watched sitting cross-legged on the ground in front of him. Over and over Lawrence repeated his training, until when he offered his hand, Lady did not bite. She cuddled. The training reminded me of the time Sonja's father slapped him over and over because they were Untouchables. I doubted if Sonja cuddled his Father after his beating.

"Now it is your turn to train, Missy, if you want to hold monkey."

"I have to hit her? I don't want to hit her!"

"Then she will not love you."

"She will love me if I hit her?"

"Yes. You must hit her, so she knows you want to be friend."

I did. Just like Lawrence. It took several days of half hour sessions, and many bites. Lawrence was always there, holding Lady's rope, and telling me what to do next. None of the bites were as bad as that first bite, and after just a few confrontations, they turned into half-hearted nips. I winced every time I smacked Lady, and only hit her hard enough for her to know I was serious about being her friend. I didn't mention the training to my parents in case that would change their mind about keeping Lady. I blamed mosquitoes when asked about the red splotches on my arm. Lawrence's way did not make sense to my American values. *Back home, in the States. everyone is kind to their pets. And pets love their people back without being slapped around. But I have heard that people "break horses." Is that the same as Lady's training? I don't like Lawrence's way, but it works. And after all, Mother and Father told me I should make do with the way things are done in India.*

Finally, Lady loved me. She sat on my shoulder with her arm around my neck. She ran the length of her tether to me when she saw me coming. She sat in my lap while I fed her bananas. She searched my hair for bugs. We were great pals.

I took her breakfast each morning. I sat beside her while she nibbled away on whatever John had allowed that morning. She used one hand to scoop the food up. She held it just below her chin, took a sniff, and then chewed it, one bite at a time. Even though she chewed with her mouth open, (one of the things I was continuously reminded never to do), I bragged about my monkey's good table manners.

We scribbled in the dirt together with small sticks. She sometimes tried to copy my doodles. She played hide and seek with me by jumping up into the tree she was tied to and hopping from branch to branch, stopping to peek through the leaves at me every so often. My favorite time with her was when she nestled on my shoulder and patted my face. I hugged her and kissed her a lot. She smelled like warm clean fur. Lawrence did a good job keeping her clean and bathed.

However, Lady attacked anyone trying to hold her unless she knew them. She bit. She scratched. She pulled hair. Daniel told all the mothers in the servants' compound that no children were ever to be near the monkey. They were not allowed in the garden anyway, but just in case he told them it was a very strict rule and they would have to leave the compound if they did not follow it.

Lady didn't bite Patty or my parents because Lawrence and I "introduced" them to her. When Lawrence was sure I was ready, I invited the three of them to come out to where we kept Lady tethered to her own mango tree. With Lawrence holding Lady's rope, just in case, I hugged her to me while moving close to Mother. I used my calmest and most soothing voice. "See Lady. See? Mother is good. Mother is good." Lady snarled and hissed, just once. I gave her a little reminder tap, then hugged and petted her while standing close to Mother. When Lady relaxed, I held onto the back of her neck and her little hands and put her on Mother's shoulder. Lawrence stood nearby, keeping the rope not quite taut, but ready. Still holding Lady's hands and neck I crooned, "Mother is good. Mother is good." One little monkey hand got away from me, and she tangled it in Mother's hair. But she didn't pull.

Mother stood very still through the introduction. She did not reach for Lady's hand but said to me, "That's fine, Dear, Lady and I have had enough time together."

Next was Patty's turn. When I put her on Patty's shoulder, the monkey chattered happily. I let go of her hands, and she started looking for bugs in Patty's hair. Patty giggled, but said after a minute, "Okay. It's Father's turn."

Father knelt on one knee so I could reach his shoulder and still hold Lady. Lawrence held the rope with both hands and spread his feet apart ready to tug her away in a flash. Lady chattered the minute she got on Father's shoulder. She leaned against his neck and rubbed her head against his cheek. When I let go of her hands, she put one arm around his neck and moved as close as she could to him. She patted his head with her other hand, chattering all the time. He laughed, lifted her off of his shoulder gently and handed her back to me. He stood and nodded. "I think she fancies me."

Mother said, "That monkey is no Lady" and they both laughed at some stupid grownup joke.

"Well, good job you two." Father said to Lawrence and me. "Now we are all friends."

Lawrence reminded them. "Sahib, Memsahib, Missy, only touch monkey when Missy or me with you. Please Sahib. Monkey scared if you not trained it."

Father answered, "I'm not exactly sure what that means, but we'll all be careful to have one of you around when we come to see the monkey. He looked at Patty and Mother. "Right, Girls?"

All went well with Lady until one day she got off her tether and ran into the servants' quarters, shrieking, grabbing food, stuffing it in her mouth and crashing dishes and baskets to the floor. She charged at small children. When mothers ran around grabbing their children, shouting at the monkey, and calling for help, Lady screeched louder.

Daniel, Lawrence, and I ran after Lady. Mother followed trying to calm everyone down. Daniel caught Lady by pulling her off one of the women's shoulders.

That evening, I slunk into the living room for Children's Hour and plopped into an armchair. With my eyes squeezed shut and all my fingers crossed, I repeated over and over to myself, *Please, please, please, let Lady stay.* Mother finished telling Father the story of Lady's attack on the servant's compound with, "I was able to calm everyone down, Bob. All the broken things are listed and will be replaced with things much better, plus I will add extra toys, clothing, food, and an envelope with rupees to each basket. They were all so frightened, it was heart wrenching. But Daniel assures me there won't be any complaints made. Thank heavens for baksheesh! Another international incident avoided!"

Father cleared his throat. He looked at me, then Mother as he said, "Well, Deedee, this is a problem. Betty, what do you think we should do about the monkey?"

Mother had been standing all through her story. Now she walked over to me and patted my arm. She said, "Lawrence has assured me he will make sure she doesn't get loose again. I think it would be good if Deedee showed all the compound children how the monkey eats and draws so they won't think of it as a monster. And then Lawrence should tell them not to be afraid, the monkey won't get loose again, but that they must **never ever** bother the monkey, that only he and Deedee can touch her, and to remember that our garden is off limits to them. Daniel told me that he and Lawrence believe one of those children untied the monkey and poked it with a stick and that is what brought all this on."

"Hmph". Father took another sip. "So, it wasn't negligence on our part?'

"Not according to Daniel and Lawrence." Mother smoothed my hair and said, "Everyone knows how careful we must be with Lady. Right, Deedee Bug? And Honey, I need your help tomorrow. There are a lot of baskets we need to pack and deliver to the compound."

"So." Father looked at me and said, "Monkey stays, and you are at your Mother's disposal as long as she needs you. No playing with the monkey until all jobs are finished. But if ever there is a next time, Lady goes."

I hugged them both with tears running down my face. *Oh no! I've inherited crying when I'm really happy, just like Mother.*

But Lady caused another problem a few weeks later when the bossy twins came to play. Jeff and John were blond and blue-eyed, a head taller and a year older than I. They lived two compounds away. Both sets of parents were thrilled that an American family with children near in age lived so close.

I was not so thrilled. The twins ganged up on me. They out-ran, out-bicycled, out-jumped, and out-organized me in every game. My role in whatever scenario they set up was the least desirable and usually meant fetching and carrying for them. It seemed they were always soldiers or pirates on an adventure and I was the nurse, or cook, or prisoner, back in the base camp. Lady kept me company, riding on my shoulder, patting my head, and chattering. Best of all, she hissed at the twins if they came too close.

One day Jeff blocked my way. He announced, "We have a new rule. No monkey allowed in camp unless it rides on our shoulders too. Give her to me."

"No, I can't. You know the rule. My mother told it to you. I'm the only one because she's trained so I can. You aren't."

"You always say that, and you're just saying it because you're selfish and want her all to yourself." Jeff reached for Lady.

I stepped back. "She's my monkey and you get away!"

John had sneaked up behind me. He grabbed my arms and pulled them behind my back and pressed on my wrist to force me to let go of Lady's rope. I stumbled backward and shouted, "No! No! She can't be loose!"

But she was. Jeff had already run across the garden with her squirming and twisting and screeching in his hands. He stopped and put her on his shoulder. From Jeff's shoulder Lady sputtered a mixture of growling and hissing.

John still held my arms. I started kicking backwards towards his legs. "You have to let me go, John. Please. She's scared. She'll bite him."

And she did. She climbed off Jeff's shoulder and onto his chest at chin level. She bit him right on the chin.

John let go of my arms and ran to his brother who had collapsed on the ground crying. Lady had her hands in Jeff's hair and was pulling it, looking for another place to bite. John reached his brother and kicked Lady. She tumbled by his foot.

I called as I ran toward her, "Here Lady. Here Lady. Come Lady. Be good Lady. Please don't bite." I called all the way to where John, with his back facing Lady, bent over Jeff. I reached out to my monkey, but she jumped onto John's hunched over back and scrunched down and bit his rear end.

The twins ran home yelping and rubbing their wounds. I stepped on the end of Lady's rope and pulled her to me, but I didn't pick her up until she stopped showing her teeth. After I hooked her back up to her tree, I rushed to tell Mother everything that happened.

All four parents met that night. I was not invited.

Mother came to my room after the meeting. She stood in the doorway and said, "Things are as good as could be expected."

What does that mean? Can Lady stay? Please, please. I held my breath.

Mother continued, "The boys confessed that you told them 'No' and that they took the monkey from you. But sadly, Honey, they will not be coming to play that often, and when they do, Lady may not be anywhere near you. Is that clear?"

I nodded yes and licked the tear of relief that had made it down my cheek.

"One more thing, Deedee. You did the right thing coming to me so quickly. It gave us a chance to figure things out before hearing from the Jacksons. We were able to keep everything friendly. Lt. Col. and Mrs. Jackson agreed that it was the twins' fault, mostly."

"It was **all** their fault!. They're mean and bossy." I jutted my chin out.

"They were very wrong to hold your arms and grab Lady, true. Also true, I suspect, is that you wanted to make them jealous of you and the monkey. Maybe that was your way of getting even. Think about it."

Mother left to get ready for dinner. I thought about what she said. Maybe Mother was right about me trying to make the twins jealous. But I wasn't sorry they got bit. I kicked the leg of my bed. *It served them right. I can see that telling the truth right away is important, but I am still mad and hate, hate the awful feeling in my stomach from John holding my arms and stopping me from doing what was right.*

Goodbye

THE TIME CAME WHEN MY FATHER'S POST IN INDIA WAS over. His new assignment was Paris.

"But we just moved here," I wailed.

Mother agreed. "What a shame we have only had five months in this perfect house. Especially after enduring all that time in The Taj, to have to leave this. But Paris, well… that really is something special."

I stamped out of her room with my loudest "Hmmph!" instead of saying what I was really thinking. *Why do we have to go to stupid Paris? It's probably just full of dumb grownups and we won't have a garden with trees for me and Lady to climb.*

Two weeks before our departure my parents sat me down for a talk. I knew it was going to be serious because we met in the formal drawing room. We used to call it the living room before Mother replaced its embassy issued furniture, which she said was stuffed with rocks and the color of mud, with pieces abandoned by the English as they left India and were now sold in the bazar as precious antiques.

Father sat in one of the pale green brocade armchairs. Mother motioned for me to sit beside her on the silky grey couch. Patty plopped down on her other side. I stared at pink roses in their silver vase on the coffee table, bracing for whatever scolding was coming. *Maybe it's more about Lady and the twins.*

Father cleared his throat. That meant "Listen very carefully." He looked at me. There was no twinkle in his eye. I squirmed. *Maybe I'll have to eat dinner alone in my room like after the lizard fell in my soup.*

Father stared at the floor, cleared his throat again, then raised his head to look directly at me. He began in a gentle voice, "You know we are leaving India soon. Lady cannot come with us."

I took a breath, but before I could let out a screech, he added, "And she will be happier here, in her own land, anyway."

My mother soothed my hair and murmured across my brow. "We will take her to the jungle. You've been there. It's not far away, and it's full of monkeys. She will be free at last. No more tethers."

I wiggled out of my mother's arms, off the couch, and jumped up and down screaming, "NO! NO! NO!"

Father 's voice changed from gentle to loud and firm. "It's final. She isn't coming with us. It's not possible. It's out of the question."

"No! No! No! I hate you. I love Lady." I ran from the room into my bedroom and slammed the door. Enormous sobs started in my toes and burned all the way up my throat and out my mouth. I collapsed on my bed.

Between heaving breaths, I heard Patty on her way to her room. She was crying, and yelling, "You're a big meanie. Lady has to come with us. She's our family." Her door slammed.

Mother came into my room and sat on the bed beside me. "I know this hurts terribly, Honey. But there is nothing we can do. India has rules about monkeys leaving India, and France has rules about monkeys coming into France."

I lifted my head and said between gulps of air, "You could give them all baksheesh. You like baksheesh now. I heard you say so. You know you could."

Patty ran into my room. Her face was puffy and red. She flung herself on the bed next to me and started to cry again. She looked up at Mother and said, "Yes! Give them baksheesh."

Mother sighed. "We can't do that, Honey. Besides, believe me, my dears, Lady will be much happier here."

She started to rub my back. Usually that calmed me down. Not this time. I pushed her hand away and kicked my legs up and down on the bed. I screamed at her, "Go away! Go away!"

Mother looked down at the tangled wailing mess Patty and I had twisted ourselves into. "I'm going to leave you two now, but I'm very close by if you need me. We love you very much. We are so sorry about this. It hurts us too."

"Ha!" I threw a pillow at the door as she closed it behind her.

Father scheduled our drive to the jungle for the next Saturday morning. This gave me three days to change his mind. Tantrums weren't working. I had a new idea which I presented at dinner two nights later. In my most reasonable and grown-up voice, I suggested, "Why don't we skip Paris and just go home to the States with Lady. We'll all be happy there, Lady too. It's where we belong, and we won't have to move ever again."

Father answered, "I have been assigned to Paris. That's where the State Department thinks I am needed, and my job is to serve our country to my best ability. That is where we are going, period."

Saturday came. Kulwant Singh drove up to the front steps. Mother, Patty, and I climbed into the backseat, and Father got in the front. Lawrence placed Lady in my lap, and then handed me the tether. We drove out of town to the jungle with Lady sitting on my lap facing me and patting the tears running down my face. Kulwant Singh knew where to find a pack of monkeys like Lady. We pulled over on a dirt shoulder.

The jungle. Not lush like in Tarzan movies. A mesh of dark and light shadows where banyan roots and gnarled limbs snaked over each other on bare patches of ground or twisted up toward the sky. Isolated clumps of banana trees swished their droopy leaves when a breeze wafted past. And yes, I could see bunches of monkeys eating and playing together not far from us. They sat on their haunches in loose circles, facing inward, grooming each other, clucking, squeaking, scolding, and barely giving us occasional glances over their shoulders.

Kulwant Singh got out of the car and opened the front door for my father and then the back door for Lady and me to join them. Patty sobbed in Mother's arms. Mother's face had shiny lines where tears were running down. They stayed in the car.

I hugged Lady and cried goodbyes to her. My father held my hand while Kulwant Singh took Lady from me and walked with her to the pack. She didn't bite him because she was looking at me, chattering over his shoulder. Kulwant Singh put Lady down near the other monkeys. He walked back to us and, with a slight bow, opened the doors. Father squeezed my hand and said, "Good brave girl." His face was still and sad. We climbed in.

"Please drive slowly so I can watch her make new friends," I begged between gulps of air. We eased away. I knelt on the seat, facing backwards, to watch out the rear window.

Mother reached across Patty who was still on her lap. She rubbed my back and murmured, "I know this hurts, Darling. You are such a good strong girl. We're proud of you." She shifted in her seat to be able to pat both Patty and me.

"Stop! Stop! Stop!" I screamed. "Lady's here!"

Lady scrambled behind the car. She caught the bumper, climbed up the trunk, and clawed the back window to reach me. I pressed my hands against the back window and wailed, "Lady, Lady, Lady!" Patty stood in the seat beside patting the window and crying along with me.

Mother said, "Oh Bob, we have to let her in. We can't do this. Stop!"

Father told Kulwant Singh to stop. When the car came to a halt, he turned to Mother.. "Betty, we must do it now. There is no more time, and no kinder way, even for the monkey, in the long run." He turned away and took a deep breath.

My mother nodded and held me tight. She murmured into my hair, "Honey, she will make friends right away. As soon as we're gone."

That didn't help. I wanted my monkey. I pounded the back window. My whole chest hurt.

After a nod from my father, Kulwant Singh pried Lady off the back of the car. We all stayed in the car while he carried her, hissing, biting, screeching, and nearly knocking his turban off. He threw her, tossed her through the air, hurled her right into the middle of a clump of monkeys, then raced back to the car, jumped in and slammed the gas pedal to the floor before even closing his door. We lurched forward to full speed, leaving a wall of swirling grey tail pipe exhaust and yellowed dust behind. I pressed against the back window and saw Lady growing smaller through the cloud of dirt. Running after our car on her hind legs, arms stretched out toward me, screaming.

When I could no longer see her even as a speck, I hunched down in the seat in the tightest ball I could make myself. *I'm never going to stop missing*

Lady. Never. I'm never going to speak to Father again. I hate the Foreign Service. I'll hide and stay with Daniel and Kulwant Singh and they'll get Lady back for me. I'm never going to stop crying. It's like a big bleeding forever scar. I hate that there has to be goodbyes. It isn't fair, and I hate it when Father says Life isn't fair.

Our impending departure loomed over our beautiful home. Without Lady, the garden seemed shadowed with emptiness. I sat with my back against her mango tree and cried for her. Sometimes I thought I heard her chatter from the branches above, but when I looked up, I knew there was no magic return.

A few days before leaving for Paris, Patty playfully grabbed the turban Kulwant Singh set aside as he washed our car. She put it on her head and skipped around the dripping car with Kulwant Singh chasing her.

"No! Missy. Stop! No!"

We left our dear household and Lady behind, but thanks to Kulwant Singh's turban, Patty and I each took a full head of lice to France with us.

PART III.
PARIS
1948

Hotel de Paris

WE COULDN'T HELP BUT SCRATCH.

We had different ways of doing it. There was the whole head at once with the fingertips of both hands rubbing back and forth, and up and down, with our fingertips. This usually evolved into wild circles with fingernails digging in. There was the more refined method of selecting one particular area to scratch with forefinger and thumb. However, soon that one itchy spot became another, and another, until our little girl hands jumped about our heads like hungry chicks pecking for worms. We often gained satisfactory relief by tracking offending parasites as they crawled across our scalps and nabbing them, then pulling them right out of our hair. Holding tight to the tiny squirming creature, we noted its size, and then squished it dead.

We arrived in Paris for the last days of June. While Father, using the required American Embassy procedures, searched for more permanent housing, Hotel de Paris served as our home. According to Mother, the only thing noteworthy about our hotel was its name. "Well, I wish I could say 'quaint,' Bob, but honestly, this is a very plain hotel. I know we will make do, but really, it is…" She took a deep breath for emphasis, "Well, it is … basic. "

We occupied two adjacent rooms, the large one for our parents, the other Patty and I shared. The communal bathroom was down the hall. Each of our rooms had a narrow balcony with wrought iron railings. Because the hotel was situated on a corner, from our third story balcony we looked down on a wide avenue and a narrow side street. The side street was tightly lined with one- room shops and open produce stalls.

"We will make do," Mother said the day we moved into Hotel de Paris. She repeated it while standing with Father on the narrow balcony outside their room. Patty and I sat cross-legged on our balcony which was close enough to theirs for conversation between the balconies.

Father pointed to his right. "The Tuileries are just about four blocks away, almost straight down that street over there. A nice little walk."

Mother pointed to the side street with all its little shops, "And we can easily pick up things for breakfast, even lunch, right there."

"Making do" evolved into a daily routine. The four of us started our day with a breakfast of bread, butter, jam and fruit. "Very French" according to Mother. We ate in our parents' room around a table so small our elbows bumped. After breakfast we spent several hours with Mother doing "school time" which consisted of the home-schooling program our parents had mailed to us from the States. Mother explained, "As soon as we are settled in a real home here we will find a French school for you. Meanwhile, this will fill in the gaps, so you won't fall behind."

Next our routine turned to getting "presentable" for our walk to the Tuileries, four blocks away. We represented our country here too. Appearance was important. Once in the park we were free to run up and down the wide paths. After the first week of Tuileries-exploring, our mother bought us little boats to sail in the pond like all the French children seemed so delighted to do. We sat politely and smiled as our tiny crafts bobbed up and down, going nowhere. We, the outsiders, didn't understand why this entertained the French children.

But we did understand why they liked the Punch and Judy shows. We were never sure when the puppets would appear. Some days we left the Tuileries disappointed. On the days we happened to be there at the right time, we laughed until our sides ached. We didn't understand a thing the characters shouted in French, but we understood they beat each other unmercifully. Sometimes with loaves of bread, sometimes with shoes, or flowers, or even sticks. When Father asked us how our day when we returned from seeing Punch and Judy, Patty said, "Guess what? French kids laugh just like us."

Laughing together with the French children let us feel less other.

Our days ended with efforts to get rid of the lice.

The fact that her children had lice appalled our mother. When we rubbed, scratched, captured, and squished in public, she whispered, "Stop that right now! Take a deep breath and think of something else." Because we had no refrigerator in our rooms, the rolls, fruit, and other food we needed meant almost daily shopping on the side street by our hotel. Mother tried distracting us from preoccupation with our itchy scalps as we trailed behind her while she shopped. "Here Deedee, hold these packages for me. Don't drop them. Careful. Use both hands. Patty, pick out three apples from this nice man's stand. You need both hands to hold them. There, that's right. You can carry them home, just like that." When we scratched anyway, she sometimes walked apart from us, looking anywhere but in our direction.

Mother spoke some French, but she did not speak it well enough to explain her current need to the man wearing a white doctor coat who stood behind the counter in the apothecary shop. Struggling to say she wanted something to treat two heads of lice was not only difficult for Mother but also humiliating. She lifted her chin at the end of each labored sentence. I think she was trying to restore her dignity with each lift. When her limited vocabulary regarding insects in the hair failed her, she sketched a single louse on a scrap of paper. The man behind the counter shrugged and called the other shop attendant over to decipher the "femme americaine." Patty and I leaned against her sides as she added a head of hair to her drawing.

I wanted to help. I said, "Mother, I could take one out and show him for real,"

"Hush!" Her fingers twitched like she wanted to pinch me. I scratched all the way across the top of my head using the forefinger and thumb method.

"Ah!" said both men as they watched me. The first man walked to one of his cases and came back with a bottle of thick liquid." Voila!" It was the same color as the Navy pool in Singapore.

Mother thanked them in French and English and ushered us out of the shop as quickly as possible. That evening both parents poured over the directions that came with the bottle using the French-English pocket dictionary Father carried in his briefcase.

Patty and I hated the treatment. Mother took us into the bathroom down the hall and wet our hair. Then with towels around our shoulders, we returned to our room where she rubbed the "shampoo" into our hair until our scalps were saturated. We sat still for an hour mopping up drips working down our faces. We squeezed our eyes shut because obviously it if killed lice it couldn't be good for eyes. We took turns asking, "Is the hour up yet? At some point during the wait I usually managed to remind my sister, "It's all your fault for putting on Kulwant Singh's turban and giving them to me." Sometimes she pretended not to hear, sometimes she cried, and Mother reminded me that we both had them now and that was the point.

The lice did not seem to mind the procedure as much we did. The bottle lasted for three days of treatment. By the third day our heads barely itched. Then, ten days later we were back to serious scratching. This meant another embarrassing stop at the apothecary and starting all over again.

One Family Sunday Outing day, Mother pleaded particularly hard. "I love you dearly. And I am doing everything I can to get rid of the lice. I know they itch. But today we are visiting Notre Dame. Please, my loves, please don't scratch while we are in the church."

Mother held each of us by the hand as we entered the cathedral. "I want you close beside me to share this. It will be our memory forever," she whispered. She stood between us smiling up at the sunlight flowing through stained-glass windows. Father followed close behind and he stared up at the windows too. Mother sighed and said, "Look, Girls. How beautiful! I think this is how God's voice would sound if we could hear it."

Father smiled at us. And winked. "Remember, your mother is a poet," he whispered.. I worked my hand out of Mother's loose grasp so carefully I didn't think she noticed. Patty watched me for a second and then did the same. No matter how much we didn't want to, we had to scratch. Even in Notre Dame.

Mother turned from the windows to watch us scratching. She shook her head slowly and sighed. Her eyes looked like tears were hiding in the back of them.

"Betty! Where are you going?" my father asked when she abruptly turned to leave the church.

"Away," she said. She walked toward the entrance without looking back.

Patty grabbed Father's hand. "Is Mother mad at us?" she asked.

He shook his head to say "no." He led us aside from the crowd of tourists and said softly, "She's taking a break. Waiting for a place to live, keeping you two happy and healthy in two hotel rooms, home schooling, battling lice, attending diplomatic functions...everything...It's all difficult but she'll be back."

Father ushered us around Notre Dame to see the organ and to point out where the hunchback lived. Once I thought I glimpsed Mother walking in a group on the other side of the church, but I wasn't sure. I had all my fingers crossed. Fifteen minutes seemed like forever. Strangers' whispers echoing across the pews emphasized the vastness of the cathedral. *I wish we were in our garden and playing with Lady and not in this big old church. It's so big* Mother *might be lost. Maybe she's looking for us but can't find us. If she doesn't come back soon, maybe I should shout where we are so she can find us. What if she doesn't love us anymore because we have lice?*

Suddenly, there she was, right in front of us, holding her hands out in front of her, one for Patty, and one for me. I knew then that she would love us forever.

Detectives

AFTER OUR WALK IN THE TUILERIES, A SHORT NAP TIME WAS next on the schedule. As soon as Mother fell asleep, Patty and I spent our nap crouched on our balcony. That was when we discovered that the small side street running past our hotel was a secret assignment location for detectives.

My sister had a better eye for detail than I. She was the first to notice the same undercover agents interrogating suspects. "There's a detective," she said, pointing towards the street. "That one always wears the same hat. See her?"

"Where? I don't see a hat on anybody."

"Right there. Look! She's questioning the man with a cane. Right by the apple store. See?" Patty pointed again.

"Oh yes. She does have a little hat on. But now she's leaving."

"She'll be back," Patty assured me. "There's another one. With yellow hair. I saw her hair yesterday. Now she's following Scottie. They must be on the same case. Like Nancy Drew."

"Scottie?" I asked.

Patty nodded. "I named the hat one Scottie because her hat is plaid like the Scottish skirts Mother got us."

"Oh. Then let's name the yellow hair Blondie."

Patty agreed.

Within a week we had named five detectives: Scottie, Blondie, Black Hair, Bootsy, and Ruffles. They questioned suspects up and down the side street. Sometimes some of them were absent for a time, but they always came back to the crime scene. Patty and I figured there must have been a lot of robberies in the little fruit and vegetable stands up and down that street. There was a doorway a block down from the markets that we decided was police headquarters because the detectives often took suspects in there. We couldn't tell from our perch if they handcuffed anyone no matter how hard we squinted.

Our discovery was exciting because shopping on that street was part of the late afternoon after nap time. Mother led the way armed with three shopping bags, and a schedule that included returning to the hotel in time to greet Father when he arrived after work. Then we would once more get presentable for going out to dinner, usually to a nearby restaurant called Les Caveaux.

Following Mother in and out of the same small shops daily became an adventure because my sister and I were on a mission to break the detective team's code. We knew they had a secret signal to contact each other. From our balcony we had noticed Scottie stopping short during her patrol, then turning into a shop to join Blondie briefly. This happened several times with different detectives. We knew they were signaling each other to discuss an important clue. When we walked on the street, we never heard them call to each other. Yet right in front of us, one of the team would suddenly turn and join another.

My sister had the eye for detail, but I had the good ear. Careful listening uncovered the signal. One of the detectives would click, like a rider does to urge a horse to trot. "Tzlicccck, tzliccck." The clicking summoned the nearest teammate.

It wasn't long before we mastered the signal. We hid behind groups of customers or a fruit stand and clicked. If a passing detective heard the click, she stopped, searched for her associate's face, looked puzzled, and then moved on. Our sudden disappearances disconcerted our mother.

"Girls, don't knock the pile of apples over. Try not to touch everything you pass."

"But everyone else touches everything," I reminded her.

"I know. I know. But they are buyers."

"So are we. You buy things here all the time." I could hear the whine in my voice.

She sighed. My mother, the great sigher. She sighed when she was tired, when she was upset, when she was pleased, when she thought of something but didn't want to say it out loud, when the three of us cuddled up while she read to us, and when she was happy and content. I understood most of her sighs. This sigh meant she gave up the argument.

We ran our fingers over apples, celery, oranges, lettuce, whatever was just sitting out in the open for the entire world to touch. We didn't touch the chickens hanging from their heels. Their heads and beaks met us at eye level. We often stood in front of them and stared into their little unblinking eyes while scratching our lice.

I thought it scary and strange seeing dead chickens hanging upside down. Stores back home never hung up dead chickens. I supposed it was another one of those "different culture things" I couldn't do anything about. I secretly wondered if their dead eyes saw through my hair right to the lice. I knew the French people passing me on the street did. They turned their heads and looked at me, with half smiles, as they passed. Perhaps I was as out of place to them as the dead chickens were to me.

One day Ruffles caught us. She came into the market where our mother was buying fruit. Patty and I dropped some oranges on the floor and while pretending to be busy picking them up, we clicked. Ruffles looked everywhere for her signaling teammate including behind the row of fruit stands where we were scrunched down as small as we could make ourselves. She stood over us, hands on hips, glaring down. The ruffles on the front of her blouse were stretched across her chest. I could see a lot of her skin puffing out, moving up and down with her breath. I was surprised because up close her face wasn't as pretty as her blouse with its rows of pink and white ruffles. I wondered why she painted red slashes across her cheeks. She didn't blink. I looked away first. I figured she was a strong police-trained fighter. She leaned down and said something to us in a sharp whisper voice. It probably was a warning not to interfere with important police business.

Patty and I refrained from clicking for at least a week.

We kept our discovery a secret from our parents until the night they decided a family walk after dinner would be a lovely way to end the evening. Although we had been in the hotel for two months, this was the first time we visited the crime scene at night. Our mother and father strolled ahead, arm in arm. Patty and I lagged behind, looking for an opportunity to test our clicking skills in the dark. Patty nudged me and silently pointed to Scottie patrolling just ahead of our parents. I took a deep breath for volume. I let it out with my loudest "Tzliccck, Tzlicck. "

Scottie whirled around. Our parents had to draw up quickly because she was right in front of them. Face to face. She grabbed my father's arm and spoke to him rapidly in French. His face turned red. He shook his head from side to side stammering, "I don't speak French. No Francaise."

That surprised my sister and me because we knew he read French newspapers every day and spoke it well enough to get us wherever we were going. Our mother surprised us even more. She never ever caused a scene in public until now. She snapped at Scottie. "Go away! Get out of here! Allez vous!"

People passing by slowed down. Scottie kept speaking only to Father. A small crowd began to gather. Scottie's voice became sharp and loud. She gestured to the crowd. Some of them snickered.

Mother yanked Father's arm. They turned together. Father cleared his throat.

"Come girls. We are going back to the hotel. Quickly now."

We protested together. "But what did Scottie ask you? What is she investigating? We have been trying to figure what case they are working on for weeks. Tell us. Please. Please."

Our mother answered through her teeth. I had never seen her talk with her mouth hardly opening at all before. She almost hissed. "We'll discuss this later. On with you. Lead the way. Go. Now!"

Back in their room, Father paced back and forth in front of the bed. Mother stood by the little table. She started rearranging the fruit bowl on the table, but sometimes poked the pears instead of gently moving them to another position. She talked louder than usual. "The nerve! The very nerve! I was beside you. Arm and arm! A horde of locust. Really! That's what they are. Dirty, filthy pros…"

Father interrupted her. "Betty, careful. The children." He stopped to face us where we sat up straight on their bed, with our legs hanging still over the side and our hands folded in our laps. I didn't want to interrupt this conversation because we might learn more about the detectives from it. I gestured "shh" to Patty. She nodded.

Father asked, "Girls, what did you mean by 'case?' Who is Scottie?"

Patty and I spurted out our story. "We know about the secret investigations…" I began.

"We've been watching. All the time," Patty added.

"From the balcony," I explained. "Detectives. We even learned…"

"Their secret code," Patty finished for me.

Father held up a hand like a stop sign. "Whoa. One at a time. From the beginning."

We told our story, tumbling over each other's words. Both parents stared at us, listening without a word. Father coughed once or twice, and raised his eyebrow, the way he did when something interested him. Mother stopped fiddling with the fruit and leaned against the breakfast table. Her mouth seemed to stay open in a little round shape, and she patted her heart several times. We finished by telling them the names of the detectives. Then they looked at each other and burst out laughing. Mother laughed so hard she had to sit down in one of the chairs at the table, holding her sides.

Father blurted out "Oh to be eleven and seven again!" Then he said, "No more tracking the detectives, or making signals. Promise you won't interfere with their work ever again."

When we were alone at bedtime, I whispered to Patty, "They didn't say we couldn't still watch them."

I guess Father thinks we need to be careful not to get in trouble with the detectives, I wonder if he forgot the balcony watching on purpose so we could still have something to do cooped up in the hotel.

A package arrived from Aunt Doreen that added a new activity to our bedtime ritual of war on lice. Although Patty and I hoped for something more exciting, it contained four fine-tooth combs and a long letter to Mother with a note for Patty and me. Mother read our part of the letter out loud; "My poor little dears. What a fight you are going through! These combs will help you win. The shampoo may kill all the grownup lice, but they lay eggs called nits that are little white specks stuck on a strand of your hair, and very hard to see in a head of long hair like yours. Maybe you should think of shorter hairdos, my dears. When nits hatch, they turn into grownups who make more babies nits to hide in your hair. So have your mother and father help you use these combs every night to get rid of the nits. It takes about ten days for them to hatch. Work hard for those ten days on combing, and I think you will win the battle."

Mother and Father patiently combed our long hair with the fine-tooth combs just before we hopped into bed. Any bugs riding the comb out of our hair were dipped in a bowl of alcohol and soon layered the bottom of the bowl in shiny black.

We had special shampoo washings as often as our mother thought was safe for our scalps. Sometimes the lice were gone for over a week, but then they crept back again.

Mother tried to cheer us up. "It's because we haven't found all the nits yet, and they hatch. We'll get them. Don't worry, my little Lambie Ducks." Lambie Ducks meant she loved us to pieces. But sometimes she looked around the hotel room, with her mouth in a sad bend. One evening I heard her say, "You know, Bob, I don't know how it could be more difficult. I miss India terribly. I don't know how much longer we can do this."

I agreed. The twin beds in our room filled up the space so much that I could step from the top of one to the other. In our parent's room, we could run all the way around three sides of their bed without touching the walls. Running around the table without knocking any chairs over became our greatest challenge. We tried out the running feats and tag possibilities only when one of the hotel maids baby-sat us on evenings our parents had to attend diplomatic things.

Mother fussed the whole time she dressed for a party because the bathroom was down the hall and she had to walk back and forth in various stages of hairdo and make up.

Our suitcases were stuffed under our beds. We bundled our laundry up for the hotel to do, but if it wasn't back in time, we hauled a suitcase out from under the bed and found something else to wear. Our dresser was small so most of our belongings were crammed in the suitcases under our beds.

Sometimes when I went into our room, I wanted to kick and scream I was so tired of it.

Here there was no Kulwant Singh to take us places. We had to walk everywhere. Sometimes we took the bus. Father took the bus to work. On Sundays we took busses or trains to visit important places like Versailles. I missed Lawrence hanging around behind me so I could explore places almost on my own. Here we couldn't go anywhere without Mother, which must have worn her out because it meant she couldn't go anywhere without us.

The Taj didn't seem so bad anymore. I missed our bungalow and garden. I missed my monkey. I missed Daniel and Kulwant Singh. I wondered where home was. *Maybe India is home. No, the States is because they speak the same language we do and there's neighborhoods full of friends we can play with. I wish we were home somewhere.*

Patty and I still squatted out on the narrow balcony during nap time. We watched the streets, the people, the sky, and tried to peer into rooms next to, above, and below us. We had no idea of what our neighbors looked like, or how many there were. We only knew that windows opened and closed, and lights turned on and off. That was until, during our afternoon balcony time a few weeks after the evening stroll when Scottie got mad at Father, Patty elbowed me and said, "Deedee! Look! It's snowing." She was looking upward through the grated bottom of the balcony above ours.

"It can't be. It isn't that cold," I argued.

Patty pointed at our feet. "There's white stuff coming down. Look!"

She was right. I could see layers of something white spread across our balcony floor grating.

Patty picked up a handful of the white stuff and said, "It's paper! Pieces of paper. See? There's parts of pictures."

"Ha! You're right. It's torn up paper. With pictures." I scooped up a handful.

Patty handed me a scrap "Here's a face. It's smiling." It was part of a woman's face with thick straight bangs going across her forehead all the way from one ear to the other.

I shifted through the pieces my sister held. "Here's a neck and shoulders. Maybe they go together." They did.

We searched through the torn papers to match the puzzle pieces for the rest of our lady. We dove into our new mission, full steam ahead, delighted to be a busy team solving a mystery once again.

"I have it!" I shouted. "This one is the right shape. It must go at the bottom of the shoulders." When we put the papers together we were shocked. The pieced-together woman was naked! Parts that should be covered by underwear were right there, staring at us. We both gulped. After studying the picture, without looking each other in the eye, we dove back into the layer of paper on the balcony floor. We matched another few pieces.

I held the new picture up to show Patty. "I think this is a man because he has hair on his chest, like Father. This part fits right under the chest, except it looks like more hair at the bottom of his stomach with something red sticking out. What is it?" We hunched over studying the new image intently. My back began to tickle in a way that told me I was doing something I wasn't supposed to be doing and that someone was watching. I checked to the right and left. No one on those balconies. Behind me I could see through the door that our mother was still napping. There was a scraping sound above. I looked up but no one was there. The creepy feeling grew.

"I think we should show Mother." I whispered.

Patty agreed. We climbed up on her bed and tapped her face to wake her up.

When she opened her eyes, she frowned for a second, but then looked at us closely. "What is it girls? Why are you upset?"

We showed her the pictures and explained how we found them. She grabbed them from us and gasped, "Dear God." Then she rushed out to the balcony without even straightening her hair. She looked up. We were right behind her and looked up too. I could see a big pair of black shoes with trousers going up from them, and a man's face bent over the railing grinning at us. Then the shoes backed away and we heard the door above slam shut.

Mother pulled us back into our room with her and slammed the balcony door shut. She put her hands on her cheeks and said, "Oh My Dear God! She turned to face us. "No more going out on the balcony. Ever. Never. Do you understand me? Never!"

Both Patty and I started to cry

"We're sorry, Mother," Patty sobbed.

"We didn't mean to do anything wrong," I added. I was crying for a double reason. One, I had not seen my mother this upset before, more than the night Scottie talked to Father. Two, I loved going out on the balcony. And now I never could. Never.

"I'm not upset with you two. You did nothing wrong." Mother hugged us both and told us to clean up and dress for dinner.

When our father returned to the hotel after work, Mother met him in the hallway before he reached our rooms. Patty and I tried to listen to their conversation through the closed door. We heard her say, "This is the last straw," and "We swore to keep them safe," and the word "Paris" a few times. The rest of their long conversation was too soft to hear.

At dinner Father asked us questions about the pictures. Patty and I sat side by side, facing our parents across the table. The lighting in Le Caveaux was dim. Father kept his voices low so no other guests or waiters could hear our conversation although I don't why he bothered since everyone else spoke French in there anyway. I know the waiter didn't understand English or Mother's French because one night we got green beans instead of artichokes.

"Is this the first time things have been dropped on the balcony when you were there?" Father asked.

"Yes." We answered together.

"Have you ever seen the person who lives in the room above ours?"

I shook my head. "No. Well, just today when he leaned over."

Patty piped up. "Maybe. There was a man standing up there sometimes when we were watching the detectives. But I didn't see his face."

"Did he ever talk to you?" Mother held her breath waiting for us to answer Father's question..

"No. I didn't even know he was there." I turned to my sister. "Patty, you never said."

"Cause you would've said I was a fraidy cat."

Father interrupted, "Girls. Girls. No arguing, this is important. Do you know what he looks like?"

"I only saw his shoes, and some legs in them the other times." Patty's mouth was all squeezed up getting ready to start crying.

Our mother patted our hands across the table "Never mind." She said, "We will be moving soon."

Our father nodded in agreement. "Absolutely. The first chance that comes up."

Within a week we moved into a "petit palais" in Sainte Germaine En-Laye, a town just outside of Paris.

The Empty Room

WHEN WE FIRST WALKED THROUGH THE GATE TO OUR NEW home, I pictured what it was like long ago when there was a king and nobles before they got their heads chopped off. There must have been acres of garden in front where the street was now. Maybe like Versailles but smaller. In my imagination two guards wearing puffy short pants patrolled the gate. Horses clippety clopped past them pulling fancy carriages right into the courtyard where we stood. As royalty, draped in silks, stepped out of the carriages, a whole line of servants bowed to them.

The picture I conjured at age eleven in that courtyard was far removed from the reality of Paris in 1948. Instead of prancing horses and flowing silks, what passed us in the streets were proud and resolute faces above worn clothing. Mother said she could feel an enduring togetherness among the Parisians that would lead their country to recovery from the devastating humiliation of Nazi occupation.

No one greeted us that first day at the petit palais. There were no grounds or gardens, only the courtyard. The building was a three-story square U-shape, now divided into three separate living units. The center part of the U that stretched across the entire back end of the courtyard, was ours. The embassy had mentioned to Father that a French family lived in the left wing, and a Danish family was in the right wing.

Mother stood in the courtyard between Patty and me with an arm around each of us. She said, "This will do quite nicely. I don't know if the embassy ever was going to come up with a place in Paris for us. The commute will be worth it in the long run, Bob. Don't you think?"

Father didn't reply at first. He stroked his mustache. Then, shaking his head side to side, he said, "Betty, Girls, we are very lucky to have a place to live. There is a serious housing shortage in Paris now after the war. Generations of families are living together in tiny substandard apartments. Don't complain. The embassy did a miraculous job finding this for us."

"But it doesn't make sense that we can't at least talk to anybody else who lives here. Why is that a rule?" I asked.

Father shrugged his shoulders. "We aren't exactly sure. But the embassy made it very clear that was a condition of our moving here. My guess is probably the other families own their wings and insisted on no intrusions as part of the agreement when the embassy took over the middle section. They probably think Americans are loud, ill mannered, and too friendly. Let's prove that stereotype wrong."

While our father commuted by train back and forth to work, Mother had a new making do schedule in place. "So, my dears, we will be walking a little way to shop in the little markets here too. It will take time to get a staff in place." She kept a pot of left-over bits and pieces simmering on the stove night and day. "This is what the French do, and they make wonderful soup, you know," she assured us. Most of the time it tasted alright.

The best thing about this house with rules was that our third floor was a cavernous room with floor to ceiling windows and a polished wooden floor. It was completely empty except for a grand piano. Patty and I had lots of free time. We were not in school yet although soon we would be going to the French girl's school not far down the street from our new home. Mother was waiting for the lice to be completely gone before enrolling us. She would continue with our home schooling until then. We heard the girls singing and laughing at recess and looked forward to joining them. Meanwhile we played tag, marbles, jacks, and catch in a room so big the noise we made bounced off the bare walls in faint echoes. Sometimes Mother drifted through to remind us, "Girls, this is a ballroom, not a playroom. A magnificent place where grand parties were held with ladies in silk and velvet dresses dancing the minuet until dawn."

When Patty left me alone in the room, I danced and sang, and pretended I was the Goddess Diana tending fawns and other baby animals in the forest or in the jungle fighting Sheer Kahn with Mowgli. I practiced shooting my pretend bow and went on imaginary adventures with my twin, Apollo, hunting down evil Gods and monsters. I was getting used to finding things to do on my own.

Banging the piano keys with both hands as loudly as possible or running my fingers up and down the keyboard like mice chasing each other was another of my favorite pastimes in that wonderful room. The best times on the piano were when Father joined me on weekends. He played the piano well. Mother told me that once Father had a job playing the piano on a ship. He taught me how to play chopsticks with him and he soon tracked down a piano teacher for me. Monsieur came twice a week. Practicing scales and simple pieces assigned by Monsieur was a joy. My favorite piece was a funeral march. It reverberated through the great ballroom. I loved my ballroom kingdom and my time in it. There were times when I was lonely but Christmas was coming, the lice would be gone for good, and I would have a bunch of new French friends.

But the lice lingered and in November, Father got word he was transferred again. This time to Vienna. We left France late December, after only six months.

Mother sang songs and smiled all the way in the cab to the train station in Paris. "Just think, Girls, we're taking the Oriental Express from Paris to Vienna! The Oriental Express! Just like in the movies." She added, "A few of those nasty lice are still with us, but let's pretend you just got them. I want you to tell anyone who asks that you got them on the Oriental Express. That has a nice romantic ring to it."

Father scowled and cleared his throat. "Betty, there is a line between poetic license and truth."

I think Mother is tired from the lice. I think she's tired of "making do." But she sure is good at it."

Patty and I were excited about another train trip. We were happy about leaving Paris because we didn't have playmates there, and Mother promised us that the U.S Army Dependent School in Vienna was full of American children our ages. She promised I wouldn't even miss the ballroom in the palais that much.

PART IV.
VIENNA
1948

U.S. Occupational Forces

WE ARRIVED IN PARTITIONED AUSTRIA IN LATE DECEMBER 1948, and once again started our lives in the new post in a hotel. The Cottage Hotel. I could tell it was fancier than the "basic" Hotel de Paris because it had a beauty shop on its ground floor. However, I didn't get much of a chance to explore our new surroundings before my throat became so sore that each swallow came with wincing and groaning. Along with a high fever and flushed face. This time the Army Hospital was nearby, and I had no choice. I had scarlet fever.

Mother stayed with me as long as she was allowed when two orderlies met us to escort me to my room. She moaned holding me tight before they whisked me away to the children's ward. "Oh, my darling, I am so sorry. First Yellow Jaundice. Now Scarlet Fever!"

I locked my arms around Mother's waist and said, "I don't want to go! Why do I have to go with them? Why can't you come with me?"

"Honey, the Army will take good care of you. They won't let us go with you because Scarlet Fever is contagious. But Patty and I will come to your window every day and write notes and draw pictures for you. The nice doctor promised to put you near a window so you can see us."

Walking backward between my captors in order to see Mother standing where we left her, I shouted to her. "Will I throw up all the time like in The Taj? Will I have to eat that stupid no fat stuff again? Why do I have to go to the hospital? I don't want to go! I want to stay with you." The orderlies turned down into another hallway and I lost sight of her blowing kisses to me. Too tired to throw a significant tantrum, I dragged my feet and cried the rest of the way down two more hallways to my room. I hated the Army. They took me away from my family. The worst thing in the whole world was being separated from my family.

The room had two beds in it, but no one else was there. The orderlies showed me which bed was mine. There was a small table between my bed and the window. I sighed in relief. *At least the doctor kept his promise and I can see Mother and Patty outside there tomorrow.*

The Army was not only serious about Scarlet Fever but also they went to war against my lice. Two nurses came into my room. One sprinkled powder in my hair. When she stopped, the other wrapped a towel around my head. Like a turban. They both used the sink in my room to wash their hands. As they started to leave I called out, "Wait!" I stood up and touched the towel with both hands. "How long do I have to wear this towel around my head?"

"Until the lice are gone," the powder nurse answered.

"It itches!" I tried to scratch through the towel.

"Don't scratch!" The powder nurse's voice was sharp. I didn't like her.

The other nurse explained, "You don't want the DDT in your hair to get into your scalp. It will only itch for an hour or so, and then again later if the nits live through hatching. It will be on as long as any lice can possibly live."

"But you must NOT scratch!" The powder nurse scowled at me.

When I walked down the corridor to the bathroom, heads turned my way and stared. Looking in the bathroom mirror, I could see my headdress did not look as neat as Kulwant Singh's turban that started this whole thing. It was bulkier, taller, and stark white. I worked hard not to cry on those trips back and forth in that long hallway.

The doctor in charge of me also stared, sometimes at my headdress, but mostly at my feet. He asked why I taped pencils to my toes when I was in bed. I explained the fourth toe on each foot curved inward and I was using the time to straighten them with pencil splints.

He put a hand to his chin and leaned over my feet to look closely at my splints. "Well," he said, "Well, well. I haven't seen that before. You may have an invention there. I think you might grow up to be a doctor one day."

"My father says that too." I called after him on his way out of the room. He smiled and nodded. I liked the doctor even if he was part of the Army. *How come some nice people belonged to bad things?*

Besides working on straightening my toes, I practiced piano on a cardboard keyboard. My mother sent in a steady stream of art supplies, puzzles and books. My time in the empty ballroom had taught me how to enjoy time alone, but the best part of my day happened when Mother and Patty appeared outside my window. We blew kisses hello and goodbye. I showed off my drawings, completed puzzles and books read. One day, about ten days after I entered the hospital, Patty had a new haircut. It was short and curly. I liked her long hair better but I nodded at her so she would think I liked it.

When I was released after two weeks, the doctor detained my mother in a long conversation at the exit.

"Let's go!" I tugged at her hand.

She smiled at me, but it was not a real smile. "Just a minute, Dear, the doctor is telling me how to keep you well." Her face didn't look as soft and rosy as it usually did. She was standing as tall as possible and keeping her back stiff and straight.

We hailed a taxi outside the hospital. Once inside and on our way, I asked, "What did the doctor say, Mother?"

"Oh, just the usual thing about baths and regular hours. He thought maybe you would like to have a new hairdo. A cut and permanent. Maybe like Patty's new hairdo."

"No! I want my hair like it is!" I moved my head side to side, so my hair swished back and forth, way past my shoulders against the middle of my back. I liked the way it felt, like a silk cape. I liked it when Mother combed and braided it for me. *The Goddess Diana has long hair. I don't want short hair like a stupid boy.* I slapped my hand against the taxi door. "Why? Why does the doctor care how my hair is? They put that awful stuff in so it would be good again."

Mother patted my arm. She said softly, "Honey, there is a possibility that a few nits are still left. The doctor wants to be sure they are gone forever. A permanent will end this whole nightmare for good."

I was too happy to be out of the hospital to make a bigger fuss.

Mother made an appointment for me at the Cottage Hotel beauty shop. She told me about it at breakfast in the hotel dining room the next morning an hour before it began. "Look how lucky you are. A grown-up appointment in a fancy hotel beauty shop. And going to it all by yourself!"

I stabbed the roll on my plate to keep from yelling and hissed across the table, "Why can't you come with me? I don't want to go alone. It's like the hospital. I want you to come with me."

Mother reached across and held my hand. "Come, come. You're my big brave girl. You'll do fine on your own. It'll be as easy as pie. You'll see. One. Two. three, and you'll have a beautiful new hairdo."

More than anything I wanted to stay near Mother after being away for so long, but I also wanted her to be proud of me. I took a deep breath and headed for the beauty shop. Mother said it would be as easy as pie.

The beauty shop ladies didn't agree. The one that started cutting my hair called another over, and then another. I fidgeted in the chair. My feet dangled in space. I wiggled my legs to keep them from going to sleep. The women poked through my hair whispering in German. One left the room. She soon returned with an older lady who wasn't wearing a pink work coat like the others. I figured she was the boss. She picked up the telephone on the front desk and dialed.

Her voice boomed through the room. "Frau Carr, your kinder hast... (words I didn't understand). I don't think my mother did either because the boss snapped her fingers at one of the women in pink standing near me. The pink lady left the room, then returned with a dictionary.

The boss continued. "Your kinder hast, (she squinted at a word in the book)... nits... in her hair.. We do not work with lice. Verbotten! You must come. Take her away." I didn't hear what my mother said but the boss listened quietly. When she hung up, she spoke to the hairdressers in German. I recognized the words "doctor" and "U.S. Army."

I kept checking the entrance, but my mother did not come as requested. My insides felt sick. *Why doesn't she come?. They don't want me here. Like I'm Untouchable. Come on, come on, Mother, please. I'm going to close my eyes and count to twenty. Please, please be here when I open them.* But she didn't come.

I sat with tightly wound dripping stinky rollers all over my head under a large dome that blew hot air on me from the neck up. All the time my inside head was full of thinking. *I wish I could run away and hide. Maybe Mother is hiding from the ladies because she's embarrassed about me. It isn't fair! I wonder if Patty got her new hair cut here. I'll bet Mother came with her if she did.* This last line of thinking made tears in my eyes. Then it got worse. *Maybe they didn't miss me when the Army took me away. Maybe even Mother doesn't want me around. That's why she sent me here alone.* When my tears spilled over, the dryer's hot breath whisked them away.

A pink lady finally came and freed me. She led me to a chair, removed the curlers and combed my hair, and then handed me a mirror. A fiery red face stared back at me. *Oh no! Scarlet Fever again! Can't be! Maybe the dryer burned me!* Then I realized I was bright red because I was so mad I was going to explode. I wanted to kick my mother for not coming into this horrid beauty shop with me. I hated my hair. It was curly all over and so short it barely covered my ears. When I moved my head side to side, no hair swished across my back, or even my neck. There was a drawing of Christopher Robin in one of my books. My hair looked just like his.

I ran out of the beauty shop and up to our room. Mother was waiting for me outside our door. She held her arms out. I fell into them sobbing. She kissed my forehead and smoothed back my hair and then held my chin to look at my hairdo. She hugged me close again and said, "I am so sorry I couldn't go with you, Darling. I know it was embarrassing and scary. It was awful waiting up here for you, but not as hard as what you did. The doctor explained that the chemicals in the permanent solution were the only way to get rid of lice for good, but he felt the beauty shop wouldn't do it voluntarily. So, I told them the permanent was the U.S. Army's Doctor's orders. If I had gone with you, they might have argued more in person than on the phone.

She held me at arm's length to look at my hair again, then said, "I like it! And it will be so much easier to take care of. Best of all, the lice are gone for good now!"

Lice brought with them invaluable lessons: what it feels like to be considered repulsive, how the fear of abandonment and rejection can imprison you, and how sustaining it is to know you are loved unconditionally.

Three days after my return from the hospital, we moved to a house in the outskirts of Vienna. It came with a lady caretaker and a dumb waiter. Even Father did not know why the house had a caretaker that we had to pay but who did nothing but glare at us whenever we encountered her. I thought her face looked not only mean, but also slightly green. Father shrugged, "Somehow she was requisitioned along with the house, and we just have to put up with her." The dumb waiter served a purpose at least. The kitchen was on the bottom floor of the three story house. The dining room was on the third floor. Mother prepared meals downstairs, loaded them in the dumb waiter, pushed a button, and we joined her upstairs to eat. Then the process was reversed for clean-up.

Two months later, maybe because of the caretaker and inconvenient distance between the kitchen and eating area, or maybe because Patty and I were caught trying to ride the dumb waiter, or most likely because of his commute into Vienna, Father seemed pleased to announce we were moving again. Mother added, "To a much nicer house in a lovely part of Vienna."

Father smiled in agreement and added, "We are going to buy a car and get a driver so everything will be easier."

I reminded my family in my firmest voice, "I hope this time I'll have a room of my own."

A week later we were in our new house, close to the heart of Vienna.

The Villa

VIENNA IN JANUARY 1949 WAS COLD, BLEAK, AND GREY. The French sector, the British sector, the Russian sector, and the American sector. The city was "reduced to a stricken whisper" according to Mother. In our sector, the American sector, jeep loads of helmeted GIs whizzed past, and MPs directed traffic. The conquerors.

When we walked in the city, Vienna's people shuffled past us in dull clothing and sloped shoulders. As they passed us, they turned to stare at our backs with cold unfriendly eyes. Mother said once they had an empire but now staring was all they had left.

The sense of otherness fell on me harder than ever. Here I was not only different, I felt hated. My clothes were too new and my smile too bright. My country ruled our quadrant of the city, but I was an intruder. I knew that in India we were foreigners too, but I didn't feel hated there. Father explained people were too busy building a new India to be annoyed with us. But Mother said the Raj was resented, and sometimes she wondered if we got lumped in with it. In Paris, I didn't feel unwanted. The people there seemed friendly but sad. France was grieving but grateful to us for our help in freeing them from the Nazis. In Vienna, we were occupiers. The whirl of my parent's life as members of the diplomatic community in Vienna was completely different from the lives of the everyday people who wanted their country back.

Mother referred to our new house as a villa. Father never corrected her, so indeed it was a villa. It came with a history. An Austrian duke built it for his mistress who was half Jewish. The Nazis seized it when they set up headquarters in Vienna. Now it was the requisitioned property of the U.S. Army Occupational Forces. Many of the original furnishings remained with the house despite the changes of masters. Somehow Frau Vundra, the fierce little witch who lived in an apartment in the basement, accompanied the villa through each transition. Frau Vundra, like Green Face in our previous residence, was caretaker but in no way connected to us. Instead of green, I saw her complexion as lavender and dark purple. She made it clear she did not like us one little bit by turning her back to us and marching away if we chanced to pass her in the basement. Her quick disappearances were punctuated by a sharp slam of her door.

We missed Daniel, Lawrence, Kulwant Singh, and and even John. Our new cook here, though as territorial as John, seemed to me a dim and faceless figure lurking in the shadows of the kitchen which, as usual, was off limits. Of course, Patty and I explored it on Sundays, his day off.

The most exciting thing about that kitchen was the door in the wall across from its main entrance. That door was the entrance to our new driver's room. His name was Peter. At twenty-two, he stood straight and tall. He slicked his blond hair straight back. He held his handsome head high at an angle as if he were acknowledging a salute. Besides being our driver, he was head of our staff and in charge of setting up and serving at our parents' cocktail and dinner parties. When our parents weren't nearby, he snarled at us. Patty and I had quickly identified Peter as our enemy.

At first our parents were amused by Peter. My mother remarked, "My, my, Peter certainly is poster material for the Aryan race."

Within several months, they were not finding Peter amusing. Patty and I were hanging around in the little sitting alcove off their bedroom, waiting with my mother to greet Father when he came home. We sat very still on the dark blue velvet love seat that was one of Mother's special treasures. She discovered it the first day we moved in and declared, "It's Biedermeier! Biedermeier! I'm sure the Duke picked it out himself for his dear love." If we were well-behaved and quiet, we sometimes got to stay for this special time before their rounds of diplomatic functions began. We could hear the gossip of the day and discussions of the strategy for the evening ahead.

After Father arrived, Peter knocked at the door and entered without waiting for an answer. He carried a small round silver tray with two martinis. There were no drinks on the tray for my sister and me. This was not a Children's Hour time because our parents were on their way out. Mother turned her back to Peter when he came in. Father noticed and raised an eyebrow in question, then turned to Peter.

"Thank you, Peter." Father lifted the two martinis off the tray.

"Yes Sir," snapped Peter. He clicked his heels together, turned sharply, and left the room, not closing the door behind him. Father handed Mother her drink, then crossed the room and closed the door.

Mother whirled around to face him. She said in quiet even tones, like she was trying not to wake someone up, "See what I mean? I don't know how much longer I can put up with his attitude, Bob. He looks at the children and me with utter distain. He's arrogant. When he opens the car door, he's almost as proper as Kulwant Singh, but then I swear he comes as close to slamming it shut as possible. Sometimes I even suspect he's giving a Hiel Hitler salute when our backs are turned."

Neither parent sat down although each had a preferred Biedermeier chair nearby. Mother stood still with her hands clasped at her waist. Father paced back and forth a few times across the tiny space. He smoothed his mustache, then reached out for Mother's hands.

"Let's give him more time to get to know us, Betty. His English is very good and a big help to me."

"Alright. But if this keeps up, you're going to have to talk to him about his behavior. Promise me." She withdrew her hands and shivered. "And to be honest, Bob, I suspect he's a Nazi, and proud of it, and it makes me sick to think we have one of them in our house. That we are making life easy for him. If he is one of them, I don't even what to imagine what he did during the war. I certainly don't want my children near him if that's the case and..."

Father interrupted her. "Now, now Betty. Don't get carried away." He shook his head at Mother. "I know he looks the part, but he assured me he was grateful to the Americans for saving his country when I interviewed him. And, yes, of course I will talk to him about his manner." Peter seemed to try to be polite to Mother after that, but he still scowled at Patty and me. We still counted him as an enemy.

Peter's room became Patty's and my first secret target for exploration in the new house. Peter had Sunday off, just like the cook. But finding a safe window of time to sneak into his room proved difficult because now we had a car and Mother and Father continued the tradition of Family Sunday. We returned from our outings around five Sunday afternoons. At six, Mother took over the kitchen to cook a light supper. We all helped carry it into the dining room and back into the kitchen again when we finished. Patty and I were in charge of carrying the knives, forks, and napkins back and forth, but we were not to carry the requisitioned Meissen China that had remained with the house. Father and Mother stacked the dirty dishes neatly by the sink. When all was cleared, Mother posted herself at the kitchen door. She took a deep breath and gave the room one last check.

"Bob, make sure the stove is off. Deedee, check that the refrigerator door's shut. Come Patty, it's time to leave. Don't fiddle with the spoons. Peter will be back soon. We don't want him to think we've left a mess."

I guess she didn't worry about what the cook thought.

Patty and I knew there would be no sneaking through the kitchen after clean-up. Bedtime and Peter's imminent arrival were two firm obstacles. We schemed in our room at night. I had an idea. "We could do it early in the morning, before they wake up."

Patty stared at me open mouthed. Then she bounced on her bed in agreement. "O.K. Tomorrow? Can we do it tomorrow?"

"No Silly. Tomorrow's a school day. Everyone gets up early on a school day. Besides, Peter is here. Except on Sunday. It has to be on a Sunday."

Patty bounced some more. "Oh. OK. Next Sunday? Can we do it next Sunday?"

"Next Sunday for sure. First one to wake up gets the other up."

Patty had a lot of questions. "What do you think his room is like? Do you think he has a girlfriend picture? Do you think he has a gun?"

"Father would never allow a gun in our house. What makes you think Peter has a gun?"

"He acts like a soldier. Soldiers always have guns. We can look for it, can't we?"

"Sure. And I'm going to look for things he stole from the house. Like silver boxes and Father's shirts. Remember how in India when we were at The Taj and the cook helper had all those stolen things from our house in his quarters? Mother saw them when she took food there for their sick baby. Mother said it was just something we had to put up with and not to make a fuss. But I am going to make a fuss if I can find something stolen in Peter's room because he's mean, and Father will fire him."

We plotted and giggled all week. We practiced sneaking downstairs. We imagined creeping through the kitchen and opening Peter's door.

Sunday morning Patty jumped on my bed. "Wake up! It's time to find Peter's gun."

I slid out of bed. We started downstairs. One quiet step down. Carefully onto the next. So far no creaks to give us away. Two steps down. Three steps down.

Father's voice rang out. "Girls. Where are you going? You still have your pajamas on." He stood at the door of his bedroom, fully dressed, with his hands on his hips. He held several papers in one hand and a pen in the other. We had forgotten that he got up early to catch up on work before our family picnics.

"We're just going to the kitchen," I answered.

"Get dressed. We'll have a snack before we leave this morning. Your mother will need your help after breakfast packing our picnic.

Patty kicked my bed when we got back to our room. "Now I can't find Peter's gun and get him in trouble, so they'll make him leave. Now we will never get to serve Peter right."

"We will. Don't worry. This is our secret mission, and sometimes secret missions take a long time." I was determined not to give up. *I can make do and wait. I hope my seven year old sister can too.*

Under the Stage

"STOP IT," I HISSED.

Since our failed attempt at Peter's room, our shared room was now a battle ground. The configuration of the room alone was enough to cause problems. It was a 14 by 12 ft rectangle which normally would be big enough. However, one wall had a six-foot-long, four-foot-deep platform attached to it. It was two and a half feet high and centered on the wall, leaving just enough room for a door on each side. One door belonged to our closet, and the other opened into a linen closet which was about half the size of our room. The wall opposite the platform had three tall windows with radiators underneath them—a fire hazard if furniture was placed against them. The best arrangement we came up with was to butt the heads of our beds against the face of the platform. This left only a lengthwise crack separating our beds.

The comradery in planning an invasion of Peter's room was on hold the night Patty lay sideways across her bed tapping her heels in the crack between our beds. "Pat- pat- pat. Pat-pat-pat. Annoyance bubbled in the bottom of my stomach.

"I said stop!" I crammed my foot on the side of her bed and give the whole bed a shove.

She remained silent but tapped harder and faster. My annoyance turned into anger that spread up to my neck and turned it red. I shouted, "Tomorrow I'm going to make a fence out of cardboard from the moving boxes Mother saved. A fence right down the middle between our beds, and you better not dare to ever even breathe on my side."

"Hah!" Patty blew a puff of air across the gap.

"Stop it!" I screamed. "You're a brat! A horrid spoiled baby brat! And this is a horrid room. I hate it. Hate, hate, hate it!"

Mother's voice as she entered our war zone was the gentle purr she used to calm us down. "Now, now. We can hear you all over the house. And this is such a lovely room. Look how tall the windows are." She walked over to the windows and beckoned us to join her. "Look. You can even see your favorite pickle store from here." She put an arm around each of us and herded us to the opposite side of the room. She used both arms to indicate the platform. "And on this side you have something extraordinary. A little stage of your very own! I never heard of a bedroom with a stage. Goodness. Imagine that! I think this must have been a special room the Duke planned for his lady-love because she liked to sing." She guided us of one side of the stage and pointed to a door. "And this little linen room gives you extra places for your toys and books, as long as you don't mess up the linens. Now no more fighting tonight."

Patty turned to face me. She said, "Mother's right. It's much better than the stinky hotels and the Taj."

I nodded. "And the palais and Green Face's place. But it isn't as good as our bungalow."

Patty agreed.

After Mother left, I stared at the stage. *It doesn't make sense. If this is a special room the Duke built for his lady love, why does Marta have one in her room just like it?* Marta was our live-in maid. Her room was next to ours, right behind the wall with the stage. Her bed was on top of the identical platform in her room. She placed a stool with two wooden steps beside the stage so she could climb into it easily. I knew about her stage because sometimes when our parents were out and Marta baby-sat us, she invited us into her room to color or do puzzles on the floor while she lay on her bed and read. We loved Marta. She smiled almost all the time, she was eighteen, she twisted her long blond hair into a roll at her neck, and her eyes twinkled. *If I put my bed on top of the stage, like Marta's, Patty's bed wouldn't touch it. Nuts! Patty won't ever go along with that. She sings and dances up there and makes up plays we all have to watch.*

I had another idea. Move the stage! I made a plan.

First: Check the stage's size to make sure it will fit in the new place planned for it.

Second: Write all the measurements down so it doesn't have to be measured over and over.

Third: See how it is attached to the wall and figure out how to unattach it.

Step Three ended up being a big surprise. The platform was not attached to the wall! A ruler moved smoothly between the stage and the wall from one end to the other. *I can move it right now. I'll be as far away from Patty's bed as possible!*

"Patty! Patty! I have a great idea." I pointed at the platform. "We can move the stage right beside your bed. Look! Where my bed is. They'll just change places. You'll be able step on it right from your bed."

"You can't move a stage." Patty shook her head. "They're supposed to stay. So you can jump on them." She climbed on to it and jumped up and down making sure her landings were heavy.

"Hey! Stop that noise for a minute. I want to show you something. Get down. It's something strange."

She got down and moved beside me. "Okay. What?"

"This one moves. I tried it before. When I was measuring. We can pull it away. See?" I wiggled the platform back and forth.

She watched for a what seemed like a long time before she shrugged, then joined me. We tugged. The stage moved forward inch by inch. As soon as there was enough room for us to fit behind it, we sat with our backs braced against the wall and pushed with our feet until the stage was as far out in the room as our legs were long. We rose to begin pulling and pushing it toward Patty's bed.

"Look!" Patty pointed to wall behind us.

"Can't! *I'm* busy pushing. Come on, help!"

"No! Look! A fairy door! In the wall, there! Behind my stage."

I rushed to where she was kneeling. Yes! She was right. I could see a thin slit outlining an opening.

"Let's find out if it opens." I knelt beside her and reached toward the slit.

"No! Don't!" Patty pushed my hand away from the door. "Maybe we should ask first. What if the fairies don't want us? Sometimes they do bad tricks." She shuddered and whispered, "What if there's a monster or a skeleton?"

"Ha! Don't be such a fraidy cat." I pushed the door inward. It opened easily.

Pitch black nothingness poured out at us, giving no hint of what was inside.

No problem. We knew where flashlights were stored.

Marta caught us each armed with a flashlight, dashing back upstairs. Marta wasn't like Peter. She liked us. "Was machen zie?" she asked.

"Playing detective," we shouted through a tangle of giggles over our shoulders. We raced to our room, slammed the door behind us, and collapsed against it in a heap of excitement.

When we were sure she wasn't following, we crawled through the little doorway. We could stand up on the other side in a narrow passage. We flashed our lights everywhere: walls, ceiling, and floor. The passage made a sharp left turn, then continued straight ahead for about eight feet. We muffled our coughs as the stale air pressed against us. In the middle of the long straight- away, our lights showed another small door. It was the same size as ours. It had a heavy wooden latch bar across it. I guessed it opened into Martha's room. We checked the wall at the end of the passageway. It was solid. No more doors. Only an old shoe and a torn dirty blanket on the floor.

We crept back to the latched door.

We'll try that later," I whispered fingering the latch. "When Martha has a day off. You know what?"

"What?"

"I bet this door opens under her stage like ours does."

"Really?"

"I think so. She's going to visit her parents this weekend. That's only three days away. We'll check then."

"Shouldn't we tell Mother and Father?" Patty's voice sounded worried.

"Let's wait until we check where the other fairy door opens. I think the stages are in our rooms to hide the little doors."

"Why?" Patty's voice sounded more worried.

"Don't know."

Patty was still and quiet. She sniffled. Then she grabbed my hand "Maybe Peter's room has a secret tunnel too. Maybe he hides his gun in one."

"Yeah. I'll bet. Now we know what to look for." On the way out, I discovered that our hidden door had a wooden bar for locking it from the inside also. I made Patty cross her heart, spit, and step on it not to tell until we checked where the other door led. We pushed our stage back in place to hide our secret.

Saturday evening, because it was Marta's weekend off, Peter was our designated babysitter between driving our parents back and forth to a dinner party. Knowing his baby sitting consisted of his going to his room and slamming the door shut between rounds, we edged our stage out from the wall just far enough to slip under it, flashlights in hand. Patty helped me lift the wooden bar off the door in the passageway. When we crawled through it we were indeed under Marta's platform. Her stage didn't wiggle away from the wall like ours because her bed was on top of it. That meant she didn't know about the secret passage. We were the only ones in the whole world who knew!

Patty was bursting to tell Mother and Father. Once again, I made her cross her heart, spit, and step on it not to tell them until we were on our picnic the next day. We were going to a park with a Merry go Round and other rides and I didn't want to miss the fun. They might get too busy with our secret and cancel the outing if we told them sooner.

When we arrived at the park and began to unpack our lunch, I heard faint music like merry- go-round music, but before I could locate its source, Patty blurted out our secret. Her announcement stopped everything.

Father's eyebrow almost reached his hairline. "What? A tunnel in your room?"

Mother crossed her hands on her chest. "Oh Bob, do you suppose the rumors are true?"

"What rumors?" I asked.

Our parents looked at each other. Mother leaned toward me and patted my arm. "Never mind, Dear. Let's enjoy our lunch and then go home and see your tunnel."

The Villa's Secrets

OUR PARENTS INSISTED ON SEEING OUR DISCOVERY AS SOON as we got home. I was surprised by how interested they both were. Interested enough to each crawl into the passage. Patty and I led the way. We all had flashlights. I showed them the latched door, and how it opened into Marta's room.

Father explored the end of the hallway. "Betty. Take a look at this." He shined his light on the old shoe and blanket.

"Oh, No!" Mother shook her head back and forth. "I didn't think about that part of... This makes it too real. Oh. Oh."

"Makes what real. What real?" Patty squeaked.

Mother shook her head. "Bob, I have to get out of here."

We all left the passage quickly. Once back in our room, Father turned and stared at our fairy door. "Hmm. It is obviously big enough for adults to climb through. And I would guess, when it is latched from the inside, it is practically invisible.

Mother had tears in her eyes. "It breaks my heart that people had to live in such fear."

"What are you talking about?" I didn't understand their conversation at all.

"Were people afraid of monsters?" Patty asked.

"Yes Dear. The worst kind of monster. They were afraid of mean soldiers."

Patty gulped and ran to safety by throwing her arms around Mother's waist. Mother hugged her and reached for me.

"No, no, Dears. You don't have to be afraid of anything now. We are safe. Very safe. The mean soldiers are gone. That is what the war was about. That is why our army is here. They made them go away."

"Were the mean soldiers the Nazis?" I asked.

"Yes Dear. They were. And I am afraid our lovely villa has a story to tell. It seems the Duke protected his love with a secret passage where she could hide if her Jewish heritage became a problem."

"Why?" Patty asked.

Mother sighed and stared at the floor. She spoke softly, "The Nazis tried to get rid of the Jewish people because they blamed them for everything that was bad. That way they could think of themselves as everything that was good."

Patty pointed to our fairy door. "If the lady heard soldiers coming, she ran into our room and went through the door to hide?"

Father ruffled her hair. He said, "Yes Honey, we think that is the sad story this house has to tell.

I went to bed that night with a feeling that something was missing. *That can't be the whole story. I'll bet there are other places to hide because what if she was in another room, or downstairs?*

I became adept at tapping on walls to tell when there was a hollow space behind them. Patty often joined me. Within two weeks we had a new find. It was in Father's study. Three walls of this small room were wallpapered in a print of tiny blue flowers. There was no fourth wall because that side opened into their bedroom. There was a suspicious softness in the wallpaper around a shape that I felt for certain was another secret doorway. Patty agreed.

We ran to tell Mother about the new discovery. She felt along the soft path in the wallpaper. "Hmm. I see what you mean. Oh dear! This is very odd. Your father will be home soon. Don't do anything more until he sees this. But wait to tell him until he has his drink in hand. Promise."

It was hard to wait, to sit still on the blue couch while Peter delivered the evening cocktails. As soon as Peter left the room with his usual flourish, Patty and I descended on Father, pulling him toward the papered wall in his study and talking loudly over each other to explain what we found. He put his drink down on the desk. I took his hand and put it on the hidden door's edge. He felt around, up and down, across the top and bottom several times. He stood back with arms crossed, squinted his eyes almost shut, and stared at the wall.

Patty and I held hands and squeezed little messages back and forth. That was how we contained our excitement while he concentrated. Father retrieved his cocktail and sipped it, still staring silently at the wall. When he finished his drink, he nodded at us. "You girls have something here. Let's find out what it is. Betty, where's that fancy letter opener? Never knew what it was good for until now."

He had been cross at Mother for buying something so expensive and unnecessary. She smiled when she laid it in his hand. She tilted her head back and said, "There you are. It really is a lovely thing, isn't it? And so useful too." She sounded pleased with herself.

Father shrugged and began to slit the paper following the outline we all had felt. He looked back over his shoulder at Mother. "It's nice and sharp. I can say that for it."

After he had worked all the way around we could see a three quarter sized door. It opened inward. Father led the way. I followed, then Patty, who stayed so close to Mother that they kept bumping into each other. The first thing ahead of us was a flight of four steps.

We noticed this door had an inside lock also. At the top of the steps was a space about the same size as our linen closet. A window high on the opposite wall dimly lit the area. My whole family took deep gulping breaths when we saw what the room contained.

"Dear God," Father moaned.

"I don't believe it!" Mother gasped.

I clapped my hands and shouted, "It's a treasure trove!"

"Like a pirate cave!" Patty added.

Father stormed. "I had no idea.... I had better call the ... Someone... Whomever I should notify... Uh..." He cleared his throat. "I have to report this."

There were swastikas everywhere! Posters of Hitler spilled out of cardboard boxes, some the size of portrait paintings, others could fit nicely in desk frames. Two swastika flags leaned across boxes stuffed with swastika adorned leaflets. A dingy military uniform lay folded on top of one box. Three soldier helmets stood stacked next to it. A ragged cloth doll and tiny china tea set with roses painted on the cups nestled in one box, along with a jumble of toy airplanes and metal soldiers.

Best of all were the honest to goodness weapons! Three bayonets and a sword! Neatly lined up on a layer of straw in a long open box. Two bayonets, about a foot long, had metal covers. Rust showed along the sides where the black paint thinned. The third, my favorite, gleamed coverless in the light. It was about eighteen inches long. Two gold braided ropes looped from its handle. They met in a hard knob with a crest on one side and a monogram on the other. Patches of dark brownish red crusted along its edge. I picked it up and started to see if I could remove the crust by scratching it off with my fingernail, but Father snatched it away from me.

"Use your head, for Pete's sake! This is not a toy!" He examined the knife, turning it over and over. He studied the monogram and crest. He walked to Mother who stood over the weapon box. She didn't look up from staring at its contents.

"Betty, I think this belonged to an officer. An important officer." She nodded and continued scanning the weapons without a word.

"Did the important officer have this too?" I held up the sword. It didn't look like an Errol Flynn sword at all. It was round, about as wide as a nickel. It had ridges running from top to tip.

Mother took a deep breath and looked away. "For goring," she whispered.

"What's goring?" Patty asked.

"Never mind, Girls." Father pointed at the sword. "Put everything back exactly the way it was. You are not to come in this place again. Everything must be just like it was. Someone will come to inspect it after I get the report in to the right place. Wherever that is." He looked at Mother. "Army or Embassy? Which?" Mother shook her head, unsure. She took a deep breath, looked at Father, then back at the weapons in their box, but said nothing.

After we returned everything to its place, Father stood at the top of the stairs and glanced over the whole area one more time. Something caught his eye. He hurried across the room to the far side where shadows created blurry lumps. He smacked into something. "Goddammit!"

"Bob, are you alright?" Mother started after him.

"I'm okay. Stay where you are. There're steps here. Didn't see them in the shadow. Four of them up to the attic. But this is what I was after. What in heaven's name is it doing in here?" He came back to us carrying a long pole with a bright red triangular flag at its top.

Mother let out a small snort of laughter.

"Betty! None of this is funny. It's a very serious matter. This looks like a communist flag!"

"Oh Bob. I have to either wail or laugh! I hope you didn't get hurt. But honestly! Think of it. This beautiful house has put up with so much and stayed elegant. What stories it has. First the Duke, then the Nazis. Could it also have seen the Russians?"

We left the secret chamber. Mother and Father headed for the sitting alcove in their room. Patty and I followed as invisibly as possible. We wanted to hear everything they had to say about our find. Father paced back and forth, trying to figure out who to notify and our mother sat in her usual Biedermeier armchair looking into the distance, distracted by some worry of her own.

Father stopped his pacing and headed for the phone. "I'm going to call Col. Brown, the military attaché to the embassy. A reasonable fellow. I think it's a good place to start."

Mother rose and went to him. She put her hand on his arm. "Oh don't, Bob. Don't call anyone. They might take the house away from us. It has kept its secrets. We can do the same."

He brushed her hand away. "Are you suggesting that we keep this cache of Nazi propaganda a secret? Really, Betty! You aren't looking at the big picture."

Mother rolled her eyes up at him. She patted his cheek. "What is the big picture? What does it matter? This little bit of spill over? This little pile of old boxes someone left behind? What difference does it make to anyone? Bob, we can just quietly get rid of some of it. Or leave it for the next tenants to find."

Father shook his head. "I'll think about it. Your idea is tempting because I really don't want to get mixed up in some kind of a Embassy-Army big to-do over what you call a pile of forgotten leftovers. I'll give it a few days."

Then he turned to face Patty and me standing behind the loveseat, not invisible after all. "And you two are not to go in there again. Thank you for showing it to us. Now you mustn't mention it again. Forget about the whole adventure. Is that clear?"

We nodded and crossed our hearts. But our fingers were crossed during the promise. If Mother or Father noticed, they didn't mention it. So, the new rule wasn't really a rule. Whenever we got a chance afternoons after school, when our parents were busy with their day and the Marta with her work, we sneaked in the room by using the attic stairs and played with the helmets and toy soldiers and tea set. We didn't disturb the Hitler stuff and we never touched the bayonets or sword.

Our secret visits were well kept until we made a big mistake one day when, to make more room for our game and avoid continually tripping over the pole, we hung the red flag out the window. Our house stood on a corner formed by a wide avenue and a little side street. The window opened above the busy avenue. An M.P. jeep heading down the avenue passed under the window. Its occupants looked up to see the communist flag flying from an American Embassy home.

Four M.P.s marched to our front door and demanded to speak to the master of the house. He was at work. Mother faced them alone. Patty and I lurked behind in the hallway.

"Oh My! Sargent, I had no idea." Mother called us to join her on the doorstep.

"Girls, did your little playmate who came over this morning bring a flag with him?"

Patty was leaning against her on the left. I stood beside her on the right. We both turned our heads and stared at her. Neither of us had any idea of what she was talking about.

"You know, your little friend, Hanzi Prock." She turned back to the M.P.s who stood. two in front, two behind, shoulders back, heads up, arms straight at their sides, not moving. I don't think they even blinked. Mother shrugged her shoulders, spread her arms out in a "what can you do with children" gesture, and explained, "He brings the strangest toys when he comes to play."

She put one hand on Patty's shoulder, then her other hand on my shoulder. She gently pushed and turned us so that we ended up in front of her with our backs to the soldiers. I think she didn't want them to see the disbelief on our faces. Or maybe she did it to form a wall of little girls between her and the U.S. Occupational Forces. She said to us, "Girls, I know you were all playing in the attic this morning. Hanzi must have hung his flag out the window." She looked over our heads at the military formation on our doorstep. "I'll take care of it. Sorry to have bothered you."

The leader stepped forward. "Ma'am, we need to come in and inspect the premises."

"Oh, that isn't necessary. Girls, go take care Hanzi's toy right now. Thank you, Sergeants." And she closed the door.

Patty tugged Mother's skirt, "But Mother…"

Mother interrupted her with a sharp movement of finger to the lips for silence. She put her ear against the thick front door. I didn't think anyone, even Mother, could hear through it, so I knew we were in a serious situation. She finally eased the door open a crack. We all peeked. The doorstep was empty. She closed it quickly and let out a loud "Whew!".

Patty finished her sentence, "But Mother, we don't know Hanzi Prock."

"Who is Hanzi Prock?" I asked.

"He is a friend when you need one. Now go take care of that flag, quickly. Then we need to talk. Come to see me as soon as you finish."

We did. We joined her in Father's study where a new bookcase stood blocking any trace of a door to the secret room.

"You were not to be in that room at all. I know that is where you were playing because how else could that flag have been hung out the window?" She put her hand on one of the shelves and tugged lightly; the bookcase did not budge. "How did you get in there?"

I explained we could go up the regular steps leading to the attic. Once in the attic, we crossed it to a door that opened at the top of steps leading down to the hidden chamber. "Remember the steps Father tripped on? But honest, we never touch the swords. Just the helmets and toy soldiers and doll dishes."

Patty repeated, "Honest. We never do."

"You are little monkeys. I suppose even Hanzi Prock didn't know how upset the soldiers would be when he hung a Russian flag out the window."

Patty tried truth again.. "But Mother, we don't know a Han…"

"Never mind, Dears." She motioned us out of the room by flicking her wrists in shooing gestures. "I'm sure you have schoolwork to do before dinner time."

I had some things to think about. *Mother isn't following Father's truth rule with Hanzi Prock. Poets get away with stuff, I guess. Maybe I'll be a poet.*

My exploratory tapping continued. Our parents had a built in closet in their bedroom. One evening when they were out, a few weeks after the secret room discovery, I tapped its walls. Sure enough, one end, the one closest to the outside of the house, sounded hollow. I gathered Patty and flashlights and we went to work. Patty held the clothes back so I could see the end wall clearly with my flashlight. We were not surprised to find another fairy door.

In we went. It was dark and musty and about the same size as the one behind Marta's room. Our lights flashed up and down the space. A disappointment. Nothing of interest. Only a bunch of old tattered paintings in fancy curly cue frames lined up along the outside wall. Boring. Like the ones in the museums our parents dragged us through on some of our Sunday picnics. Women sitting in chairs, dressed in velvet and satin gowns full of ruffles and lace. Men wearing long coats looking cross and important. The only painting I liked at all had a lady with two children and a puppy seated on the floor by her chair.

We wanted to tell Mother and Father about the discovery that night, even though it wasn't very exciting, but Marta made us go to bed when it got close to eleven. We had to wait until Children's Hour the next evening, when as soon as Peter left our drinks, I blurted out, "Guess what? We found another secret passage!"

Patty pointed at their closet. "Right in there." Patty got up and went to Mother and took her hand, tugging her toward the closet. "Don't you want to see? We found pictures like in the museum."

"Yeah, and they're just as boring," I added.

Father laughed. He said, "It would be hard to top your other discoveries." He threw his head back and finished off his cocktail, then went to his desk and fished out two flashlights. Patty and I had our two with us. "Okay. Lead on McDuff. Let's see what's so uninteresting."

Our parents followed us through the fairy door and into the passage.

"See!" I flashed my light down the row of portraits. "Nothing but this old stuff."

Mother took a deep breath. "Look, Bob!" She pointed to the first portrait. Then the next. They both shined their lights on the third, then the fourth. They walked without a word down the whole line, shining their lights into each painting. They were so slow examining the paintings that I wanted to stamp my foot and shout "Hurry up!" Instead I walked to the portrait of the lady with children and puppy and said, "I like this one best, but it's torn too."

Mother and Father looked at each other. Father started to speak, but Mother put her hand on his arm to stop him. She said softly, "Let me tell them." She put her arm around me and pulled my head away from looking at the picture to nestle against her chest. "Oh Honey. The pictures are not torn. They have been stabbed. Each one has been stabbed through the heart."

"Stabbed? Like with a sword, stabbed?" I asked. Both parents nodded yes. "On purpose?" They nodded again. I peeked at my favorite painting. *Yes! She's right.* What I thought were just old tears were holes speared through the lady's heart, through the children's hearts, and even the puppy had a wound ripped through its heart. I burrowed into Mother's warmth. Patty joined our huddle whimpering.

Father swept his light up and down the line again. "Who did this? Who in God's name would do this?"

Mother patted our backs. "Let's leave this awful secret forever."

Once we were back in their bedroom, Father resumed pacing. He tugged on his chin all the while. Back and forth, tug, tug. He muttered, "So deliberate. So precise."

"So filled with hate," added Mother. She shook her head slowly side to side, sighed, and then looked up at Father. She said, "Oh Bob, they're probably portraits of people who lived here. People who lived in this house and loved it as much as we do." She slumped in her favorite chair. She looked pale against its dark blue velvet cushions.

Father stopped pacing and looked at her. "I wonder, were the paintings stored there, discovered, then methodically stabbed, or were they hanging on the walls, slashed first, then stored. The Nazis? Or someone after them?"

"You certainly are not suggesting our boys did this!" Mother's cheeks turned red. Her voice sounded gravelly. She bolted out of her chair to stand straight and stiff.

"War is a fearsome and unpredictable thing, Betty. Soldiers can become filled with uncontrollable hate for the enemy. I think maybe they have to be, to fight in wars like this."

"Not our boys. No! If anyone besides the Nazis, who are certainly responsible for this, then… remember the red flag …"

"We don't know for sure that flag is Russian, Betty. Or that Russians were in this part of Vienna."

Their voices grew loud and strained. An uncomfortable feeling crept up my legs and through my back, like a swarm of tiny spiders crawling over me. I had to make everything safe again. I said, "You could ask Frau Vundra. She's lived in the house forever. She knows everything."

They stopped talking. Father raised an eyebrow in surprise. Mother took a long deep breath and said in the soft purr she used to stop Patty and me from fighting, "That's a good idea, Honey. I'll ask Marta to talk to her tomorrow."

"I agree." Father clapped me on the back "Good thinking, Detective Deedlebug."

Frau Vundra, the witch in the basement. A crabby gnarled woman who came with the house. When my father asked why we inherited her, the quartermaster sergeant barked she had been with the house ever since it was built. And we were to keep her on but not to expect any services from her. We were also to pay her caretaker's wages. Army orders.

Once I knocked on her door. She creaked it open only wide enough to stick her head out. She turned her head so only a part of one side of her face loomed in the space. Several children clumped behind her, whispering. I assumed they were her grandchildren. Or maybe children she stole and used for slave labor. Whether they were there for good or bad reasons, I just wanted to see what it looked like inside and play with the children, but all was dark and forbidden beyond her door.

When friends came to visit, we played in the long wide basement hallway. A rickety Ping-Pong table rated it far above the velvet and satin living room for entertaining playmates. If we entered the area on tiptoe, we occasionally caught the old woman puttering about. When this happened, she stared at us through slatted eyes. She held the stare long enough for a pall to settle over our games. Her mouth never moved from its downturned disapproval. She ended her stares with a sharp turn towards her rooms and slammed her door shut so hard it echoed.

Marta told Mother that Frau Vundra said the Russians came through the house and slashed the pictures and stole the silver ware. When Mother told Father, he said, "Humph, that's what she thinks we wanted to hear. Just like all the Austrian ex-military I meet say they fought on the Russian Front. We'll never know for sure."

But Mother, Patty, and I squeezed each other's hands and whispered, "It was the Russians."

Already the Cold War had begun, Patty and I knew the Russian sector of Vienna was a bad and forbidden place. Father explained that the Blockade of Berlin had been a foreboding shadow over the future of Austria. Keeping it from being gobbled by Russia, or blockaded was important to our government and Father, PHD in economics, was involved, but I didn't know the details of his job. Like all diplomats, he kept his work to himself. We only knew he worried a lot and worked long hours and was tired when he got home.

The Drivers

SOON AFTER DISCOVERING THE HIDDEN PAINTINGS, PATTY and I accepted that the upstairs was all tapped out. We turned our attention downstairs. We had not forgotten our original quest, Peter's room. I saw an opportunity to explore it one rainy Sunday afternoon. We were on a family outing to another museum filled with chairs covered in petit point, intricately carved tables, and walls heavy with gilded framed faces. Impatience and boredom rolled through me. *If only we were home, we could try Peter's room again.* I began plotting possible ways to make that happen. I settled on becoming annoying in little ways long enough to get on everyone's nerves until they'd be glad to leave.

First I sneaked up behind Father and tapped him gently on the shoulder, then darted to his other side so he wouldn't know who did it. But he did.

"Deedee, behave yourself!"

Next I tried the same trick on my mother. She didn't flinch but reached her arm out to the side I had switched to and hiked me up against her. Imprisoned by her soft but steady grip, we walked together, stopping along the way to admire three more of those portraits that stared down at us with unblinking eyes.

When freed from her, it was time to concentrate on Patty. If I could upset her to a whine, maybe our parents would take pity on her and we could go home. I crept up behind my sister and blew on her neck.

"Stop it!" she hissed.

I faded back and drifted innocently beside Father. Patty glared at me and took Mother's hand.

Good beginning. Now it was time for the next move: standing as close behind Patty as possible without touching her and taking steps when she did so that my legs shadowed hers. She jabbed her elbows back to get rid of me.

"Ouch! Patty just hit me."

Mother put the back of her hand against her forehead. "Girls! This fussing must stop! Bob, I have a headache. Let's go home and take a nap."

Father grinned. He put his arm around Mother and pulled her close. "Great idea."

Back at home, Patty was furious with me when we were sent to our room for quiet time too. She shouted, "You got everyone mad, and blamed it on me! I'm not going to talk to you or do anything you say for a whole week."

I put my finger to my lips. "Shh! This is our chance to get into Peter's room. That's why I did it. It's part of our plan. While they're asleep, we can explore Peter's room. At last!"

Our parent's bedroom door was closed. We crept past it, down the stairs just like we practiced, and across the kitchen to Peter's door. It was not locked. It took nine months, but at last, we were in! His bed looked like a military cot, all corners sharp and a pillow laid squarely in the middle. Nothing stashed under the bed. Books lined a small shelf. Clothes hung from a row of wall hooks. No closet to investigate. No picture of a girlfriend. The only interesting thing about his room was a loft above his bed. A thick wooden ladder leaned against it.

In the loft, we found a jumble of newspapers, boxes of clothes, and several piles of magazines. Patty began rifling through the boxes. She looked up at me to say, "I know he has a gun. I'm going to find it." She continued searching the boxes while I moved the magazines to tap the wall they blocked. The cover of the top magazine stopped me. A naked woman sat open- legged on a foot stool. I picked it up and stared. It felt icky and ugly in my hands. I didn't want it to touch me. I threw it. It landed with a different page open on the floor by Peter's bed. The new page showed two naked women kneeling beside a man wearing only army boots.

"Patty, he has horrid pictures too, like the man in Paris. Let's get out of here!" Patty looked where I was pointing and without a word, she scrambled down the ladder and out of the room. I picked the magazine up, climbed the ladder to return it and be sure the boxes were like we found them, then followed her, slamming Peter's door behind me. We ran upstairs and sat cross-legged in front of our parent's bedroom door, waiting for them to wake from their nap so we could tell them what a terrible man Peter was, and watch them make him go away for good.

They jointly scolded us. According to Father, we had "crossed the line." According to Mother "Investigating our part of the house was one thing, but invading others' privacy is completely different." Our sentence: Grounded for two weeks in our room, with each other, to "think about things." No playing with friends after school. No ballet classes. No piano lessons. No family picnics. And most dire of all, no sessions at Sgt. Buckley's Riding School.

The next evening, Patty and I were not allowed to join our parents during their cocktail time. After Peter entered with their drinks, we pressed our ears against the closed door eager to hear the words, "You're fired!" but heard only murmuring voices. Father's mostly, reasonable and calm. Now and then Mother joined in, a little more hurried and urgent, but also too well modulated for us to have any idea of what she said.

Then Peter started talking. We could hear him through the door. He got louder and louder. We heard him say "You Americans! You! You make me your servant. I drive you here, there. I serve your parties, your drinks. Whenever you say, I do. You! But the Nazis send me to school. To be a doctor. A doctor! Not a servant for Americans!" We heard him coming toward the door and moved back from it just in time. Peter flung the door open, then turned to face my parents. He raised an arm in the Nazi salute. "Heil Hitler." He clicked his heels together, turned sharply and marched down to his room.

We heard a door slam in the kitchen. Father joined us at the top of the stairs. He explained, "Peter will be gone by tomorrow. It will be difficult until we find a new driver. Your schedule will be affected. You are grounded regardless."

Missing Tuesdays after school and Saturday mornings with Sergeant Buckley and his horses hurt us both to the very bone. He ruled the U.S. Army stables filled with magnificent horses requisitioned from the Nazi's and Austrian nobility before them. Spoils of war. The stables nestled against the Vienna Woods in a little town on the outskirts of the city. Because the reservation list for horses to ride was clogged with adult requests, Sergeant Buckley organized a riding school to give kids a chance to ride too.

Sgt. Buckley had a lot of rules. They matched his crisply pressed jodhpurs and jacket with medals glinting on a proud jutted chest, shiny riding boots, and gleaming leather crop rhythmically tapping against his leg demanding respect and homage. He was, after all, the last Master Sergeant of the U. S. Army Cavalry. We worshipped all five feet two inches of him.

We learned feeding, grooming, caring for tack, saddling, and riding English style. Even jumping. I learned how to get off a horse when it started to roll, how to get back on even though I was scared, and I surprised myself how, with dedicated effort and determined practice, I could meet a mentor's expectations.

Now, thanks to nasty old Peter, we would be stuck in our horrid bedroom, missing four precious sessions with Sgt. Buckley!

Irving replaced Peter. Unlike Peter's slick blond head, Irving's hair sprung from his scalp in black curls. He was younger than Peter, just twenty. Unlike Peter, Irving smiled when he greeted us. He often wore lederhosen. Once he tied Patty's ribbon at the end of her braid when I refused to help her. Best of all, he went with us to buy pickles from the little store across the street. The store people were much nicer to us when we were with Irving than when we were alone. We got to pick out the biggest pickles we could see in the barrel.

Seven months after Irving became part of our household, there was a commotion in our entrance hall one afternoon involving him, Marta, and the cook. Mother hurried down, after forbidding Patty and me to step beyond the top of the stairs. We watched from above when several men rushed through our front door. They carried Irving out on a stretcher. A siren blared in the high- low-high-low wailing moan so different from siren sounds we knew in the States. Patty and I sat on the top step, crying because of the unnerving siren, because we liked Irving, and we didn't understand what happened.

Irving returned from the hospital several days later, shrunken and pale. Mother asked him to meet her in the living room for a little chat. She surprised us by coming straight up to our room after her talk with Irving. She sat down on the edge of my bed and folded her hands in her lap. "Girls, I'm sorry to tell you. Irving isn't well yet and he needs to go back to his home to get better. It will probably take some time, so we'll be hiring a new driver. I know you like Irving and will be sad to see him go. He's leaving tonight, but if you hurry, you can write quick little note telling him how nice he is and that you hope he feels better soon."

We scrambled to finish our notes in time. Marta was waiting for us at the top steps. She grabbed the notes from our hands and said, "Stay here. I take the notes." She hurried downstairs. That wasn't like her. She usually smiled and laughed with us. And explained things to us, sometimes in German, but mostly in English now.

Patty poked me. "Do you think she's mad because she's going to miss him? Maybe she's his girlfriend and it's a secret."

"I don't think so. She has a boyfriend. She sees him when she visits her parents. Remember? She told us and showed us his picture. Shh! Here she comes."

"Marta, why are you upset?" I asked as soon as she reached our step.

She made a tight line with her lips. And wiggled her head side to side. She said, "I know you like Irving, but he is sick. Sick in his head. He took gift. He tells your Mother he will take gift again. Better he is not here to do that."

Patty asked, "What is gift?"

Marta motioned us to join her in her room where she kept a German-English dictionary. She ruffled through the pages, then pointed to the word "Poison." I knew my eyes had popped open as wide as Patty's. "He took poison?" I asked. Marta nodded yes.

Marta nodded again. "He take enough, next time, I think. He is too sad because his girlfriend married, not him. He is a dummkopf."

Cristoff followed Irving. Round, not so young, and Greek. I suppose Father thought a non-Austrian driver would work out better. My mother found the Greek annoying, mostly because his girth filled our little fiat when our family of four plus chauffeur set out on a jaunt. She said "We look like an over-stuffed cabbage rolling down the street. There is no dignity to be had in this!"

Vienna offered more than secret passages and errant chauffeurs. Mother and Father were immersed in the diplomatic social scene throughout our year and a half there. Our parents' presence was required at a cocktail or dinner party almost every Friday and Saturday. Patty and I waved goodnight to them as they left looking splendid in the dress requirements of the evening.

Some invitations called for semiformal wear: a white jacket and black tie for Father, a floor length dress for Mother and her mink stole when the weather permitted. For formal occasions Mother helped Father into his cummerbund while Patty and I giggled from our perch on the little Biedermeier sofa. He allowed us to pull his tails once a piece, after cautioning us each time to "Use your head" before doing so.

Mother had four gowns to meet the formal requirement. A sleek black sheath which neither Patty nor I liked because we didn't approve of the low-cut front. We scolded, "Your top- parts will fall out if you bend over."

Another had a dark green velvet bodice and paler green full satin skirt that rustled as it swept across the floor. We had things to say about it too. Patty gave her opinion, "That's your Holiday dress and you shouldn't wear it if it is not a holiday."

I added, "You look like a Christmas tree."

There was a summery blue organza with off- the- shoulder sleeves that ended in little puffs on her arms. I thought she looked like a fairy godmother in it. Finally, her 'best -of-all dress,' in our opinion, was the pale pink lace floated over a deep rose taffeta.

Patty and I marveled at Mother in her elegant formals, hair swept up and fastened in place with a jeweled comb. We loved her earrings, necklaces and fancy high heels. "Does this look better or do you like these best?" she asked as she held up earrings for her three admirers to vote on. Then she donned the pair she had always intended to wear regardless of our vote.

One evening Patty and I watched from the little sofa in their room as our parents practiced waltzing. Mother bubbled with excitement. "A ball, Girls! We're going to a ball at a palace where we will waltz to Strauss until dawn!" Then she turned her attention back to Father. "Immer links, my darling, immer links. Always to the left."

They waltzed around the bedroom, and around their empty chairs in the alcove, and in small circles right in front of our sofa. All the while Mother hummed *The Blue Danube*. When comfortable that their waltzing was tamed to a natural flow, they invited us to join them. Patty hopped onto Father's shoes and away they whirled. Mother's hand on my back pushed me in the right direction while she kept cadence. "One, two, three. One, two, three. Turn, turn, turn to the left. Always the left. Immer links."

Sometimes before our parents left for an evening out, Patty and I listened as they rehearsed whom they should notice at the parties they were attending, who it would be important to talk to, who to avoid if possible, and who should be seated next to whom at the dinner table. Above all, they anticipated what to listen for in the conversations they engaged in. Their presence at these events was an essential part of Father's job. He explained to us that in the daytime he did paperwork and went to meetings about how to make things better in Vienna and the world, and in the evenings his job, and Mother's too, was to represent our country and listen to representatives from other countries.

Playmates

ONE OF THE BEST THINGS ABOUT VIENNA WAS THAT I HAD lots of playmates at last, thanks to a real school, the first since leaving Washington D.C. I entered the second semester of sixth grade and completed seventh grade in the school run by the U.S. Army. I got used to the taunts of "Embassy Snob" and learned the retort to that was an equally dismissive "Army Brat".

Jimmy and Otis were my favorite classmates. Our gang of three rode our bikes on afternoons not taken up by the riding school or piano and ballet lessons. Sometimes we pedaled to the city ice rink and skated. The Austrian children did not invite us to join their skating games. We made up our own, paying attention to our parents' warnings of not to be loud and boisterous. By now, we were immune to cold stares.

Sometimes we ventured down the bumpy dirt paths in wooded areas near our houses. There we rode ferociously, either racing against each other, or chasing imaginary creatures.

Sometimes, when we dared, we went on "our secret mission." Otis led. We rode single file and in silence to the turn- off where a sign posted at its entrance read, "Access by permission of the US Army Only."

"Stay here." Otis would order in a sharp whisper. He checked the one-lane road on foot to make sure it was deserted, and that only one car was parked at its end. We knew our mission was a "go" if Otis returned quickly. If he took longer, we knew he had to hide because there were more visitors than just the one car and our adventure was postponed.

When Otis came back with a "coast is clear" assessment, we did our best to become invisible. Communicating with hand signals, we rode on the grass bordering the graveled lane because the sound of our tires crunching against rock would give us away as we approached our target, the place where Otis's father worked.

His father's car was parked at the end of the lane in front of a single-story brick building. A ten-foot-high mound of earth covered with tall grasses and weeds rose behind the building. No normal windows interrupted the brick walls, but high up, just below the roof line, light and air were allowed in through four transom windows that faced the mound. At ground level, we couldn't see in at all, but we knew what to do: climb to the top of the mound.

That meant passing through a space we considered dangerous and scary. Otis motioned us to leave our bikes every time we reached this area. "He commanded, "No riding bikes in the graveyard." We tiptoed past twelve rows of oblong lumps of earth. Two flat white sticks crossed in a tee at the head of each lump. Tiny silver ball neck chains looped over the top of each upright stick. It looked like each stick was wearing a necklace. A small rectangle hung, like a charm, from each chain. Sometimes the dull metal charms rustled in the wind. They were bumpy because numbers and letters were punched up in tiny ridges across their surface.

After sneaking through the graves, we wiggled up the slope on our bellies. When we reached the crest we each made a part in the unmown grass and weeds to allow a line of vision through the transom window and down into the room where Otis's father did his work. We watched him as he bent over a thick wooden table shaped like a fat figure eight. On the table a pale human body lay stretched, with its arms spread outwards in the upper circle and legs forming a vee in the bottom circle. He operated on the body, and sometimes he pulled things out of it.

When we tired of watching from the top of the rise, Jimmy, Otis, and I crept back through the graveyard, keeping low to the ground and using our secret signals, looking for clues of anything we could imagine hiding between the lumps of broken earth. Perhaps it wasn't the wind causing the charms to rattle. Perhaps it was ghosts, aliens, enemies, robbers, or murderers.

The silver necklaces fascinated me. I decided to take three home because, after all, there was no point leaving them there for murderers, robbers, and enemies.

That evening at Children's Hour, I joined my family in the usual gathering place, the alcove part of my parents' bedroom. Both Father and Mother were already seated in their usual chairs, and Patty took up more than her space on the little sofa. I held my newly acquired jewelry in my outstretched palm. "Look what I found!" The three rectangles dangled down from my fingers. I smiled, waiting for my parents to be enthralled as I was.

Instead, they stared at my hand as if it held a snake. Mother gasped. Father leaned against the back of his chair and clicked his tongue against the roof of his mouth, shaking his head side to side, eyes closed.

I felt a chill crawl up my back. I knew I had crossed a line again, this time more seriously than the invasion of Peter's room. It seemed forever until Father opened his eyes and looked at me.

He rasped, "Where did you get those?"

I didn't want Otis and Jimmy in trouble. I didn't want to give away our secret missions. "I just found them." I crossed my fingers beneath the necklaces hoping that would be enough of an answer.

"Exactly where did you just find them?" Father's voice was louder and less of a rasp.

"Just somewhere."

Father stood. He crossed his arms. His eyes seemed to narrow and grow brighter at the same time. "Young lady, you will tell me exactly where you got these. Now!"

My words fell out in sour lumps. "I found them where Otis's father works. They were just hanging there on sticks."

Father looked at Mother. "Otis?"

Mother's eyes were full. She blinked several times before telling Father, "Otis is a favorite playmate. He's a nice boy. His father is in the army medical core, I think." She took a deep breath.

She turned to me. "Honey, where does Otis's father work? Is it near an army graveyard?"

"I guess so. He cuts up dead people. Sometimes we sneak up on the hill and watch. There're some graves behind his building. But nobody cares about it. There's lots of weeds around. The Army is bossy about everything being neat all the time. So maybe they don't belong to the Army."

Mother pointed at my necklaces. "And the sticks you took these from?"

"They're stuck at one end of the graves. Like this." The necklaces banged against my forearm as I made a cross shape to show her how the sticks were pounded in.

Father stared straight at me. "Oh, my God! How could you do such a thing?"

I covered my face with my arms and sobbed. "What did I do bad? I don't know why you are so mad. I didn't mean to do anything bad."

Mother got up and walked to me. She hugged me and patted my back until I could control the heaving sobs. She said, "Oh Honey. I can tell you have no idea about what you have done." She looked at my father over her shoulder. "Bob, calm down. Let's see if we can fix this."

Patty started crying too. "Deedee didn't know she did a bad thing." The only thing Patty ever got into trouble for was butting in and defending me when I was in trouble.

Father barked at her. "You stay out of this!"

I felt like I had fallen in a deep pit with slippery walls and I could never get out.

Father sank back down into his chair. "Unless you know where to return these, what you have done is unforgiveable." He didn't seem angry anymore. Just sad. His eyes closed, his eyes brows went down in the middle above his nose, and skin around the bottom of his mouth wrinkled.

Hope flooded me. *I can be forgiven.* "Yes! Yes! I know exactly where they were. They were in a row together. I know where. Honest."

Father opened his eyes and turned his head towards me. "You will return what you have stolen, and then you will never go there again. Do you understand?"

"Yes. I promise. I didn't know... I didn't think I was stealing. I thought I was finding them."

Mother took my hands in hers. She folded our joined hands over my necklaces. "Honey, you are holding something very precious. They are called dog tags. All soldiers wear them around their necks in case they are injured, or worse, in battle. The tags tell doctors and families about the soldiers they belong to. The ones you took belong to American soldiers that died here, in Vienna. Their families need to know which grave someone they love lies in. When you take the tags away, the soldiers are lost to their families forever."

I went alone on the scariest mission of all, ashamed but determined to make things right again. I whispered over and over " I hope their families find them, I hope their families find them."

It must be awful, awful to not know where your family is even if they are dead. I couldn't sleep for a lot of nights after that because of bad dreams and thoughts.

Mother vs. Army

A FEW WEEKS LATER, FATHER ANNOUNCED HE HAD RECEIVED notification that we would be going back to the states in June for Home Leave. He cleared his throat and gave a quick nod and added, "It is long overdue." He explained that the State Department planned for its foreign service families to return to the states every two years. This would keep them in touch with the culture they were representing to the world. We had been gone for three and a half years.

Two months before we were to leave Vienna Patty got the mumps. Big swollen hamster jowls that made her cry. Soon I felt tiny hurtful bulbs growing under my ears.

The Army ordered a "Quarantine" sign to be put on our front door.

Mother did not comply. A quarantine sign on the door was "unseemly." She muttered "Strangers don't need to be informed about our state of health.

The army seems to be getting bossier and bossier with embassy personnel lately."

True. At school name calling had grown more combative. Now "Little embassy snot" vs. "Big stinkin army brat" floated across the playground.

Mother was not enamored with the military. She bristled with hostility the day a Master Sergeant, dripping in braids and shiny badges, rapped the back of his hand on our front door. She did not invite him in. Patty and I (in pajamas because we were resting as the doctor ordered) huddled behind her, wondering what the army was up to this time, and why this stiff man stood on our doorstep.

"What can I do for you boys today? Mother asked, looking past the sergeant to a line of three young soldiers standing at attention behind him.

"Madam, I have come to repossess the Meissen China you are harboring." He waved a paper in front of her face.

"You may not come in this house." Mother answered.

"Sorry, Ma'am. Inventory must be accounted for before you leave. My men need to take possession of the goods now. This is an order of the US Army."

"One moment please." My mother retreated into the house. Soon she returned carrying a rolled paper. "By Order of the US Army you may not enter this house." She held her paper up for the Sergeant to see. "We are under quarantine."

"For mumps!" she added.

The sergeant barked an order. The men turned and marched away.

"They sure left in a hurry" I noted.

Mother rushed toward the kitchen calling for Cristoff. "Yes, they did, rather. And now I must hurry. I have an emergency trip. Make sure Marta knows you are in her care while I am gone."

She returned a few hours later laden with boxes and bags. She called for us to join her downstairs. "No time to lose. I need Marta and Cristoff, and anyone else in the house. Both of you. Come!"

She whisked off to the dining room. The tureen from the sideboard was handed to Marta, a stack of blue and white platters to Cristoff. Patty and I received small stacks of dishes and bowls. The relay began, up the stairs, to our bedroom, and under the stage and into the secret passage. Soon all the Meissen china was carefully stacked away, out of sight to any prying Army eyes. Meanwhile, our mother was busy neatly stacking the new Meissen replicas in the sideboard cupboard. The replacement tureen completed the switch. She stepped back, turned to us, and smiled.

"Now I am ready for the U.S. Army."

Adrenaline began to wear off. The swollen lumps on my neck started to throb. Patty looked about to cry. She placed her hands on each side of her neck and winced when she swallowed. I put my arm around my sister's waist. We stood as close together as we could.

I had questions. "But Mother, won't they know it isn't real?"

Patty asked, "Won't God be mad at you?"

"Aren't you kind of lying?" I asked. Remembering her story about getting lice from the Oriental Express and that Father wasn't pleased with it, I added, "What will Father say?"

Mother stood straight-backed, hands on hips, head high. She snorted gently. "Nonsense. If I thought there was one knowledgeable or appreciative bone in their bodies, I wouldn't have to do this. I shiver to think of those beautiful dishes banged around in a mess hall. They deserve to be loved. We will put them back when it is safe. They need to stay with their villa. God and your father will understand, you'll see."

We enveloped Father the minute he walked in the door that evening. He herded us upstairs to our "Children's Hour" meeting place. Mother sat in her usual Biedermeier armchair chair watching with a smile while we poured out our story.

"Will we all get in trouble?" I asked

"Are you going to make her give the real ones to the Army?" Patty tugged at his coat sleeve and looked up in his face for answers.

I felt a glimmer of possible vindication for my recent crime. *Is tricking the army as bad as borrowing necklaces? Will Mother be grounded? Will Father get fired?*

"Will they put Mother in jail like in India?" Patty ran to Mother and wiggled onto her lap.

Father listened as the barrage continued. He stroked his mustache. When there was at last a lull, he put his hands behind his back and rocked a few times on his heels.

"I think it will all work out, Girls. Don't worry. Besides, I have no control over your mother. You know that. The Army probably suspects that. And Patty, I'm sure God knows it." He nodded at Mother. "And thank you for the heads-up phone call, my dear." There was a twinkle in his eye.

She nodded, "You are most welcome."

It felt good knowing my parents worked things out together. Father seemed to agree with Mother that special things that belong to the house shouldn't be taken away from it. So, keeping them here is sort of honest even if the dishes the army took weren't real. *I think this is one of those things Father calls complicated.*

U.S.A
HOME LEAVE
1950

"WE'RE GOING HOME AT LAST!" I YELLED TO PATTY OVER
our stacked suitcases at the head of the stairs.

She took a uneven breath, then shouted back. "But Marta can't come."

Darn! How come I'm sad right on top of being excited? I didn't want to
leave Marta either. Or my gang. Or our wonderful house with all its mys-
teries. And our riding school. I thought of the older kids at the ice rink who
picked us up after a fall and asked "ist alles gut?" And how much fun it was
to walk across the street and buy pickles. I would miss all the good times that
took away the meanness of Peter and Frau Vundra's bad manners, the faint
lingering fear of Nazis and the bossiness of the U.S. Occupational Forces. But
Patty was right. We would miss Marta most of all. Marta is the good side of
Austria, Peter is the bad side.

"We're going, like it or not, so like it!" I whispered to myself. And then
yelled back to Patty. "I know, it's sad she can't come with us. But we can have
all the cokes we want. And milkshakes. And no one will stare at us."

"Are we going back to our old house where Father gave us airplane rides?

"I hope so. I don't want to stay at other people's houses. And you'll be
able to roller skate with us all up and down the sidewalk this time because
you're almost nine now.

She shouted back, "Yipee! The same as you when we went to India."

"Girls! Less shouting please." Mother came out of her room with a pile of clothes to pack on her arm. "Deedee," she said, We're going to stay with friends. Patty, the house we rented in Washington house belongs to someone else now. But maybe we can visit the neighborhood. We'll only be in Washington as long as it takes the State Department to talk to your father about things. Then we're going to California to visit all your uncles and aunts.

We were met in Washington by friends who whisked us off to their farm in Virginia where we were staying during Father's debriefing. Patty and I slept on cots in the living room where the grownups gathered to sip for a "night cap." We were lulled to sleep as they reminisced about times before we were born. Each morning at breakfast, we had standard questions ready "When are we going back to our neighborhood? Will you get us roller skates so we can join the kids? Why can't we go TODAY?"

Mother mumbled about it being a long and complicated trip back to the neighborhood in Washington from the farm in Virginia by bus. One day rolled into the next for over two weeks until Father called a family meeting in his and mother's borrowed bedroom. Patty and I brought a bag of potato chips to the meeting and chomped away while waiting to hear the reason for the summons. Mother sat on the edge of their bed, one moment looking up at Father, wide-eyed, and the next frowning at us for rude chomping noises and greasy fingers touching things in a home that did not belong to us. I realized that going from diplomite to houseguest did not change the fact that good behavior and manners were top priority.

Father began, "My debriefing is finished." He paused, rocking back on his heels, hands clasped behind his back, smiling the smile that Mother called "his cat that ate the canary smile."

Mother took a deep breath and held it, waiting. When she finally let it out, she said, "And?" Father kept smiling. I'm sure if Mother had been holding a fan right then, she would have snapped it shut. She took another deep breath and let it out in a huff which she followed with another "And?" Then she blurted out, "Bob, do you know our next post yet?"

Father nodded yes. His eyes twinkled. His smile spread.

Patty and I had too many questions to wait through his pause. "Where? Will we like it? Will there be kids and a school like in Vienna? Will we get to ride horses there? Will the bossy Army be there too? Can I get a monkey again? When can we have real milkshakes like you promised?"

Father laughed. He spread his arms out to the side and announced, "We are going to Tehran."

Mother stood and clapped her hands together. "How wonderful, Bob! How exciting! Persia! Home of Omar Khayyam, and magic carpets. Rich history. Beautiful art. The Middle East this time! How lov..." She looked down, suddenly silent. Something was wrong and scary. She took Father by the arm and led him across the room, away from my sister and me.

Patty looked at me. Her eyes were shiny. She reached for my hand. I felt a warm surge of love; she was my very own person to share scary things with forever. We squeezed comfort signals back and forth and held our breath to hear our parent's hushed conversation.

Mother asked, "Persia? Oh Bob." Her voice trembled. "Or is it Iran? Is it safe? Are we pushing our luck? Are things stable there? Are we making the right decision for the girls?"

Father's voice was smooth and comforting. "Yes, Betty, or the government wouldn't allow family. We've gone through hardships, and more will come, but just think! They've seen the Raj leave India. Gandhi's death. Lived through lice in post war Europe. Sailed boats in the Tuileries. Rode in the Vienna Woods. We've kept them safe and happy. For God's sake, Betty, there is no better life we could give them."

The room fell silent. Patty and I froze. We didn't want to be noticed and sent away. Mother broke the stillness with two long sighs. She began talking so each word stood out, by itself, like she was using capital letters. "O.K. But I have some requirements before we go. This time we **Must** have quarters ready when we get there. I can't face another long hotel stay."

Father answered softly, "I'll do my best."

Whew! Patty and I let our breaths out. With a happy squeeze signal, we let our hands go.

Two days later we piled into the car and headed for California. Patty and I established our separate kingdoms in the back seat. We shoved each other's arms when they crossed invisible territory boundaries and slapped any hand that crept into the wrong side. We guarded our floor space behind the front seats by kicking each other's bags that were stuffed with things to do during our back seat journey..

"You are taking up more than room than your share."

"Am not. You are sitting to close to the middle."

Father interrupted the bickering twenty minutes into the drive. "That's enough, girls. Stop it! We've a long trip ahead, and your Mother and I want to arrive in California with some sense of sanity. You won't be cooped up in the car the whole time We're going to visit some famous places along the way."

Mother turned around from the front seat and leaned toward us. "You'll love them. My favorite is Carlsbad Caverns in New Mexico. And then before you know it, we'll be in California, I packed an Atlas in one of your bags. It has maps of everywhere we're going. See if you can guess where our first stop will be."

After four days with stops, we reached boiling hot New Mexico. We stood in the sun waiting to go into the caverns. A guide walked up and down the long line of visitors saying things like, "It won't be much longer. So sorry you folks have to wait. Today is unusually crowded because the Boy Scout Jamboree is joining us. Just a while longer folks." I wondered why Mother liked this place. I was sweaty and sticky and tired of standing. *Even the back-seat is better than this. What's a boy scout jamboree, anyway?*

The dusky coolness was heavenly when we finally stepped inside after waiting over an hour. Down, down, we circled the steep sides of the huge cavern. Down into what had to be the center of the earth.

Tingles of excitement traveled into my chest and down my arms along with the cool air. But not because of the enormous rock spears below or the ceiling of gigantic rock icicles above me. I stared at the boy scouts, not the rocks. Tall blond boys. Medium sized boys with freckles and lots of muscles. Younger boys with surprised faces. Boys everywhere. Whenever one stared back, lightening flashed in the pit of my stomach. *Boy oh boy! Where did that come from? It's new, and I like it!*

Mother's voice, loud enough for anyone listening to hear, interrupted my thrill. "This, my dears, is Dante's Inferno. And I will not go forth meekly. Nay, I shall be a prancing pony as I descend into the bowels of hell." The word "nay" sounded horse-like. She blew a kiss to Father and said, "I'll meet you at the exit." My dignified, wise, comforting mother began prancing through the line ahead of us! *Right in front of the boy scouts! How could she?*

My face turned as hot as it was with Scarlet Fever. I stopped scanning boy scouts and stared at my feet. Father cleared his throat. His forehead wrinkled. He held Patty's hand to keep her from running after our mother.

"Make her stop!" I said. I stomped my foot.

Father sighed and shrugged his shoulders. "I have no control over your mother. Don't worry, she's playing. She'll be fine, and so will you. Mothers get to play sometimes." He smiled like he was amused.

An hour later, we met her at the mouth of the cave where she had been waiting for us. She kissed each of us on the forehead, including Father, and we continued our drive to California.

Our parent's families were scattered across California from Berkeley to Los Angeles. At each stop, Patty and I remembered our best manners, shared couches and beds, and listened to Mother telling our hosts about our life and adventures outside the States. She varied the stories and the details. Patty and I chirped in when she told about going to jail in Delhi. The telling of Gandhi's death and Lady screaming after our car brought tears to her listeners, including me. The Detective Ladies in Paris and Secret Passages in Vienna were included at each stop. Father joined in, straightening out facts that got tangled in poetic license or when he explained a bit about what the world was doing at the time. I began to remember our adventures the way she told them, true or not.

We stayed with Aunt Doreen for an extra month when Father left for Iran ahead of us to arrange housing. By watching Mother distribute the little gifts she had carefully chosen for each host and relative, Patty and I learned that good manners included thank you gifts for hospitality. Patty saved her allowance and bought a baby goose as a house gift for Aunt Doreen and Uncle Calvin. It imprinted on Uncle Calvin, following him in and out of the house and around the garden, leaving a trail of loose greenish-brown droppings behind.

A month later Aunt Doreen and Uncle Calvin took us to the San Francisco Airport. We were teary about leaving the comfort of being in our own country, and our big warm California family, but at the same time, Patty and I were excited about having our own home again. I think our hosts had split feelings too. They were sad to see us go so far away again, but they also planned to stop by a farm on their way home where Loosifer might find some new friends.

PART V.
TEHRAN
1950

Downtown

FATHER HAD A HOUSE WAITING FOR US NOT FAR FROM THE city's center. An American family had rented the house before us. Their departure and Father's arrival overlapped. They asked Father if we would mind inheriting their dog and the gardener. Lulu could not go with them because of the quarantine laws in their new post, and Gassam was old, finding a new job would be difficult

Lulu was a toy Pomeranian, caramel and white with a sharp fox like nose, and a sharp yippy bark. Lulu and I tolerated each other. Patty and Lulu loved each other. We also inherited our predecessors' cook, Jamal. Once again, the kitchen was out of bounds.

The two-story house had a flat roof. It hunched down behind a high earthen wall painted ivory white. All the houses in our residential neighborhood were hidden behind high walls. A grilled gate opened from the courtyard garden into the street. Four raised planters, each about the size of two picnic tables, divided the courtyard into equal sections. The rest of the garden was all brick, either as pathways around the planters, or as the sides of the planters. Inside each planter, flowers and shrubs grew in precise rows, trimmed into precise shapes. Patty and I quickly discovered the best way to enjoy this insanely tidy garden was to tightrope walk around the top of the planter walls, and leap from one planter to the other without touching the paths between. In one corner a small round basin with a rusty water pump interrupted the ridged symmetry of the garden. This was where Gassam filled watering cans. There was no hose.

We invented a game of tag that had as many rules as the courtyard had corners and ledges. Lulu joined in, yipping and bounding down the pathway as we lept on and off the ledges in ten second spurts. The game led to arguments as well as exhaustion.

"You are burned up because you were on the path for more than ten."

"Was not."

"Yip, yip, yip, yip"

"Were so. Lulu, be quiet!"

"You counted too fast."

"Did not."

"Girls, come in. There's far too much noise out here."

Father reminded us again that we were representatives of our country. Noisy courtyards jarred the neighborhood.

Outside our front gate the jube trickled along both sides of the street. This open gutter trench ran next to all the city curbs in Tehran. It gathered run-off from the houses and businesses it passed. It served as a convenient hand washing station. Kabob preparation took place in carts straddling the jube. Donkeys stopped their caravan by abruptly turning to the jube to drink. Young men sometimes used it as a urinal. I watched passersby pause to lean over the jube and place a thumb against one nostril. Then they blew their nose out the uncovered nostril into it.

"Who needs a handkerchief when you have the jube?" my mother asked under her breath as we watched from our gate way one day.

The beauty of early morning calls by vendors as they passed by our house enchanted Mother. She often stood by an open window to listen. She sometimes crept outside to stand behind our gate to be closer to the morning symphony. Some voices praised their merchandise in slow deep minor tones from the backs of donkeys. Some rippled praise for the goods they carried atop their heads. Some urged customers to buy in high frantic staccato while pushing their carts up and down our street.

"Listen carefully, Girls," she urged us. "These are sounds you will remember as part of the mysterious East, of Aladdin and Scheherazade."

Now that family had arrived, hiring household staff became an important time-consuming chore. Father called a meeting to discuss solving a major part of the staffing problem. The four of us stood together in our new living room. There was no seating because the allotted embassy furniture remained stacked in a corner waiting for Mother to decide on a temporary room arrangement until our own household goods arrived from wherever the State Department had stored them during our home leave.

Father started the meeting with, "I think Gassam could do a lot more than water and trim the garden. I think he should be our head houseboy."

Mother pursed her mouth into an unspoken "Oh?" and crossed her arms.

I pictured Gassam as he pumped water into the little basin, swooped it up into a watering can, and poured the right amount on each plant. His head was balding on top. His chin was bordered with a fringe of grey, but the calf muscles below his baggy shorts bulged. His tanned arms, well-muscled from pumping and lifting cans of water, looked extra-long to me. He did not look like a proper head houseboy, elegant and crisp as Daniel, or as formal as Peter, or as young and smiley as Irving. I covered my mouth not to giggle at how out of place he would look in our dining room, lugging a watering can in one hand and juggling a platter with the other. Patty caught my eye. She must have been thinking the same thing because when our eyes met, we couldn't help but burst out in short, stifled snorts.

Father continued as if there had been no reaction. "I know it's risky. Serving a formal dinner is as foreign to him as Mars is to me, but he's eager and loyal. We can train him, Betty. It'll be hard, but worth it for us and for Gassam in the long run, after we leave. There's a lot to say for loyalty."

"Head houseboy, in shorts, and three words of English?" Mother shook her head.

Father crossed his arms over his chest and rocked back on his heels. His voice sounded like he was patiently telling me why I couldn't slurp spaghetti at the dinner table. "Now hear me out, Betty." Father explained how Gassam could be coached by a well-respected houseboy of one of our fellow embassy families and we would easily supply the proper clothing.

Mother continued to stare into space. "Hmmm."

"Think of loyalty, Betty. Dependability." His voice lowered. "We need someone we can count on."

They exchanged a long look that became a silent conversation secret from Patty and me.

Mother sighed.

Father nodded. He went on as if he had won that round. "Besides Gassam, we will still need to find a permanent driver to replace the one on loan from the embassy. and an assistant houseboy.

"Stop! "Mother uncrossed her arms and held them in front of her. Her palms, fingers up, faced Father. She looked like she was fending off something approaching that was unpleasant. "We will not have an assistant houseboy. We need a maid instead! Someone I can depend on to help me and take care of the girls."

Father nodded again. "I guess that's a fair compromise. Agreed."

This was a huge promotion for Gassam. He grinned and bowed whenever he saw any of us. His head bobbed up and down as he said, "Yes Sir, Yes Sir, I do Sir." Then off he scuttled, his slip-on house shoes flap, flap, flapping as he hurried to complete whatever mission he was on.

Mother started interviews for a maid a few days later. She asked Patty and me to join her in case we came up with an observation she missed, or a gut feeling. Sometimes Gassam was called in to help with what translation he could manage. The need for a maid was growing urgent. Gassam couldn't clean house, garden, and butler all at once. And Mother wasn't pleased leaving us in his care when she needed to "make the rounds" with Father in the evening. Plus, it was out of the question that he readied her wardrobe selections for upcoming events.

When the latest candidate left the room, Mother tapped her foot and snapped her fan open and shut. She was running out of time and patience.

"Well girls, any ideas?" she asked.

"None stick out one way or the other," I offered.

Patty asked, "Why do they look like they're wearing ghost costumes that have little flowers all over them?"

I asked, "How can they do anything if they have to hold that cover thing shut over their mouth all the time?"

Mother scoffed and shook her head. "It's called a chador. I don't think someone part of a household must dress like that inside. It certainly is a lot more freeing and coloful than what women here used to have to wear —a heavy black shroud with only a slit at eye level. But…"

And that is when Gassam came flapping into the room.

"Sir. Sir, please, Sir," His head bobbed more vigorously than usual. He flung himself down in front of Mother.

She took a step back and gasped. "Gassam! What is it? What's the matter? Is someone hurt?"

"No hurt. Sir. Please. My wife make good maid. My wife. She come. Big worker. Please Sir."

"Your wife?"

"Yes Sir. Very good worker. She come please."

In the evening, with the temporary driver's help, Father joined Mother in questioning Gassam about his request. For several days the pros and cons of hiring Gassam's wife dominated our parent's conversation.

And that is how Fatima came to join us.

Because Gassam was sixty, we expected his wife to be grandmotherly, although we understood they had young children. It turned out she was barely twenty. Her long black hair hung from a middle part down to the small of her back. Her body seemed to be put together in a series of small rounded mounds.

Fatima and Mother formed a close bond although neither spoke but a few words of the other's language. Mother told us Fatima had been fourteen and devastated when he parents arranged the marriage six years ago. Fatima's salary went to Gassam. At pay time, she stood beside him while he held out his hand to collect her money which he then put in his pocket.

Mother fumed about this during a Children's Hour. "Can you imagine! He doesn't even let her look at it, much less touch it. Swish! Away it goes, her week's hard work."

Father tilted his head and raised his martini glass. "That is how it is, here. We can't change the world, you know."

The bottom of my stomach felt angry. I pounded my fist on my thigh. "I don't like the way everyone bosses women around here. It isn't fair. I'm glad I'm American. I wish I could change the world."

Mother smiled at me. "I agree!" Then she huffed, "And I, I can at least make Fatima's world better."

She went about this by developing a business understanding with Fatima. Fatima received bonuses secret from Gassam in a form he would never suspect. Mother bought eighteen caret gold bangles for Fatima but wore them on her own arms. That way no one questioned either of them as Mother bought bangle after bangle, or sometimes traded a few in for more a substantial gold bracelet. From time to time, Fatima made "withdrawals" by taking one of the bangles, but mostly she smiled when her growing fortune jangled passed her in safe keeping on Mother's arms. But I worried about what would happen to Fatima when we got transferred again and Mother handed over all the bracelets. *Father said we would be here for at least two more years. Maybe Iran will treat women better by then.*

Gassam, Fatima, and their sons occupied two rooms in the servant's quarters which were strung along the garden's back wall. Ali was six, and his younger brother, five, who had a name that started with an R but we couldn't pronounce it right, so Patty and I called him Razor. The little boys lugged watering cans around the garden under their father's instructions.

One day Patty and I tried to teach them our tag game. Ali and Razor stared at us as we babbled English while demonstrating leaping, counting, and running. Suddenly Ali turned to Razor and shouted something in Farsi. Both boys began running up and down the paths at top speed. Patty and I took to the ledges for safety. We watched from above as they sped around and around. That is when we noticed the top of their heads. Each had four or five bare whitish circles, about nickel size, branded on his closely cropped head.

Something wasn't right. We described it to our parents that evening at dinner. Father looked across at Mother.

"Ringworm, you think? he asked her.

She sighed. "I'll arrange for a doctor's appointment. Meanwhile, Girls, don't play with them until we are sure it's not contagious."

Besides coping with the challenges of our new home, Patty and I also were adjusting to our new school. I entered eigth grade in the Presbyterian Missionary American Community School. Each morning the students gathered in the chapel, listened to a short sermon, sang a hymn or two, then two by twos marched from the chapel to classes singing *"Holy Holy Holy, Lord God Almighty."*

The school puzzled me. Community School was a two-story building big enough to house one class each of Kindergarten through Tenth grade. While the kindergarten squirmed with over twenty-five children, the tenth grade eked by with seven or eight students. The Army school in Vienna had kids all over the place, and two or three teachers for each grade all the way through the twelfth grade. Here there wasn't even one eight grade teacher I could claim as my own. I walked around the upstairs hall from classroom to classroom, teacher to teacher.

I bombarded my parents with questions about this set-up one Children's Hour shortly after entering the new school. There was no alcove or special sitting room off my parents' bedroom in this house. Here we held our Children's Hours in the large formal living room. When our household goods arrived, Patty and I had the same Biedermeier love seat to perch on, and my parents had their favorite dark blue velvet chairs from India. *Our smaller meeting places were better. Everyone was closer. Oh well. Any Children's Hour is better than none. Another adjustment! It's like I always have to adjust. And now this school…*

This evening I chose to sit in a boxy embassy chair because I felt like kicking something and didn't dare attack the love seat. I drummed my legs against the new grey slipcover and asked, "How come I don't have my own classroom? I don't even have a desk. Why does Mr. Swan have to teach all the grades history, instead of just be my teacher?"

"Mr. Swan?" asked my father. He raised an eyebrow and smiled. I blushed.

"He's the nicest teacher of all," I explained.

"I see." said my father.

I was quick with more questions. "And why does the tenth grade have only five students? My class has fifteen kids, and someone said it is the biggest upper class ever. What's big about that? Why do I have to sing "Holy, Holy, Holy" every morning?"

Mother and Father shared a look over their martini glasses. Mother left her chair and sat on the arm of mine. She patted my shoulder. "Well, Dear, "Holy, Holy, Holy" is because it is a missionary school and they need to be sure you are getting some religious instruction. You change classes and teachers because the teachers specialize in their fields. You'll get used to it, and like it even better than the other way."

I didn't have time to think about that because Patty slipped to the edge of the sofa and said, "But I have my own teacher. And I never get to see Deedee because she is upstairs all day and at lunch she doesn't even say hello to me."

"Oh Dear." Mother left me and gathered Patty up. I crossed my arms and glared at Patty with the wrinkled-up face look that usually scared her into being quiet. I wanted my parent's attention. I wanted them to fix this thing for me.

Father tipped his head to the side and grinned at me. "Your school is kind of a launching pad. The reason there aren't so many kids in the upper grades is that parents send them off after their sophomore year to other countries, to boarding schools, so they will be ready for university. I understand most of the older students there now are from international backgrounds." He looked at Mother and raised his shoulders like he was asking a question.

She nodded, "That's what the principal explained when I asked why some of them seemed so..." She hesitated, then finished, with "mature."

"Most are there to perfect their English after attending other schools before this one. I could tell the missionaries are pleased to have some influence on them, as well as the tuition money." She turned to me. "And Honey, I think there are at least eight tenth graders."

"I don't get it!" I whacked the backs of my legs against the chair. I missed the backyard schooling in New Delhi, where my mother was the boss. I missed the lessons with just her and me in Paris. *If I can't have things to myself, I want a big crowd of kids my own age. And a teacher who cares about me, like in Vienna.*

But my parents were right. Within a month, life at Community School seemed the most natural way to do things. And now I had a best friend, someone my own age to do things with instead of my baby sister. What a pair we made! Jenny—tallish, well rounded, blue-eyed, honey blond waves of hair resting on her shoulders, and me: small, wiry, long brown braids, and green eyes that no one notices because they crinkle up when I smile.

As Father had guessed, I had a big crush on Mr. Swan. It was as if a bunch of the boy scouts from Carlsbad Caverns were rolled into one young missionary. Jenny had a crush on him too. We planned for extra time with him by going to his classroom after school to ask him to explain the homework or to return a book we had "accidently" taken out of class.

One day I felt angry with Jenny and didn't know why. I rushed into Patty's and my bedroom after school and slammed the door shut to keep Patty out. "Go away! Stop following me!" I yelled through the door when she tried to get in.

A minute later, Mother walked in. "You seem upset." she said softly. What's the matter?"

"I don't know. I feel like ants are in inside me, crawling around, and I'm mad."

"Did someone say something that upset you? One of the kids? A teacher?"

"No." I took a deep breath.. "Well, maybe. I think I'm mad at Jenny."

Mother sat down beside me on the bed. "Did you two have a fight?" She soothed my hair off my forehead.

"No. She doesn't even know I'm mad. I guess it's because she's so excited about her dinner tonight." My throat began to get that hurting feeling.

Mother put her arm around me. "Why in the world does Jenny's dinner upset you?"

Now it was hard not to cry. I forced words out of my mouth, one at a time, to keep tears away. "Because of her family. They're missionaries like the teachers at school. And all the kids eat with their mom and dad even when they have guests. Jenny doesn't have to eat upstairs with her little sister like I do when you have guests. And her family invites other missionaries to dinner. And Jenny gets to sit next to Mr. Swan tonight."

Mother hugged me, then patted my back. She said, "I'm sorry you feel left out, I don't think you're mad at Jenny. And I think you're envious of her family right now. That's certainly understandable. There're so many rules our family must follow because we are in the diplomatic service. But don't let something as petty as envy spoil your beautiful friendship. Believe me, good friends are precious."

I knew she was right. I felt honored that Jenny was my best friend. The next day I safety-pinned our skirts together so we wouldn't be apart all day long.

The crush on Mr. Swan, and envy of Jenny's family began to fade when I discovered Alex. He was in the ninth grade. Oh! The thrill of sitting at a window in my classroom and adjusting the angle of the windowpane just enough to catch a reflection of him seated next to a window in his classroom. Electricity ran from my head, somersaulted through my stomach and jolted out of my feet whenever we both happened to be checking the reflection at the same time and our eyes met. Wow!

I never wanted to miss a day of Community School because it meant being away from Jenny and Alex. But there were days we couldn't go to school or were fetched home early. On those days. drivers lined up in cars in front of the school. Students waited behind the closed doors until their family car gained first place. Then they rushed out. The car zipped away and the next in line quickly took its place in the loading zone.

Demonstrations. That was the dreaded word that sent us scurrying home or kept us away from school for the day. Sometimes Mr. Mosaddeq led these demonstrations, and other times the Tudeh party called for them. Either became potentially dangerous to us as foreigners when angry crowds gathered near our school, or marched past it chanting and shouting in Farsi.

"Why are the crowds so angry? Why do they hate us?" I asked Father one evening during Children's Hour after our new driver, Emmanuel, had whisked us home from school that afternoon.

Before he answered my question, Father began pacing back and forth in front of the couch. He had more room to pace in this living room than in our smaller meeting places. I knew his pacing meant a long answer. He began, "It's complicated. I'll try simplifying it, but I don't even understand it completely myself, and my job here is to understand it. Like I said, complicated. Let's take Mr. Mosaddeq first. At the most basic level, it boils down to oil. Mr. Mosaddeq doesn't hate us as much as he hates the British. He's angry with them because of they're extracting and selling Iran's oil and keeping the money. True, they built the facilities, but Mr. Mosaddeq doesn't think that's a good excuse. He wants to take the oil back, nationalize it and the facilities. So, probably what he's saying to the crowds is that they need to get their oil back and he's probably scolding the British for taking it. There! That's a big simplification. Does it help?" He stopped pacing and waited for me to answer.

"Not really." I said. "You didn't explain why the crowds are angry with us. We're not British." Patty snorted at me. She left, then came back with a coloring book. She probably wanted to kick me so I wouldn't ask questions and there wouldn't be more long answers. Mother leaned her head against the back of her chair and closed her eyes, except when she took little sips of her drink.

"Hmm." Father nodded at me. "You're right, I didn't. It's because our country is very friendly with the British, and usually we take their side of everything."

"Kind of like best friends? I asked. I was proud of me. Listening to Mother tell our stories in California I realized that she and Father added a lot of stuff about what was going on outside our family. Now I was keeping the promise to myself to learn more about what was going on in the world around me.

Father picked up his drink and took a few sips, put it back on the coffee table, and said, "Usually. Long history there."

"Okay." I said. "So, what about the other demonstrations? The ones when the Tudeh party marches right past of our school, yelling, and some of them shaking their fists? Is that because of the British too?"

He started pacing again, but this time with his hands clasped behind his back, a signal he was deep in thought. "Umm," he said. "No, not the British. That one's because of us. They're the communist party here in Iran, and our country doesn't want communists in Iran or anywhere. I think the Tudeh party suspects we are out to do them in."

"Are we?" I asked.

Father spun around to face me. "In any case, remember that a crowd can become a mob, and a mob becomes a vicious beast that no longer needs a reason to attack. Stay away ..."

Mother opened her eyes and said, "That's enough talk for tonight. Gassam's here to tell us dinner's ready." She finished her drink, got up and walked to the coffee table to put it on the tray beside Father's as Gassam appeared in the doorway.

Spooky. Somehow she must have seen Gassam coming even with her eyes closed. Maybe she heard his shoes flapping. I don't think Father wants to answer my question and she's in cahoots with him.

Father's explanations didn't keep the hot prickles crawling in the small of my back whenever I heard the rumble of chanting in the distance. When the voices grew louder and closer, a cold mist of fear enveloped me. I had heard rumors that horrible things happened to foreigners when trapped in one of these mobs, like their arms were torn off or they were thrown down and stomped to death.

Except for those rare days dominated by demonstrations, life settled into comfortable habits. School, family picnics on Sunday, Children's Hour when time permitted, parties at friend's homes, and trips to The Bazar with mother and Emmanuel who had joined our household as our permanent driver.

Unlike the scattered open-air collection of stalls in India, in the Bazar small shops crowded both sides of winding pathways. Their closeness blocked full daylight; it always seemed to be late afternoon no matter what time we arrived. Merchants stood in doorways luring shoppers in with songs and chants. Mother's interests lay with the wide choice of handwoven Persian carpets. She also lingered in places where copper trays and urns gleamed through the dusky light. Fabrics, china, and tea caught her eye too. And she visited the jewelry shops to buy a bangle or two for Fatima.

Because a male escort was essential when we went to this magical place, Emmanuel always accompanied us. He was twenty five and spoke English well. His thick black hair swept back making his profile look like pictures I'd seen of carvings in ancient Assyrian frescos. That made sense because he was Syrian. Although Mother bargained well on her own, a must in the

Bazar, Emmanuel added to her success. Patty and I dropped behind, giving the two of them space for their act. When Mother showed interest in something, Emmanuel approached to stand respectfully behind her shoulder, pointed farther down the road, and said loudly enough for the merchant to hear, "Come, Madam. There is a better one, better price, over there." The merchant usually lowered his price until Mother, and Emmanuel, were satisfied. I learned from watching them that there was more to bargaining than bickering.

Under the Stairs

SPRING BROUGHT MUHARRAM. A NIGHT OF RELIGIOUS marches throughout the city. One night, on my way upstairs for bed, I noticed Gassam and Father standing close together in the front hallway. Father's voice was hushed, Gassam's head bobbed vigorously. *What in the world are they talking about?* I stood still, willing the muscles behind my ears to open wider and pull in more sound. By listening so intently, beyond their hushed voices I heard a distant rhythmic rumble.

Father looked up at me. "Go upstairs and tell your mother and sister to get on comfortable clothing, use the bathroom, then come down here. You do the same as quickly as possible. And make sure all the lights are turned off up there."

"But, …why…?" I froze in place, overcome by curiosity.

"Just do it now!" he barked. "Go! I'll explain when you're all down here."

When I entered her room, Mother looked up from her dressing table. She smiled at me and purred, "Hello, Honey. You look worried. What can I do to help?"

"Father's acting weird. He said to tell you to get on comfortable stuff and go to the bathroom. All of us. Then go downstairs. He said to turn the lights off and hurry, but I don't know why."

She put her hair brush down slowly. She took a deep breath and then said, without smiling, "Get a sweater and comfortable shoes. I'll meet you downstairs. I have to find your sister." She hurried off to find Patty. Within five minutes we hurried down the steps. Patty and I asked questions all the way down.

"Hush! Hush!" Father put his forefinger over his lips. He cleared his throat. "Quickly now. Under here." He pointed to the space under the staircase where Gassam was placing pillows and bottles of water. Father put his arm around Mother's shoulders. "The embassy just called. This is the safest place. We will stay here until it's over."

Gassam hurried away,

"Why? Why are we hiding under the stairs?" I persisted.

Patty added, "It's crowded with all of us under here."

"Hush!" Father's voice was a harsh whisper.

Outside, the rumble was getting closer. I could faintly hear one voice calling out, then a murmur of many voices answering.

I whispered, "What is it? What's happening?" I felt the familiar hot prickles in the small of my back. The world seemed to be shrinking to just our staircase and the noise growing outside.

Father glared at me, again placing his finger to his lips, more forcefully this time. His lips squeezed into a thin line. They were almost white. Mother put her hand on Father's arm. She leaned close to me and whispered, "It's a religious rite. They're mourning the death of one of Islam's holy men. The problem for us is these marches can turn violent against outsiders. The embassy warned us that young men participating get caught up in the moment and sometimes whip themselves into a religious frenzy, beyond reason. Then mob violence takes over."

I put my hands over my mouth to keep my whisper as quiet as possible, and asked, "Whip themselves? With real whips?"

Patty whispered to me, "What's mob violence?"

"Something bad and dangerous. Like angry lions that could eat us in a second." I whispered back.

Her eyes grew big and wet.

Father smoothed my hair off my forehead then patted my back. I strained to hear his whisper. "Yes, they whip themselves. With chains. Across the back of their shoulders." He shook his head and sighed like he couldn't believe it. "I've heard sometimes it gets very bloody. The embassy has notified us that their route tonight goes right down our street, in front of our gate. It's best that they don't know we live here. Or," he paused and looked at Mother, "if someone in the procession knows Americans live here, best that they think we're not home. Betty, are all the lights out upstairs?"

She whispered, "Yes. All off, curtains drawn." They nodded at each other. I think that meant everything was in order. They must have had a plan to follow in case something like this happened. My warning prickles became a blanket of ice.

We huddled. Like a guardian angel, Father stood facing us in the highest space beneath stairs. Mother sat on the cushion nearest to him. Her head rested against his knee. From our end, where the stairs met the ground floor Patty and I hugged her around her waist, burying our heads into her side. Ten minutes lasted half an hour, it seemed. I wanted to stretch. There was no room. *What if I sneaked up to the roof and watched? We sleep up there when it's too hot inside and no one notices us because everyone does it.* The leader's voice called out, and the answer was louder this time. *No. I'm going to stay as close to Mother and Father and Patty as possible. Even if I don't move all night.*

The throng flowing towards us grew louder. They would soon be crossing the street corner half a block from our house. Loud, louder, louder. Now when the leader called out above the crowd, I could make out 'Allah' or maybe 'Ali' as part of his cry. The crowd thundered in response. Their roar vibrated through our gate, through the walls of the house, through me.

A split second of silence stifled the air after the chanted response. I held my breath. The silence was broken with a muffled "Umph! Phlat!" Then cries of pain. Leader, response, silence, thud, pain. The pattern repeated, louder still now. The swarm seemed to be on top of us. The bar holding our front gate shut rattled. Lulu shrieked a few short yips somewhere in the distance.

Patty began to cry. "Where is Lulu. I want Lulu." She forgot to whisper. Mother gently put her hand over Patty's mouth.

Father whispered, "She's safe. She's with Gassam. Usually only foreigners have pet dogs here. She could give us away." Father bent to put his hand on Mother's shoulder. Her arms hugged Patty and me tight against her. We pressed ourselves into the wall under the dark stairway. Our front rattled as the chanting poured over it and into the house.

Dadedadededdah Allah.

Dededa ramram ded Ali.

Phlat!

I winced and held my breath with each phlat. Patty and I squeezed as close to Mother and into the wall as possible. She hugged us tighter. *I'm going to scream if this doesn't stop. I can't breath. Hold on, stay calm, nothing matters but being with my family.* My heart's noise made it hard to believe the swell of shuffling footsteps, bumps against the gate, brushings along the garden wall, calls and chanting were beginning to ebb. In long slow minutes the crowd faded into a few voices and soft thuds as the tail of the procession passed our house. But we remained frozen under the stairs, even when the sounds became an indistinguishable buzz in the distance.

The street settled into silence. Its stillness felt like cold sharp slaps against my skin.

Gassam appeared carrying Lulu. Lulu's snout was wrapped with a multicolored cloth. He bowed, nodding at each word. "It good now, Sirs."

Mother let go of us. I unclenched my hold on her. I breathed. My back ached from the lean into Mother. As we unwound, Patty scrambled up to grab Lulu from Gassam. She unwrapped the cloth. Lulu wiggled and wagged all over, licking Patty's face until I saw dog spit drip off my sister's chin.

Mother stretched and straightened her hair. "We are safe now."

Patty squeaked, "I don't like this scary place. Let's go home. Back to California. And take Lulu with us!"

Father paced back and forth in the hallway. "It's not that simple, Patty. But maybe we don't have to stay here where things like this take place."

I heard the whine in my voice when I asked, "Are we going to move? Do you have a new post? Again? Another new post?"., *I don't want to leave Jenny, and Alex, Why do we always have to go and leave everything? I want a home that's mine forever. Patty would be happy anywhere if she had that stupid dog.*

Father's eyebrows lowered. He cleared his throat. He spoke slowly, looking back and forth between my sister and me. "We probably weren't in real danger. Nevertheless, remember we're guests here. Sometimes being in the way, or not belonging, is enough to upset things and turn a peaceful gathering into a senseless mob. So, we were extra careful. That's all. It's over now. And no, Deedee, we are not moving to a new post."

Whew. Now, I have to get it straight before I tell everyone about tonight. I asked, "They were hitting themselves with chains? Real metal chains?"

Father answered on his way to the telephone. "Yes. I must tell the embassy all is well now. Yes, I think it's atonement. Like Catholics going to confession. Sometimes monks do things like that too."

Patty looked up from petting Lulu. "Do we ever have to hit ourselves? So the chain men in the crowd think we belong and won't be mad?"

Mother shook her head. "No, Dear. Never. But I'm sure your father will fix things so we aren't in the middle of this again." She looked at Father like she was waiting for him to say something she already knew he would say.

He finished his phone call and turned to face us. "Yes, your mother's right." He paused, then nodded his head at Mother. "Yes. It's no longer a question. We need to move." He snapped his fingers in the air, which meant his decision was irrevocable. "Yes, just as soon as I can arrange it."

"No!" I exploded. "I **won't** go! I **won't** change schools. **I want to stay with my friends!**"

Patty picked up Lulu and hid behind Mother.

Father stared at me. His face was serious, but his eyebrows weren't all squelched up. He took a deep breath.

"Honey, I know the constant changing is hard. You have both done a wonderful job." He swept his arm out to include Patty who was still sheltered behind Mother. I gulped because I could guess what was coming next. Something about counting on me to keep up the good work. And then I would feel all guilty for letting him down. But he surprised me when he continued with "We'll move to the new suburb. It isn't far. You will of course go to the same school and have your same friends. Emmanuel will drive you to school as always. Nothing will change except the house."

Mother piped in. "I think you will be pleasantly surprised. It will be much nicer and safer than here. No jubes, and no mobs marching past our door." Then she made a sad face. "But I will miss the wonderful morning songs of our street vendors."

Two weeks later, trucks came to take our furniture and clothing and Gassam and his family to the new house. I squirmed my way into our car to sit next to Mother and try to make her answer questions about the new house. She had already seen it. Although I piled up questions non-stop. she just smiled and said, "You will be surprised, and you will love it."

I thought about our move from the Taj to the bungalow in New Delhi, and from the dumb waiter house to our villa in Vienna. I realized that although change was hard in many ways, it could end up being just the right thing.

Icebox Alley

OUR ROUTE OUT OF TOWN WAS THE HIGHWAY THAT LED UP to Mount Damavand's foothills where many of Tehran's wealthier citizens had summer homes, away from the heat of the city. Fifteen minutes later, Emmanuel turned off the highway into an isolated group of walled compounds strung along narrow streets. We turned onto one with a street sign that read "Kuchee Yakchar" under larger Farsi script. Mother tapped Emmanuel on the shoulder and asked, "What does Kuchee Yakchar mean?"

He hesitated a few seconds, then nodded and said, "Madam, Kuchee means very little street. Yakchar is cold box where you keep food to stay good."

Mother laughed and leaned towards Father in the front seat. "Well, Bob, we now live on Icebox Alley."

Emmanuel stopped the car in front of a big wooden gate. The gate and garage door beside it were embedded in the eight foot high wall stretching from one end of the block to the other. There were two other gate and garage combinations built into it farther down the block. The truck drivers, their helpers, and Gassam and Fatima had already begun unloading and were waiting for the gate to open.

I was surprised to see the garage had a second story. My heart sank. "Is that our house?"

Mother laughed. "No. No. Come along."

She handed a key to Emmanuel. He unlocked the gate. A bell hanging above the gate clanged loudly as it opened.

I jerked to a stop. "Oh! Does it always do that?"

Emmanuel smiled up at the bell. "Yes, Miss, always when the gate is opening. So you know someone is coming. Only way in, except for garage." I could see Emmanuel was proud to be in charge of the gate as well as the car and garage.

We stepped through the gate onto a hard dirt path sprinkled with gravel that crunched as we walked. Father had disappeared into the garage with Emmanuel. The pathway to the house looked longer than a football field to me. I turned to Mother. "Will we always have to walk that far to get home?"

Mother nodded. "I'm afraid so, but it's worth it. Just look at the lovely big garden we have."

The garden was big alright, probably as big as two tennis courts, end to end. Little dirt paths branched off from the main one we were on. I guessed Mother saw it differently than I did because to me it looked like plain dirt with a few scraggy things trying to grow here and there. I looked ahead. The garden seemed to end at a screen of spindly trees. Beyond the trees, I could see the top edge of a flat roofed two-story house. It was greyish white like the front wall. I looked to my right and left and realized that the entire rectangle that was our new territory was enclosed by tall walls. The word "boring" rang through my head.

"Come on Patty, I'll race you to the trees."

Patty took off before I finished my sentence. Lulu ran at her heels, yipping and blocking my chance to pass her and surge ahead.

Mother called out, "Girls! Slow down! Stop right there by the well. Wait for me!"

I hadn't noticed the well until she mentioned it. No circle of fancy brickwork with a dipping basin around it like the one we just left. Only a flat circular cement edge around an opening in the ground. There were several watering cans beside it. I glanced at the garden area.

"Wow! Gassam has a lot of watering to do."

Mother caught up with us. She laughed. "Well, he has a lot to oversee. We'll hire a gardener and probably a helper too. Gassam will be the supervisor." She looked over the garden and shook her head. "Everything is so new. Not much planted yet. But it will be lovely. You'll see. You certainly have lots of space here."

Patty knelt at the edge of the well and leaned forward to see inside. "Oooh. It's so deep."

"Let me see." I picked up a pebble and started counting as I tossed it into the hole.

"Deedee! Patty! Away from the well! It's dangerous! It's not to be played with. Ever!" Mother gestured to include the cleared area around the well where the watering cans and garden tools were organized in neat rows. "This is a restricted area. Only for Gassam and the gardeners. It's Off Limits! That's why I wanted you to wait for me here. I wanted to be sure to mention this right away. Do you understand?"

"Sure. We promise, don't we Patty?" I lunged back to the path, anxious to see what the trees ahead were hiding from me.

Patty didn't have a chance to answer or move before Mother said, "Stop." She held out a hand to each of us. "Now hold my hand the rest of the way."

The closer we got to the trees, the more we could see of the house. It seemed fine to me, not anything out of the ordinary, but new and big. The path curved from the edge of the trees to the front door. When we turned that corner, we saw the most wonderful surprise imaginable! A swimming pool glimmering the whole length of the front of the house almost up to the front door! Patty and I squealed and hopped up and down hugging each other.

"Now girls, calm down. This isn't a real swimming pool," Mother warned.

"Yes, it is. Look! Look how long it is, even if it isn't very wide." I argued. Patty nodded in agreement.

"It's a reflecting pool, Dears," Mother explained. "It's supposed to be beautiful and to be an easier way for the gardener to fill the watering cans, just like the little basin downtown. Only this was made to be a part of the garden decoration as well. See the pipes at each end?"

I hadn't noticed them, but yes, a pipe with holes in it ran across the width at each end.

"They spray water towards the middle. To make a beautiful fountain."

"Yippee! We can swim under a water fountain." I said. Patty and I hugged and hopped again.

"But, listen Girls! It isn't very deep. Patty, the water will come just up to maybe the top of your shoulders. It could be dangerous it you tried to jump or dive."

"We won't!" I spoke for both of us. Patty nodded.

Mother explained we would have to wait for someone from the embassy to bring the right chemicals to make it safe for swimming. That would be another new job for Gassam.

Gassam swelled with the added importance of managing a gardener and assistant gardener, a swimming pool, and a well, along with his realm of household duties. Emmanuel's duties included the car, the gate, and the garage as well as his full schedule of family members' transportation. Fatima's job was to oversee Mother's wardrobe, keep the house clean under Gassam's supervision, and babysit when necessary. Ali and Razor were enrolled in a school nearby. The rest of the time, they stayed in the servant's quarter area behind the house.

The kitchen was built into the same back wall as the servant's quarters. We seldom saw Jamal, the cook, but we knew he did not have a family and needed only one of the four rooms provided back there. Gassam's family occupied the other three.

Our house had three bedrooms upstairs, but Mother and Father claimed two of them. One for them, and the other as a "sitting room" for the ladies after a formal dinner where they could gossip and powder their noses before joining the gentlemen again. That was the way formal dinners always ended. Mother and Father enjoyed before dinner drinks there and Mother loved to read and cat nap on the chaise lounge. It was our meeting place for Children's Hour.

Patty and I shared a room, but I didn't mind that in this house because there were many other wonderful places to be, like the living room. Half of it was filled with tropical plants under a glass roof. It was like sitting in the garden in India and two steps out the front length of glass doors was our swimming pool.

Besides, I had my own closet and a desk that Patty wasn't allowed to touch.

Emmanuel lived at the opposite end of our compound in the space above the garage. The Saturday after we moved we headed for the Bazar because Mother had a list in mind of things needed to "finish off our new home beautifully." I smiled to myself as I piled into the car wondering how Father would like the new bunch of littles that would appear after today. Once we were on our way, Mother leaned forward from the back seat, and asked Emmanuel how his new home was working out.

He nodded happily. "It is very good, Madam. I ask my wife family to come soon. When it is not so hot."

Mother raised her eyebrows in surprise. "Oh! Emmanuel, I didn't know you were married."

"Yes, Madam. I am married."

Mother asked, "Do you have children?"

Patty and I held our breath for this answer. We imagined having to share our garden with newcomers. Ali and Razor pretty much kept out of our way after the disastrous tag game in the town garden.

"No Madam. No children. Just wife family." Emmanuel glanced over his shoulder to smile at her, then turned his eyes back on the road.

Our new home seemed to be the best of all worlds. We even had American neighbors on the other side of one of our garden walls. The only thing we missed about our former home was the magic of morning melodies ringing out above the trickle of the jube. Mother reminded us again to remember those sounds. *I will remember them, but they are behind me and now it seems there is always something new and exciting ahead.*

I thought about our moves: Washington to the ship—fun! The ship to the Taj –ugh! But from there to the bungalow —terrific! Next to Hotel de Paris-- awful. and then the Petit Palais-- okay. From there to the army hospital ---horrid! The dumb waiter house—okay, but our villa in Vienna—another terrific! And exciting. Downtown Teheran —strict and scary, but this last move—wow! I decided to put a third promise on my list; Accept other thinking, Find out what's going on outside of my own life, No more fits about moving.

Christian Wives

AS PROMISED, MY SCHOOL LIFE AND FRIENDS HADN'T changed. Emmanuel's driving schedule was full, taking Father to work, us to school, Mother wherever she needed to go, and then getting us all back home. This often meant we joined Mother in the back seat when Emmanuel picked us up at school. Sometimes she'd been shopping, or attending a luncheon, or a formal tea. On these days she greeted us with smiles and questions about our day. Sometimes she sat with her head resting in the corner between the window and top of the back seat. She used her "Let's talk quietly" voice to say hello, then settled into stillness and closed her eyes. We knew she was worn out after being conscripted as a tour guide for visiting American dignitaries' wives. This happened more often than she liked. I overheard her complaining to Father, "Bob, why can't I just tell the ambassador's wife 'No.' She could find someone else to do it."

He patted her on the back. "No one else knows the Bazar as well as you, my dear. You and Emmanuel have that place under your thumbs."

A few weeks into the fall during our drive home, Emmanuel glanced back at us and announced., "My wife family come in two days." Mother leaned forward from the back so he could hear her clearly.

"That is wonderful news, Emmanuel. I am anxious to meet your wife. Please bring her up to the house to say hello after she arrives."

She related the news to Father at Children's Hour that night.

Father raised an eyebrow. "Lord! 'Wife family'? I hope his wife's entire extended family isn't coming."

Mother shook her head. "I got the impression it's just his wife, that is what he thinks of as family. Or maybe wife and mother-in-law, or sister? Let's not get too worried over something we don't know."

I chimed in, "Well, at least we know no kids are coming." Father raised his glass in salute to me and took a big sip.

Two afternoons later there was a knock at the front door. Because we hadn't heard the gate bell clang or the garage creek open, it came as a surprise. Mother opened the door and there was Emmanuel in his best shirt. His hair was slicked back wetter than usual. He beamed.

"Madam, I want to introduce my wife." Two women stood behind him. Patty and I crowded beside our mother. Emmanuel gestured to one of the women. She moved forward. "Madam, this is Miriam." Mariam looked about the same age as some of the older girls at school. She blushed, which made her cheeks look red against her pale skin. She had green eyes, like mine, and perfect arched eyebrows which I wish I had. I thought she looked like Walt Disney's Snow White, except for the kohl outlining her eyes. They looked soft and friendly inside the kohl. *Emmanuel's wife is beautiful. I wonder what kind of clothes she wears under her chador.* It was tan with tiny blue flowers all over it.

Mother shook Miriam's hand and smiled. "How nice to meet you, Miriam. Emmanuel, what a lovely wife you have." From Mother's side, Patty and I nodded and smiled.

Miriam smiled back, then retreated behind Emmanuel. He turned and beckoned to the second woman. I was surprised when she stepped forward. *Miriam brought her little sister with her.. She's pretty, but not as pretty as her older sister.* Her chador was a dark green with yellow diamond designs around the edges.

Emmanuel smiled again. "Madam, this is my wife, Hannan."

Mother jerked slightly and took a step back. Hannan dropped her head and stared at the floor. Mother recovered. "Oh, Emmanuel, you mean your sister- in- law? Your wife's sister?" She reached out to shake hands with Hannan.

"No, Madam. Hannan is my second wife. Miriam is my first.

"But, but Emmanuel, I thought you told me you were Christian. Not that it matters... I just assumed..."

"Yes, Madam." He pointed to each woman, and then himself. "We all Christian. For sure, good Christian."

"But I thought Christians have only one wife."

"Madam, I can have two wives in Iran."

Mother remembered her manners. "You are both very welcome." She shook each wife's hand again. Patty and I nodded and smiled again. When they left, Mother leaned against the front door after closing it, and chuckled. "I can hardly wait to explain to your father what 'wife family' means."

Children's Hour contained considerable stewing as well as laughter that evening. Father was amused, Mother was worked up. "Well," she said, "that is certainly one for the books. And I don't see how it can possibly work. All of them living in that one room above the garage. Mark my words, we are in for some stormy weather."

Two months later her prophecy came true when one morning Patty and I hurried toward the garage to scramble into the car for our ride to school. Halfway down the path Patty stopped. She grabbed my arm.

"What's that?" She pointed to the end of the path. A small pile of shattered crockery lay in front of the garden gate, right below the opened window of Emmanuel's quarters.

I shrugged my shoulders. "Let's go see." Just then a tin pan hurtled through the window and landed with a clang against the gravel. We both stared, opened mouthed, at the window, but saw nothing. Then we heard a woman shrieking.

Patty turned and ran towards the house. "I'm going to get Mother."

"I'll wait here so I can tell her what happens next." I squinted hoping to see into the darkness beyond the open window. I could make out shadows of people rushing back and forth across the room. A woman shouted a long angry sentence. I didn't understand one word, but I knew she was furious. Another woman's voice screamed two sharp words.

Patty came trotting down the path towards me. Mother hurried behind her. I pointed at the dishes and pan, then gestured toward Emmanuel's window. Mother said nothing. I looked up at her and noticed she was halfway smiling. She crossed her arms over her chest and nodded as angry voices tumbled out of the upper garage. Sounds of glass breaking inside the room drifted down to us. Emmanuel's voice pleaded. Mother reached for the gate bell and rang it. Emmanuel popped his head out the window.

"Yes, Madam. I am coming." The women screeched from above as he hastily climbed into the car and backed it out of the garage so we could get in. Mother joined us for the ride to school although she had not planned on leaving the house that morning.

Once in the car, she couldn't contain herself. "You see, Emmanuel. All that fighting and racket just now? That's what comes from having two wives. They fight with each other. I'm sure they are jealous and unhappy. They probably argue all the time. Obviously. They must hate each other. Two wives are very difficult. One is much better."

Emmanuel smiled. "Oh no, Madam. They like sisters. They like each other very much. They are not angry to each other; they are angry with me." He sighed and shrugged his shoulders. "I spend too much money playing cards. They need for cooking."

"Oh." Mother stared out the window for a few minutes. Then she said, "Emmanuel, I'm sorry for interfering."

Emmanuel smiled over his shoulder. "Is Okay, Madam. I will not play cards for one month." Mother was silent the rest of our ride to school. I suppose she remembered we had to accept the way other people thought.

I leaned against the back seat and thought about the difference between Emmanuel's 'wife family' and my family. *Whew! I'm glad Mother never screams at Father like Emmanuel's wives scream at him. But I can tell when they're upset with each other in a quiet way. Like when Father thinks there are too many 'littles' everywhere.* I thought about it some more and realized that mostly they aren't even a bit mad at each other. Mostly they help each other and hug a lot, too. They're a team. I wondered if Emmanuel and his wives were a team. I wondered if his kind of family worked as well mine. Mother sighed and reached for my hand. She squeezed it and smiled at me. I knew we were both working on accepting Emmanuel's way of living.

The Big Kids

I WANTED TO ASK EMMANUEL HOW OLD HIS WIVES WERE, but that wasn't polite. Or any of my business. I suspected they were the same age as most of the Big Kids. The Big Kids, led by Nicco (Greek, eighteen), included Stefanos (Greek, looked like Peter Lorre, eighteen), Zarine, (Iranian, bubbly, curly dark hair and curvy, seventeen), Tanik (Greek) and Hady (Indonesian) both seventeen, Pari (Iranian, long black braids and tilted eyes, sixteen), Antonio Luis, (Italian, sixteen) and Dara (Iranian/German, sandy hair, enormous green eyes, fifteen).

I knew there were secret things going on in the tenth grade. Jenny overheard Zarine and Dara talking about it. When the teachers were busy in a meeting or organizing events on the playground, this elite group of older boys and girls gathered during lunch break in the classroom at the head of the stairs. And they danced! Imagine what the missionaries would do if they found out! If the Iranian mullahs ever heard of such a thing, they'd probably have the kids all stoned to death! As far as I could tell, the mullahs were against anything fun, and especially girls having fun.

The first time after Jenny's news when the teachers were in a meeting at lunch time, I tiptoed up to the classroom door and pressed against it to listen. I heard drumbeats, humming, and laughing. Suddenly the door flung open and Nicco confronted me. "What are you doing here?"

"I want to learn how to dance like all of you."

He frowned. "We'll let you know." He closed the door. Swallowing a bunch of times helped the lumps in my throat not hurt so much. I was not going to give up. I decided to find ways to stay in their sight as much as possible so they would notice me and see how much I wanted to join them.

The rest of the school year passed without a nod or wink or smile in acknowledgement of my pending request.

I started my ninth grade school year with a new plan. I begged Mother to convince the principal that I was ready to take Latin a year ahead of the school's tenth grade requirement. I didn't tell Mother I wanted to take Latin because all the Big Kids were enrolled in that class and this was the last year at Community School for most of them, especially my favorites, Nicco and Zarine, who were starting their second year of tenth grade.

Latin turned out to be difficult in more ways than one, but it did make it hard for the Big Kids to overlook me and my renewed request. Latin had as many strange rules as the tag game in our downtown house. And the class moved too fast for me to linger over rules or vocabulary long enough to understand or use them. Things zipped along because most of the Big Kids had taken Latin before. Zarine and Antonio were especially good at it because they studied Latin in the German School before enrolling in our school.

Another thing that made Latin class difficult was the way the Big Kids treated our teacher. Monsieur Placard, a French Iranian national, was short and round with black hair that looked like it was glued in place. He insisted the class stand up when he entered the room. He opened and closed the teacher's manual continually when explaining a new lesson. His mouth seemed extraordinarily wet when he spoke, and sometimes dripped. When he turned his back to the class to diagram sentences on the blackboard, his rear end moved up and down with his arm motions. I think his most unfortunate habit was banging his book on the table and shouting, "Odre, ordre, silence! S'il vous plait!" He often gave the desk one final beating, pointed to the board where the day's assignment was written, and left the room, slamming the door behind him. This delighted my classmates. They carried on their conversations, and took turns doing the homework which they passed around for all to copy. I was so slow that I managed only a few bits and pieces when the papers passed by me.

The rude chaos upset me more than my slow progress. By now my parents had embedded in me that good manners included a show of respect to adults. *If only Monsieur Placard had more control!* I couldn't complain to my parents or the school because that would be tattling. Guilt gnawed at my backbone. I realized my silence meant I accepted what was going on.

One afternoon in late October on my way out of Latin class, Nicco stepped in front of me and whispered, "Meet us in the room at lunch tomorrow." I stopped in my tracks and squealed.

Tanik joined Nicco and whispered to me, "Maybe Jenny's interested?" He, like most everyone, thought Jenny was the most beautiful girl in school. *I wonder if I can get my mother to dye my hair blond like Jenny's. Mother's hair was blond after we stayed with Aunt Zelda and Uncle Hank, so she knows how.* I shook my head "No" and told Tanik that Jenny wouldn't ever do anything against the rules. That was true, but I knew I was being selfish in wanting my idols all to myself. I closed my eyes and imagined myself with long blond curls cascading down my back.

To the drumbeats of upside-down wastebaskets and rulers on desktops, I learned the samba, tango, foxtrot, rumba, and swing. The Paso Dobles was my favorite dance of all. I could hardly wait to teach it to Alex.

Alex was the main reason I wanted to dance. I spent hours floating through daydreams imagining how it would feel to be standing close to him, moving with him.

Stage One of our courtship had been ritualistic: whenever we crossed paths, he imitated my screech owl scream at the school Halloween party the first time we met. Like all the students going to the party, I was led blindfolded through a ghost walk. When I reached the second stop, I heard a deep crackly voice say, "Ah! My Lovely, before continuing, you must hand me an eyeball from this bowl of human eyes freshly carved out of the pile of bodies up ahead. Pick one or lose one of your own!" Then a hand grabbed my hand and shoved it into a bowl of round wet human eyeballs. I screeched. I screamed. I ripped my blindfold off —and there was Alex, laughing behind a large bowl of peeled grapes. Even in that darkened room, light glowed around him like the sun had just given him a hug.

A month later, we entered Stage Two —passing notes to our respective best friends, Jenny and Peter, who happened to be having their own romance. I wrote things like, "Alex is so cute, do you think he likes me?" and Jenny would accidently show it to Peter, who would relate the contents to Alex. Peter would then leak a note Alex sent him, something like, "Sure, I like her. She knows how to scream." That went on until finally it was established through our intermediaries that Alex and I were boyfriend and girlfriend.

In the early Spring we advanced to Stage Three: sitting next to each other in assemblies if possible, or nearby at lunch, or standing by each other in any convenient line. Stage Four came over summer. It involved clandestinely holding hands in the back seat while Emmanuel drove us somewhere and cheering for each other during games and races in the swimming pool in front of my house and playing tag in the living room.

Now, as a ninth grader, I was ready for Stage Five---dancing! Body contact!

The missionaries did not sponsor dancing at school events. However, some of the older students had private parties which sometimes included brief dancing sessions. Hady gave a party in late November to celebrate his eighteenth birthday. Emmanuel chauffeured Jenny, Peter, Alex, and me. Jenny and I wore long dresses. The boys were in suits. We were ushered into Hady's home by a servant all in white with white turbans wrapped in sparkling beads and finished off with feathers reaching toward the sky. We drank fruit punch on the terrace, then sat at a long formal table gleaming in white linen and crystal water glasses. Dessert was served on the terrace with soft popular music playing in the background. I kept my fingers crossed during dessert that dancing would follow. It was an elegant and grownup evening that surely followed the pattern of the diplomatic events Hady's parents and mine attended. But no dancing.

Antonio Luis's birthday happened in January. His home was also elaborate in the usual diplomatic service ways, but his party was less formal which meant buffet, coco cola, and dancing. At last! Alex, Jenny, and Peter and I were included in the guest list, along with The Big Kids. When the dancing began, I looked eagerly at Alex. He sat silent and stiff beside me. Two songs later, after clearing my throat numerous times, wadding my napkin, and imitating my mother's sighs, we were the only ones sitting in front of empty dinner plates with Antonio's younger brother and his two scrawny fifth grade friends.

"That's it!" I stormed. "You're going to dance with me, like it or not."

"O.K. but my sister only had a few minutes to teach me anything. It's your funeral." He held out his hand and ushered me to the dance floor with all the style I ever dreamed of. My heart fluttered. Alex whispered, "Sis said to escort you to the dancing just like this. Is it right?"

"Yes. Perfect."

Then we danced.

Apparently, his sister had only time for the escort lesson and the briefest outline of the two step. Alex held me at a stiff- armed distance, muttering "one-two, one-two" for dance after dance. *So much for the samba, tango, and goodbye dear Paso Dobles.*

During the Big Kids" secret meeting shortly after Antonio Luis's party, Nicco slumped at one of the desks. He didn't smile or hum popular tunes or bang the bottom of trash cans, and he didn't dance with Zarine. Nothing was normal. Everyone was glum. Zarine stood behind Nicco, patting his shoulder, murmuring comfort.

"What's going on?" I couldn't imagine what was wrong.

Silence answered me until Tanik blurted out, "Nicco has to go."

"Go where?" I looked at Nicco, then at Zarine. She had tears in her eyes. "Go where?" I loudly asked this time. The whole group shushed me.

Nicco looked at me and hunched his shoulders, and said, "To the Iranian Army. All males serve in the army when they are eighteen. I escaped up to now because I was in school and my parents had the right friends to help. But now… I'm nineteen."

"But, but, you're going to Italy for university? You said you were."

"My family waited too long. I should have gone before I was eighteen, but I wanted more English. He shrugged. "Now I will learn a lot more Farsi and, and… army life. My family has tried everything. I must go."

Zarine put her hands on each of his shoulders. She kissed the top of his head, then looked up at us. Tears covered her face. "He must go to them in three days."

Zarine shared news of his training with us for the next month or so, and then he was sent to a place far from Tehran and gone from us completely.

Without Nicco, the dancing fell apart. He had been our leader. I remembered how long ago, when we were on the SS President Polk, our gang fell apart when George and his family disembarked. I remembered Father explaining that groups need leaders to hold them together.

Winter became spring. The Big Kids still accepted me a part of the group because of Latin. In class one April day, I noticed Dara's swollen red eyes. She sat at her desk staring at the floor, at her hands, at her book, but would not make eye contact with any of us. When Pari leaned over and whispered,

"Are you going to be alright?" Dara shook her head "No" and looked away. The class buzzed with whispers.

Everyone seemed to know what was wrong but me. When M. Placard gave up silencing the group and stormed out I went to Dara. "What's wrong? What happened?" I asked.

Zarine took me by the arm. "Leave her alone. She doesn't want to talk about it."

"About what?" *Maybe someone in her family died.*

"Her parents have arranged a marriage for her. She is to be married this summer. She has not seen this man ever, but he is a friend of the family. All she knows is that he's a major in the army and is thirty-seven years old."

Dara left school at the end of the week. She had recently turned sixteen and now there was no reason for her to further her education, the rest of her life no longer belonged to her. I felt the same indignant anger in the bottom of my stomach that I had felt when Gassam pocketed Fatima's salary. I also felt sorry for Dara. She had been sunny and happy, and now it was like she died.

In middle May the school year began winding down. Final exams were scheduled for each class. I worried about the Latin final. Although I had managed to copy bits of homework passed around class, completing the assignment at home was labored guess work. I was hoping I knew enough to get a C-, not a D.

Inexplicably, M. Placard left the class shortly after he handed out his final exam. As soon as he slammed the door behind him, Zarine and Antonio Luis dictated the answers to us. I barely completed number one before they were off to number three. I tried to fill in that response, but only got the last part. I had skipped number two to catch up but now they were on number five. I gave up. I struggled through the test as best I could, erasing and crossing out answers if I caught a hint or two from the conversations going on around me. I felt a hot lump pushing inside my neck. It hurt. My mouth twitched. "I won't cry. Don't cry," I muttered through my mangled attempts. I handed in my mess of a paper and rushed to the girl's bathroom knowing I had just flunked a test! An awful gnawing ground in my stomach the rest of the day. I couldn't sleep that night. Shivers rolled up and down my back. I had flunked. I let my parents down. Maybe even wrecked my chance to go to college. "*Dumb stupid girl*" became a mantra.

Community School held an all school assembly the last day of every school year. Parents were invited. Report cards were passed out after the assembly. My stomach drew itself into a hard clump thinking about that.

Patty and I sat next to Mother and Father. Mr. Fesser, the principal, stood on the stage and talked on and on about how wonderful the school was, how great the students were, how delighted he was to see so many dedicated parents, how kind God was to us all, and how proud the school was of the students going on to higher institutions. At this point, some of the Big Kids were asked to stand and we clapped for them. He called up the chorus and we all clapped while he doled out little pins to them. Patty beamed when she returned to our seats with her chorus pin. He announced he was next calling up the Honor Roll. Jenny and Alex each received one of those prestigious pins. Not me. *Dumb stupid girl!*

Next came what Mr. Fesser called the highest honors of all, the Super Honor Roll. Plus, a special surprise award. He read out five names, and then my name.

I froze in my chair. He called me again. Mother gave me a shove. I stumbled up to the stage. How could I get on the special highest honor roll when I flunked Latin? Couldn't he tell I was a *Dumb Stupid Girl*? Mr. Fesser helped the five named before me put on their pins. Then he paused and indicated I was to stand beside him. He smiled at me, looked out at the crowd, and asked my parents to stand.

He began, "We are honoring a very unique and bright student here today." Inside my head the familiar mantra pounded: *Dumb stupid girl, dumb*

Stupid girl. I wondered who he had mixed my name up with, and how soon he would discover his mistake. I wondered if my face could catch on fire. *Dumb stupid girl.* I didn't hear exactly what he said next. Something about me being brave and honest as well as a good student. Then he explained that I, though just a ninth grader, earned the only A in Latin this year. "As a matter of fact," he went on, "All the rest of the class flunked their final exam." He cleared his throat, paused, and leaned towards the audience. "This is because, with M. Placard's help, we caught the rest of the class cheating. Cheating is not allowed in this school! He thumped the table in front of him when he said that, and then he pointed to me and said, "This young lady was the only honest student. All the other exams were identical. Hers, though not perfect, was her own work. God bless her."

I can't remember how it ended, only that I wished with all my heart to be invisible, to drop through a hole in the stage floor and disappear. In the car on the way home, shudders of nausea engulfed me. I had to tell Mother and Father what really happened. Or, maybe I wouldn't, ever. My head was filled with hot tumbling questions. "How? When? Now? Later? Never? What should I do?

I froze when Mother took my hand and said, "We are so proud of you, Darling." *If Emmanuel doesn't hurry, I'm going to upchuck over everyone.*

Father asked, "What in the world's wrong with you? Are you sick? Is this a collapse from working so hard?"

Patty started crying because I was crying.

As soon as we were home, I rushed upstairs, washed my face, and stared in the mirror. *Dumb stupid girl. Dumb stupid liar girl. Liar. Cheater. Stupid liar cheater.* I hated the girl I saw. I had to make her go away. A sigh just like one of Mother's biggest kind escaped from somewhere inside me. *Mother and Father believe telling the truth right away was the best thing to do. Even if they are never proud of me again, I have to tell them. No matter what.*

I joined my family for children's hour and explained how I tried to cheat with the rest of the class, but that I was too dumb and slow. How rude the class was and why I couldn't tell on them. How I did copy one and half answers for my final, and some parts of homework before that, and how I was a dumb stupid girl, and we had to go back to school and make them take it back!

My parents were quiet through the explanation. When I was through, they gave each other their secret language look, agreeing on something unsaid.

Mother was first. She hugged me. "Honey, school is over until next year. There is no way to undo the honor."

"No. No! It isn't true! Make Mr. Fesser take it back. I cheated. I was just too dumb. The Big Kids will hate me forever. Everyone will. I'm a dumb stupid girl!"

Mother put her arms around me. "Honey, this is far too complicated to undo. I think they needed you as an example. Yes. As a warning against any future cheating. I'm sorry it's so hard for you, but I'm afraid it is something you'll have to live with."

Father took her place. He put a hand on each of my shoulders. Then he lifted my chin to be sure we had eye contact. "Yes. I'm afraid you're stuck. This is one you owe the universe. Live up to it."

That little honor roll pin weighed a ton. I knew that in my very deepest heart.

The Gift

TWO WEEKS AFTER SUMMER VACATION BEGAN, THE PACKAGE I had secretly planned with my Uncle Don arrived. Because our mail was delivered to the embassy, the large box addressed to me surprised Father at work. He brought it home with a lot of questions.

"Deedee, I can't imagine what my brother is sending you for your birthday, and why it's so early? Maybe he thought your birthday was at the end of June, not July? Are you going to wait five weeks to open it?"

Mother crossed the living room to the drawer where she kept scissors. "Let's see what he sent."

"No!" I shrieked and grabbed the box from Father. "I want to wait." I took the precious secret to my room trusting that it held all the fishing gear and everything I asked for. I hugged myself, imagining how surprised and thrilled Father would be with this birthday present, and how the two of us would fish together. Alex promised there was wonderful fishing in nearby Mount Damavand. *Father loves to fish. He and Uncle Don fished every morning and evening when we stayed at Uncle Don's cabin in the Sierras last home leave. And they taught me how to cast.* I expected Uncle Don's bill to arrive the next day. I smiled all over, pleased with myself for saving all my money gifts and most of my allowance to pay for Father's gift. I hid the package under my bed.

On July 1, we gathered for Children's Hour to celebrate Father's birthday before dinner. When he opened my present he sputtered. "Wha, What? How?" He pulled out the rods. Each was in several pieces, tightly wrapped in cellophane. He put one together. It made a loud swishing sound as he whipped it up and down. He nodded. "Great strength." He swished it again. "And flexibility. This is a beautiful rod..."

He glanced at Mother out of the corner of his eye before asking, "Where did these come from?"

Mother's eyes widened. She shook her head and shrugged her shoulder and pointed to me. I felt my smile grow wide enough to push my cheeks into my ears. I had never been so proud.

Father held the tackle box up. "There's more. Oh my!" We huddled around him. The upper tray contained ten different flies, each in its own plastic wrapping and a jar of tiny pink salmon eggs. Beneath lures and hooks and spools of leader was an envelope. Father opened it. He unfolded a sheet of paper.

"Uh oh!" He handed it to Mother.

"What's that?" I asked. I was confused because everything I had asked for was already unwrapped.

"It's the bill," Mother said.

"Oh!" I reached for the paper. "Give it to me. I told Uncle Don to send it but I thought he would send it in a separate letter to me. I'll take care of it."

Mother held on to the paper. "How are you going to do that?" She wasn't smiling. I felt a little worry start to grow in my stomach.

"I saved. I have lots of money, just for this."

She tapped the bill against her opened hand. "Hmmh! You may need some help."

The bill turned out to be much more than the money I had saved.

Father took the bill from Mother. He studied it, then handed it back and began packing everything back in its box. *Is he going to send it all back?* I quickly blurted out about the good fishing nearby, that Alex said so, and he went all the time with his family, and how I planned that Father and I would go on a fishing trip together because he loved to fish and so did I. How Uncle Don wrote how he loved being a part of Father 's present. I ended with, "Now we have all the right things. So, we can go. Right?"

Father "hmphed," crossed his arms, and scowled at me.

Mother came and put her arm around my shoulders. She murmured, "We're afraid Don may have spent more money than is on the bill. We know your uncle will do anything for his big brother. Just like your sister feels about you."

I glanced at Patty. She nodded and said, "Deedee, I saved my allowance too. You can have my money to help."

That made Father laugh. He walked past Patty and patted her on the head. Then he came to me and mussed up my hair, hugged me, and said, "You shouldn't have to think about how complicated grownups are. And going fishing with you will be the second part of a wonderful and thoughtful present. Thank you." He kissed me on the forehead. "I'll see what I can work out at the office for some time off."

In mid-August we started our trip. To my surprise, Gassam climbed into the front beside Emmanuel. I opened my mouth, starting my protest with "Why…"

Mother interrupted. She leaned in the window by me and said, "Yes, Dear, Gassam is going too. You will need his help"

Father had arranged for pack animals and horses to be waiting for us at the beginning of the dirt trail leading up Mt. Damavand. Imagine! Horseback riding as well as fishing! Emmanuel drove as far as the road would allow. Six donkeys, tethered in single file, were waiting for us.. I looked around. *Where are the horses? And what are those big donkeys for over there?. Oh no! Mules instead of horses?*

Father, Gassam, and I each mounted a mule. Father wasn't pleased with the substitution, but he shrugged and said, "It won't do any good to complain now." We rode in silence except for the occasional donkey protest and furious tail swishing. Up we went on the winding trail past wind chiseled rocks and sporadic brush. Our camp site, though absolutely isolated from any hint of civilization, awaited us with freshly swept ground and neatly stacked firewood.

The site bordered a rushing stream. My skin tingled. I twirled and did Grande Jete's all around the perimeter of our camp. I wanted to sing at the top of my lungs but knew that would spoil the rushing water sound in this new world. I was in the mountains! With my father! We were going to fish together for five whole days!

While Father and I organized our fishing gear and tried to follow instructions on how to tie more flies, Gassam set up camp. Gassam's duties included cooking, tending to the fire, cleaning, and being on the alert for snakes and other uninvited creatures. The three pup tents triangulated the central cooking fire. Father slept in one, Gassam and the food in another, and the third was mine. As dusk fell that first night, Father and I gathered around the fire. Gassam presented us with bowls of stew and bread. Although Father invited him to join us, Gassam indicated he was more comfortable eating alone, in front of his tent.

Father showed me how to set up a toilet area and brush my teeth with just a cup of water. I was grateful for my own bathroom and dressing area. If Gassam saw me in my underwear, that would be embarrassing to death. And besides I could get my period any time now according to Jenny. She warned me that first periods always came on trips. After telling her about that conversation, Mother made a little package for me with pads and all, just in case. I certainly wanted that to be private.

As soon as darkness fell, it was off to bed. The stream's steady gurgle was jaggedly interrupted and overpowered by Father's snores and abrupt snorts. They echoed across our camp, bouncing off the ground, the rocks, the water, magnified by our isolation. I heard Gassam muttering in his tent.

"Gassam, are you awake?" I asked in the loudest whisper I could.

"Yes Sir."

"Me too! My father's snoring is very loud."

"Yes Sir."

I giggled, and I thought I heard Gassam muffling a laugh.

At dawn, Father woke me by reaching into my tent and shaking my feet. He immediately established our schedule. Our fishing day would begin with dawn and end at dusk, with time off in the middle of the day for lunch and a nap. He laid down only one rule; Fish within sight of the camp where he or Gassam could see me. It was a reasonable rule to keep me safe, even if it meant no exploring upstream or downstream on my own. I followed his rule happily the first two days of our trip.

On our third day, after his nap Father informed me he was going to try his luck upstream. I was not to follow and to stay within Gassam's sight. Did I understand? I kicked the dirt and mumbled "Yes." and put on the most pitiful face I could when he turned to wave goodbye.

I missed seeing Father nearby. I missed hearing an occasional "Damn!" when he reeled in an empty line. I missed catching him wading into the current to find a better spot, then turning to be sure I was not doing anything as foolhardy. I missed hearing the sudden swish as he flung his line as far across stream as he could. Most of all I missed just knowing we were together on our very own fishing trip. The sun started to fade. I caught one fish, a little bigger than my previous catch. Gassam stood behind me, reaching for my knife a few times, but I cleaned it myself.

Dusk was coming soon. I stood on the edge of the bank, looking upstream for Father. A tiny prickle of worry started to grow in the small of my back. *What if he's lost? What if he's hurt?* But there he was, hurrying toward me. He held three big trout strung together in one hand, his fishing pole in the other.

I ran to meet him. "Wow! The fishing must be great up there!"

Father laughed. "Just one of these is mine. The other two are a gift from a man fishing in the same spot. The strangest thing… He was using a bamboo pole with a line tied to it. And he was catching fish!"

The next afternoon Father announced he was going upstream again.

I quickly gathered up my rod and tackle box and announced, "I'm coming with you."

"No, you're not." Father raised an eyebrow for emphasis. "I hope to run into the Russian Colonel again. He wouldn't want to spend an afternoon with a fourteen-year-old."

I protested. "Russian Colonel? And I'm fifteen."

"Yes. Yes, you are. The man I ran into yesterday said he was a Colonel, and he was Russian. Nice man. Interesting. I'll be back before dinner, don't worry."

"But…" He was gone before I could promise how I would be no bother and not say a word to the Russian. *Did Father speak Russian? Did the Russian speak English? Maybe French?*

Since there was no chance for promises, the only thing to do was follow him quietly and prove my case. Gassam was busy getting gathering firewood. I slipped onto the path.

After ten minutes the trail ahead took a steep turn upward. At its crest, a tall, thin man in a floppy hat stood looking down, watching my father approach. I squinted to see a bamboo fishing pole because, of course, this had to be the man my father was scurrying to meet. No pole in sight.

It was going to be difficult to get any closer unseen. A growing annoyance began tugging at my ears. Somewhere in the distance a voice was calling. And it was coming closer.

Suddenly, as if ice water splashed over me, I recognized the voice.

It rang out clearly, "Sir Diddy Sir."

Gassam! Gassam was frantically searching for me. I hissed, "Be quiet, you fool!"

But Father heard him and swung around to see Gassam trotting up the path. He turned back to wave to the man at the top of the hill, then placed his rod and tackle box carefully in the middle of the trail before rushing downhill to meet Gassam.

Have to think. Have to think. Quick. Quick. Stay hidden and cause a frantic search or come out of hiding and face Father? Circle back to camp and pretend I was there all along? Father gave Gassam strict orders about keeping me in sight. Gassam would die before disappointing Father. And covering up is like cheating. I pictured my unwanted Special Honors pin and came out of hiding.

Father crossed his arms, scanning me from head to toe. He said nothing at first. Then, "Well, well. So much for a quiet afternoon. You turn right around and go back to camp with Gassam. Now!"

"I'm sorry. Really, really, sorry. But I only wanted to fish upstream with you. I promise not to talk or even look at the Russian Colonel. Honest." *Why is it such a big deal, this Russian Colonel? Like a secret or something?*

Father just stood looking at me, saying nothing. His silence was worse than the scolding I expected.

Gassam half crouched on the path, beat his forehead with the palm of his hand, and moaned in Farsi.

Father touched Gassam's shoulder. "It's alright Gassam. It's Okay. She's safe. It isn't your fault. I'm sure she sneaked out in a very clever way."

Gassam nodded as if he understood and stopped beating his forehead. He remained in the half crouch until he glanced up at Father who smiled and nodded. Then Gassam straightened up to his full height, turned back toward camp, motioning me to follow him. The back of his bald head gleamed in the late sunshine. I mumbled, "I'm sorry, Gassam." He didn't acknowledge my apology and muttered in Farsi all the way back without turning to look at me once..

Father returned to his fishing gear and continued up the hill towards his new friend.

On our last day, adhering to Father's schedule, we started fishing at dawn. I felt sad that our time together was ending, yet at the same time, joyful about how wonderful it was. The stream just a step away with its comforting gurgle and flat rocks to lie on and watch tiny fish swim past, casting side by side with Father, eating around our campfire at night, my own private dressing area and pup tent, but mostly, just having time with Father all to myself. I stopped midway on our way back to camp to hug Father around his waist.

"Thank you, thank you," I muffled into his shirt.

He patted my back. "No," he said, "Thank you. This is all your doing,"

After lunch Gassam folded up the three pup tents, rolled the sleeping bags into neat sausages, boxed the cooking utensils, and stacked our luggage. Father and I packed away our shiny gear. "We never used the salmon eggs," I said as I tucked them back into the tackle box.

Father grinned. "You know, the Colonel told me he fished only with worms. I gave him a few of our fancy flies. He studied them, shook his head, tucked them away in his pocket, and told me worms were better."

Everything was packed before five o'clock when the guide was scheduled to pick us up for our return trip. That allowed plenty of time for the mules and donkeys to get us down the mountain before six thirty when Emmanuel was scheduled to meet us. We would be home in time for a regular dinner.

We stood by the gear right where the guide left us. Fifteen minutes later, Father began to tug at his mustache and squint down the trail. He asked Gassam again, "The guide said five o'clock, didn't he? He understood to come for us at five, right?"

"Yes Sir. Yes Sir. Five o'clock." Gassam walked down the trail a short distance. He returned a few minutes later and shook his head. 'No see guide Sir. I go more."

Now it was closer to six. Light would hold for another hour and a half. We were cutting it close. This time when he returned, Gassam's face was pinched and pale and his brow a web of wrinkles. "No guide Sir. I find man with goats. He say guide not coming. Guide mad. Not coming. He say we to follow goats to truck. Truck go down mountain."

Father rocked forward from heel to toe. "The guide is not coming?"

"No sir. Not come."

"Are you sure? The guide is not coming because he is angry?"

"No. Not coming Sir. Guide Crazy. We go with goats to truck, Sir. Goats go now, Sir. We fast go now."

Father said nothing. I recognized that silent anger. We each packed ourselves like donkeys, especially Gassam who could hardly walk with the weight of two pup tents and cooking utensils and his bag. Father carried two sleeping bags and one tent and his bag. I carried my bag, the fishing gear, and a pot Gassam couldn't fit in.

The goats were a five-minute walk away. We followed them down the trail and onto a narrow path. Bushes tore at our loads, small sharp rocks poked our feet, and the herd of goats left dollops of poop behind them. After half a mile the path ended at a dirt road where a rusty battered truck waited.

Two men sat in the cab. Gassam spoke to them at length. The conversation grew heated. The driver stuck his arm out of his open window and banged on the door. Gassam raised both arms and shook his fists at the sky..

Gassam returned to Father. "They take you, Sir. Need dollars."

Father's eyebrow went up. He crossed his arms and scowled at the truck. "Really? Do they know I am with the American Embassy?"

"I tell, Sir. No matter. Want dollars."

Father's arms remained crossed and his eyebrow stayed in a firm upward arch. He cleared his throat. "They should be pleased to be helping us, not charging. How much do they want?"

Gassam's head bobbed. He looked at the ground, the truck, the sky, but not at Father. "Fifty dollars. He say hundred, I tell him fifty."

"I'll pay five dollars. US Dollars. That is all." said Father.

Gassam trotted back to the truck.

The driver sent back a demand for thirty dollars and gunned the motor as Gassam delivered the message.

Twenty was the final agreed sum. The goat herder insisted on being paid too. Father gave him five dollars. Then came the part of the bargain we weren't prepared for; Gassam was to sit in front with the driver and companion, but Father and I were to ride in the back, with the goats!

The men in the cab watched through their rear window, commenting and occasionally laughing as we, with Gassam's help, struggled to lift and stack our gear into the bed of the truck, on the right side, near the tailgate. Father's face flushed in shades of red with tinges of purple in the crevices of his wrinkled forehead. He stepped up into the bed and turned to help me, but I clamored in on my own. *I'll show them that I'm strong and quick, and not a helpless chador-wrapped person they can boss around.* We staked out our place, also on the right side, but as close to the cab as we could get. The wooden railing rose as high as my shoulders. Father could rest his arm on it comfortably, but I could not. I picked out the smoothest part of the lower slat for holding on. Splinters could be a problem.

The shepherd began shoving goats into the truck bed. I scanned the size of the herd milling behind him and took a deep breath realizing there were so many that there would not be enough room. *We're going to drown in a sea of goats!* However, after only four goats, the herder slammed the tailgate shut. I let out a giant "Oaf!" Father nodded curtly to show me he was relieved too. The animals huddled together in the left tailgate corner of the truck bed, as far away from us as possible. They bleated and snorted. Three kept their backs to us, but the fourth turned sideways, watching us and occasionally lowering its head with a thrust in our direction.

With no warning the truck lurched forward. Father grabbed me by the shirt just in time to stop my plunge toward the goats. I latched onto my selected gripping place and braced as we began bumping down the dirt road. When the truck veered to the left, my body slammed against the side. A right turn meant extra arm strength was needed to avoid being flung backwards across the bed. Soon I got the hang of it.

I threw my head back and whooped. "Yahoo! I always wanted to ride in the back of a truck! And with goats! Hurray! What a great way to end the trip!" Father said nothing. With his face still mottled, never letting go of the railing, he watched the goats.

Ten minutes into the ride, one, or maybe two, of the goats wet. A puddle of urine elongated into a rivulet that snaked its way along the floor of the truck bed. Though the stream changed course with each turn and bump, it crept steadily downhill toward us. I never took my eyes off it, ready to jump when necessary. We reached the bottom just in time.

There was Emmanuel, pacing up and down in front of our car. He had no idea that we would emerge from the back of that truck but when he spotted us, he ran forward to greet us. I think he wanted to hug Father. Instead, he pulled himself up to attention and gave the hint of a salute. "Sir! I was so worried Sir! Where are the donkeys and horses?"

At his mention of horses, I exploded. "They were never horses, Emmanuel! They were mules." My words spilled out in hot piles. I couldn't help it. *Enough was enough!. First mules instead of horses, then a goat truck instead of mules. I need a bath.*

Mother greeted us at the front door and mentioned a shower the minute she hugged me. On my way to the bathroom, I heard father mutter to her, "Goddamn set-up. That's what it was..." They disappeared into their bedroom.

Under the clean warm water of the shower, I thought about things that puzzled me. *Who prepared the campsite for us? Was the Russian Colonel really a chance meeting? Who did Father think set him up for the trip downhill? The Russian? The guide? Gassam? Mosaddeq? Who?*

Father changed the subject when I started asking questions at dinner. Mother smoothed my questions away by demanding details about our fishing. Father bragged about our catch and about me learning to clean my own fish. He said it was the best birthday present possible and patted my arm. But he didn't mention the Russian and he fidgeted with his silver ware during our meal. His mouth drew up in a tight line when he wasn't eating or talking.

When Gassam left the room after clearing our main courses dishes, Father slapped his dinner knife the table. He said, "Goddamn it, Betty. I hate it that there was such a catastrophic ending to such a beautiful gift. It keeps coming over me that I, an officer of the US Embassy, relegated to the bed of a beat up pickup truck with urinating goats!"

Gassam came back in with dessert. When he padded out again, Mother murmured. "I am so sorry. Dear. I know you're furious, embarrassed, and feeling humiliated. Just remember the fishing time you and Deedee had together wasn't spoiled. And in a year or so, it will all make a wonderful story."

Goodbye

PHLATT! DEFLATED. LIKE A FLAT TIRE. THAT'S HOW I FELT going to bed after dinner. *All the planning, all the anticipation, and the wonderful trip itself... Over. Done. Finished.*

Alex's visit the next afternoon ended my moping, mostly because he was Alex and we were together. Also, because I learned Mother was right, the good part of a memory stayed good, and the bad part made a good story. As we sat side by side on the Biedermeier love seat, Alex guffawed and laughed through my fishing tale. He draped his arm across the sofa back. Gassam and his assistant, our second houseboy Naveed, slipped in and out of the room, fixing flowers, dusting, and obviously keeping an eye out that no hanky panky occurred. But sometimes Alex's fingers slipped down to touch my shoulder and I melted into the back of the tiny sofa, thrilled with the tingly jolts running through me.

These were rare moments. Mostly we galloped about inside and outside, grabbing and running with items for the other to retrieve, or bumping smack into each other by accident. The pool gave us lots of opportunities to shove or drag each other in. Anything for body contact. Mother sighed and said it was like a pair of wild ponies in the house. Father called it horse play.

Patty began to fade into the background for me as I became preoccupied with Alex. She complained and cried about this to me, and to our parents. In retaliation, she wouldn't let me near her donkey. When Father and I were on our fishing trip, she'd talked Mother into a baby donkey!

Patty named her new pet Francis. Francis was too young to be ridden by humans. When Alex and I were splashing and chasing each other in the pool, Patty spent her time holding Lulu, the Pomeranian, on the donkey's back, walking up and down the pool side, then pulling Francis away if I made any gesture of approaching.

What did I care? I had Alex. Four more wonderful weeks of summer and Alex before beginning tenth grade at Community School. Nothing was going to spoil this time. I forbid myself to think about changes September would bring. Alex had completed tenth grade. The day summer vacation begun, there was no place for him at our school. We didn't talk about it, but bits and pieces began to filter through. He would be starting the new school year in—The States! He planned to finish high school in Los Gatos, California, go to college, and become an American citizen. *That's in the future. Now's what counts.*

A stupid bowl almost spoiled everything. A floor to ceiling steel pole was centered in the entry. Nearby was a stand where Mother displayed a large antique Chinese bowl. It was her most prized of all "finds", a Thousand Flower bowl signed in ancient Chinese characters. She had discovered it in a tiny shop in New Delhi. Whenever she passed it, she gave the bowl a loving tap. Alex and I were playing tag in the entry hall. Alex grabbed the pole and swung himself around in the air to escape my pursuit. His feet hit the stand. The bowl crashed to the floor. We both froze midmotion.

Alex gasped. "Sorry. Sorry. Sorry." He stooped and began gathering up chunks, calling to Gassam to get him a bag.

"What are you doing? I asked as he gently placed each piece in the bag.

"I am going to take it home. We will get another one to replace it."

"I don't think you can. It was special."

"We will. My mother knows where things are. Remember, this is our country now." Because he worked for the Shah, Alex's father, of German and Czech heritage, and his mother, from Russia, had taken Iranian citizenship when they emigrated from Europe, before Alex was born.

When all the pieces were gathered, Alex asked Gassam where he could find Mother. She was in the dining room. Alex knocked on the opened door, then entered and walked up to her. He stood straight, hands at his side, and announced, "I was careless and not paying attention and I broke your bowl. We will replace it. I'm sorry. Very sorry. I am going home now."

He turned and left before Mother had a chance to say a word. I trotted after him as he hurried to the bus stop at the corner of our street, bag in hand. "Alex. Alex. Wait. When are you coming back? Please come back. They won't be cross at you. You can come back, honest."

"Not until I have replaced the bowl," he called over his shoulder.

Through our phone conversations the next three days I learned that his mother had found a bowl not exactly like the one broken, a bit smaller, but very beautiful, and he would be able to bring it in a two more days, after he finished all the chores at home and at his father's work to help pay for it. What Alex presented to Mother was a bowl far lovelier than the one he had broken. Mother was overcome and grateful, but it made me mad. *I hate it. That thing cost me five days away from Alex and he's leaving soon.* Alex had always been acceptable to my parents, but now he became the best possible boyfriend in their eyes. At Children's Hour, Mother praised him as honest, well mannered, and trustworthy. Mother joined me in my sad countdown of days left before he had to go.

Most of the time our friends congregated at my house, but there were times when gatherings were held at other homes. Mother finally agreed I was old enough to take the bus down the hill to be with Alex and Jenny and all the others instead of complicating Emmanuel's schedule. Only in bright daylight, of course.

Besides a driver, busses came equipped with what Mother called a "spotter." Spotters hung out the front door, looking for hazards ahead like donkey trains, or passengers to stop for. Sometimes a spotter ignored my raised arm and his bus zipped past me. Most stopped, usually after a discussion between the driver and spotter and pointing at me, a lone female not in a chador. Foreign. For bus rides I felt more comfortable wearing a head scarf tied under my chin. Because the stark stares of male passengers unnerved me, I pulled the ends of the scarf across my face. I realized that sometimes a chador could be a relief, not a burden. Riding the bus was uncomfortable, but it was my first freedom to venture out of my home on my own. I was ill at ease but thrilled all the way down the hill and back up again.

During our last week Alex was quiet, His eyes focused far away. It had been arranged that he would live with a family who had a son the same age, sixteen. The only thing that slightly lifted the lead weight of his leaving was knowing Los Gatos was near San Jose where Aunt Doreen lived. When Mother tried to console me that I would see Alex next summer on Home leave, I slammed my bedroom door and threw all the clothes in my closet on the floor and stomped on them. *Next summer is years away.*

With only a week left to be together, Alex and I worked on kissing. That was a big deal. Although we didn't have much time to experiment, we found ways to work on it in secret. Mostly underwater in the swimming pool. Sometimes on the Biedermeier sofa, once or twice in the car when we were sure Emmanuel wasn't paying attention.

We promised to write every night.

The dreaded day came. Mother, Patty and I went to the airport. We stood on the tarmac apart from Alex's family. "They need their privacy. This is a difficult and sad time for everyone." Mother said. The tarmac was flat and dark with heat shimmering upward in wavy bars of light and dust. It stretched, wide and empty, from our huddled group in the designated departure zone to an airplane. I could hear the slow steady whomp, whomp of propellers. A narrow stairway jammed against the plane's belly. Alex hugged each of his well-wishers, one by one. He didn't talk. I don't think he could. When it was my turn, I clutched his shirt until Mother whispered beside me, "This is time for you to be a brave big girl. Let him go, Honey."

Alex walked slowly toward the plane. Other good-bye parties, maybe even other planes, were on the tarmac, but I didn't see them. I saw only Alex walking to the plane that would carry him across the world. He didn't turn back until he reached the stairway. He waved once, then walked up and was swallowed. Every part of me ached. *I'm never going to stop aching. I'll cry so much I'll be a puddle and melt away forever. Right here on the tarmac.*

Mother gathered Patty and me under each arm. I bored my head into her shoulder and sobbed. She smoothed my hair. We waited together watching the propellers go faster as the plane began its taxi. The three of us stood locked together until we could no longer see the tiny speck of his plane disappearing into the sky.

Several tears ran down Mother's cheeks when Emmanuel drove us home. I sat next to her and leaned into her warmth. She stared out the car window, holding my hand tightly, sometimes patting it with her other hand. She sighed.

"You are going to miss Alex too?" I gulped.

"Honey, of course, I will miss him, and I am sad for you, too. But I am thinking of what his mother said to me when I called to thank her for the bowl. We talked about his leaving. She sounded sad and I tried to cheer her. I said, 'How wonderful this opportunity is for him, and it will be so exciting for you when he comes home for vacations full of stories of his adventures and new life.'"

Mother took a shaky breath and squeezed my hand. She found a handkerchief in her purse and dabbed both eyes before continuing. "Her answer was heart wrenching. She said, 'Ah, Betty, he cannot come home. Ever. The government will never let go of him if he comes back. They will put him in the army immediately. I will never see my boy again. I am going to lose my son.'"

Mother put her handkerchief away and stared out the window. I scrunched into a ball and moaned. She turned from the window and reached around my shoulders to hug me against her and said, "It all reminds me that that it won't be long before you'll leave us to go to college. But at least I know you will always be able to come home again."

I continued sniffling through dinner even though Father assured me that in June we were overdue for home leave and a new post assignment. He said he'd arrange as much time as possible at Aunt Doreen's because it was near Alex. He mussed my hair and put his hand over his heart and said, "I promise we'll invite him on our fishing trip in the Sierras."

The school year began and with it my count down until June. There was a big change to school this year; Mother joined the faculty. She had been serious about spending as much time with Patty and me as possible.

She taught tenth grade English and Literature and sixth grade history three days a week. I think she was pleased not only to be spending more time with us, but also to be unavailable for "Guide" duty. She explained that she didn't commit to five days of teaching because her hostess and socializing skills were part of Father's job.

What didn't change were the Demonstrations against foreigners that marched past our school. The rhythmic repetition of megaphoned calls and full- throated crowd responses during these marches never ceased being ominous and scary for me, and now they seemed to be louder and more frequent. Although it meant extra time off from school for Patty and me, Father spent more time at work. Our picnics became sparse because he had "to go back to the embassy" many Sunday afternoons. He muttered to himself while pacing back and forth at Children's hour. When I asked him what was wrong, why were people angrier than ever at us, he answered, "Things aren't going well. Mosaddeq…the Shah is… Never mind, everything will work out. Don't worry. You'll be safe. Anyway, we'll be leaving in June. Hold on."

The Well

WITH MOTHER BUSIER THAN EVER, FATIMA'S DUTIES NOW centered around caring for Mother, Patty and me. The new second houseboy, Naveed, took over housekeeping as well as assisting Gassam. However, even with an assistant, Gassam needed instruction and propping up as number one houseboy/butler. This led to frequent visits from Masoud, the head house boy for the American family next door on the other side of our tall wall. He had become a regular help serving at our formal dinners, and in general around the house when extra organizing was needed. Mother had relied on his help when our neighbors could spare him when Gassam was on our fishing trip.

One day in late April , a demonstration sent the three of us home early from school. When we turned onto Kuchee Yakchar, we were surprised to see our garage door wide open. Mother leaned forward and tapped Emmanuel on his shoulder. "Emmanuel, did you leave this open when we left this morning?"

"No, Madam. No worry. When Gassam go to the market for Jamal, he leaves door open so he doesn't put packages down to get in. Then he comes back and close door. Maybe he not back from market yet."

Patty and I raced up the path. When we reached the front door, we called to Fatima to have Jamal make a snack for us.

But instead of Fatima answering, Gassam burst into the hallway. His face was dark red and puckered. He looked at us and then all over the room, rolling his eyes without blinking. "Where Mother Sir?" he gasped.

"She's coming. We ran, but she's coming right behind us." I answered. Patty and I moved close together.

Patty whispered, "He looks strange."

"He looks crazy!" I whispered back.

Gassam didn't budge from the spot where he had abruptly stopped. He smacked his forehead with the palm of his hand twice and then continued rolling his eyes in a non-blinking stare around the room, looking for Mother. When she entered the hallway, he rushed to her and bowed several times. "Madam Sir, come. Come. Oh! Oh! My room. Come, come to. Fast."

Mother walked slowly to place her purse on the entry table, never taking her eyes off Gassam. She said in her calmest voice, "Gassam, just tell me what is wrong. Do I need to call a doctor? Is someone hurt?"

"I dead, Madam Sir. I dead. Oh. Oh. Oh. Come, I show you."

"Do you need a doctor?"

"No, Madam Sir. You see."

He trotted towards his quarters in back. My mother sighed before following him. Patty and I crept behind her.

And there in his room was Fatima wailing mouthfuls of Farsi between sobs as she fumbled with her blouse. And there in the room was Masoud, the head house boy from the American family on other side of our wall. Masoud, who was such a help in training Gassam. Masoud was putting on his belt and shouting. Jamal, the cook, and Naveed guarded the doorway of the room. Masoud and Fatima were imprisoned.

Patty and I stood close together, open mouthed, elbowing each other in the excitement of watching real life drama.

"What is going on?" Mother clapped her hands. The wailing, sobbing, and shouting stopped long enough for her repeated question to be heard.

Masoud's English was almost as good as Emmanuel's. He was the first to answer. "Madam, he should not be so upset. We were measuring the rug. Fatima wants to get him a new rug. For present. Birthday present."

Gassam interrupted. "I back from food shopping. Shop quick, come soon, Madam Sir. Gate open. Fatima no hear me come." He flung his hand in the direction of his wife, then retracted it to beat his own forehead repeatedly. Fatima screamed and tried to stop her husband from hurting himself. Gassam shoved her away. Masoud, shouting in Farsi, hunched into a crouch, rocking forward, ready to tackle Jamal and Naveed, but Emmanuel trotted up behind them, making the human barricade thicker. Masoud was trapped.

Mother clapped her hands in three short loud bursts. "Quiet! All of you! Fatima, go to my room and wait for me. Gassam, I will call for you as soon as I finish with Fatima. Jamal, Naveed, go back to the kitchen. Emmanuel, go home. Masoud, leave now! Never come back!"

Masoud bolted from the room, leapt to the top of the garden wall, and shouted, "Madam, I have gone!"

Patty and I eavesdropped outside the bedroom door, but before Mother could calm Fatima down enough to understand her limited English sputtering through sobs, new shouting rang out. Running footsteps came from the kitchen, through the entrance hall, and out the front door. Mother and Fatima hurried from the house to see what was going on.

The commotion centered around the garden well.

Naveed sprinted past Patty and me on our way out the door. Emmanuel burst out of the garage and sprinted up the garden path. Jamal was leaning over the well. His apron billowed across the top opening as he shouted down into its depths. When Emmanuel joined him at the edge of the well, both men began waving their arms and yelling in Farsi. Fatima dropped to her knees, raised her arms to the heavens and undulated a cry to Allah.

"What is wrong? What has happened?" Mother called out as soon as she was within shouting distance.

Emmanuel turned to answer her. "Gassam jumped in the well, Madam."

Mother's hand flew to her breast. "You're telling me Gassam is in the well? Is that what you are saying, Emmanuel? Gassam is in the well?"

"He not at bottom, Madam. He stuck." Emmanuel thrust his hand out toward her. "Stay back, Madam!" He turned back to the well, looked in again, then back at Mother. "We need rope. Maybe wood… Broom!" He gave Fatima an order in Farsi. She ran towards the kitchen.

Mother ignored Emmanuel's command. She moved into the throng around the well and looked down. "Oh my god! Call the police! No. The Fire Department!" Cupping her hands into a megaphone while standing on tip toe, she called out, "Someone! We need help!" She leaned over the well again, watching with the rest.

I had to peek, to see what everyone else saw. Was it going to be like the man's brains on the street in New Delhi? I eased between Jamal and Naveed and peered down. I could see only about a foot inside the well. I kneeled at the edge and leaned over to get a better view. Just as my eyes adjusted to the dim interior enough to make out the top of Gassam's bald head, and a shoulder scrunched against his ear, Mother looked up and saw me bent over the opening.

"Deedee! Get away from there! Get back!"

She noticed Patty close behind me. "Girls! Both of you. Go into the house. You're in the way here. Go!" She pointed to our front door.

I backed away from rim. Mother returned to the center of the uproar. Where could I go to see what was going without being noticed? Patty sidled up next to me. Her face was a mass of lines from trying to figure out what was going on and how not to be in trouble but wanting to know everything and hating being ordered away. We had to find a place to watch! I scanned our compound. I noticed movement in the second window of Emmanuel's quarters. It overlooked the well. His wives were peering out. They looked worried, maybe even crying. *Lucky. They have a great view.* Not far from the well, in shadow, rakes and hoes and garden brooms leaned against the compound wall. *If we are very still, we can blend in with them.* Patty followed my gaze, nodded, and we backed into our shadowed hiding place. Although we couldn't see into the well, we could see and hear what was happening around it.

Emmanuel barked orders. Naveed sprinted toward the house, passing Fatima who was returning to the well. Her arms were filled with a stack of towels and a rope coiled on top of the pile. We heard Mother call down the well, "Gassam, stay still. We will save you." A muffled voice answered her. She turned to Emmanuel, "What is he saying? Is he in great pain? Can he move? Emmanuel?"

"He say he don't want to be saved. He say he is dead."

I nudged Patty and whispered, "He can't be dead if he just said he was dead."

She nodded. "You're right. He's going nuts."

Naveed hurried back from the house carrying a long-handled broom. Emmanuel and Jamal jimmied the broom handle into the well. Now Jamal took charge. He shouted, sometimes looking at Emmanuel and often down into the well at what I imagined to be the top of Gassam's head. The two men jiggled the broom until just the head of the broom showed above the well. Both men crouched down into a squat. They huddled close together, pulling the broom head toward themselves. We recognized Gassam's voice echoing out of the well.

Patty nudged me. She whispered, "Goodie. He's alive, even if he says he's dead."

Emmanuel and Jamal leaned over the opening and reached into the well. Naveed stooped behind them, holding onto their waists. The three rocked back and forth, pulling. Emmanuel inched out of his crouch. Jamal rose beside him. They both continued to pull together.

"Look!" Patty pointed at the well. "That's Gassam's arm. See?"

Fatima dropped to her knees and trilled to the heavens.

Now both of Gassam's arms and his head filled the opening. Emmanuel and Jamal each grabbed an arm, yanked, and Gassam squirmed out of the well. Fatima ran to him with towels. He brushed her off. With the help of Jamal and Naveen on each side, ready to carry him if necessary, Gassam, stumbled towards his quarters. Mother and Fatima were the last to go. Fatima slumped with her head down. Her whole body heaved back and forth. Mother went to her, put and arm around her, and led her toward the house.

Before we followed, I asked Patty, "Did you notice Emmanuel's wives looking out their upstairs window?"

She nodded. "They could see everything. They looked worried and then happy. Just like us." She glanced back up at the window. The wives waved.

We waved back, then I grabbed Patty's arm and said, "Yes. Like all of us. Hurry up, I don't want to miss anything that happens next."

We were not disappointed. There was more. We got to hear the whole scoop because Father arrived shortly after the rescue. He had requested an embassy car to come home for the emergency rather than wait for Emmanuel to drive into town to get him. Mother was waiting for him, seated on the couch in the living room. Patty and I slipped in and sat quietly on nearby chairs.

Father strode into the room demanding, "Betty, what in the world is going on? Is Gassam alive? Naveed wasn't clear when he called the embassy. I was told Gassam was dead in our well."

Mother shook her head. "No, he's alive. Bruised, but alive. He's resting right now."

"Thank God!" Father's eyebrow shot up. He hunched his shoulder, spread his arms out, and looked straight at Mother. "What in the world happened here?" he asked.

She patted the cushion beside her on the sofa. Father sat down. Mother took a deep breath and began the explanation. "Gassam came back from the store undetected. Apparently, he left the garage door open so that when he returned laden with groceries, he could unload in the kitchen before closing it. That is why there wasn't the usual creaking garage door or clanging gate to announce his arrival. He walked in on Fatima and Masoud in a compromising circumstance. He went berserk. He beat his head until I think he lost all reason."

Father nodded. He must have been remembering the same thing I was. During our camping trip when Gassam lost sight of me and blamed himself, his forehead took quite a beating.

Mother continued. "Then he jumped in the pool, I understand, to drown himself, but it is too shallow for anything that dramatic. However, the splashing alerted Jamal to something unusual happening, and he went to check the pool just in time to see Gassam run to the well and jump in. Jamal started shouting and within a minute, everyone was crowding around the well, Fatima, Jamal, Naveed, Emmanuel, and me. It seems the well narrows about three feet down. Gassam jumped in feet first, with his arms down at his sides. Like this." Mother stood up with her arms rigid and straight down the sides of her body. "He got stuck. Didn't even touch the water below. Just plain stuck the three feet down in the well."

Father smoothed his mustache with his thumb and forefinger. It was a way he had of covering his mouth when he was smiling and didn't want anyone to know. He said from behind his hand, "No! Really? Stuck?"

"Yep!" Mother kind of snorted. "Stuck. Couldn't move his arms. Got one shoulder to move. That's all."

"How did he get out?" Father coughed behind his hand.

"Emmanuel and Jamal used a broom stick to press him against one of the sides so he could get an arm loose. Then they pulled him out."

"My God. And he's OK?" Father dropped his hand. He looked around the room as if expecting to see Gassam.

"Bruised. He doesn't want to go to a doctor. I think he is too embarrassed to explain what happened." Mother clasped her hands and shook her head from side to side. She leaned toward Father. "But the real problem is what to do about Fatima. He won't even look at her."

"Hmm." This time it was Father who took a deep breath. "Unless Gassam is ahead of his culture, you know she will have to go, don't you?"

"Oh Bob. I know that, but I wish there were something to do. We only have five more weeks here. It seems a shame to send her away. Where? And to what? What about the children?"

Father stood up and rang for the bell that usually brought Gassam at a half trot into the room. Naveed appeared. "Naveed, we will have our drinks down here tonight, and are ready for dinner whenever Jamal is ready. But first ask him and Emmanuel to come back with you. I want to talk to the three of you."

Naveed returned with martinis, even cokes for Patty and me. Jamal and Emmanuel followed him into the room.

Father stood facing them.

"I want to thank each of you for the quick thinking and brave help today. Everything could have been so much worse if it weren't for you. We're grateful. I'm sure Gassam will be grateful too. There's no real way to thank you enough, but I am including an extra month's pay when we leave. And now will you ask Fatima to come see me. Where is she?"

The men talked to each other, then Emmanuel turned to Father. "She is helping Gassam, Sir. She is giving him bath and making dinner for him."

Father's eyebrow went up with a quick jerk of his head. "Oh. I see. Never mind, then." After they left, Father turned to Mother. "Well I'll be! It appears he is ahead of his time." He raised his glass in a toast. "Let's hope so. Either that, or he plans to kill her later tonight."

I gasped.

Patty ran to Mother.

"Sorry. Bad joke, girls. It seems all may hold together for our last month here after all. Even Mosaddeq and the Shah seem to be getting along right now."

I went to bed with questions. *Father mention the Shah and Mossadegh again. Are things getting more dangerous here? Mother told us Fatima hated marrying Gassam, that she begged her family not to make her and ran away but they found her, so why wasn't she glad he might be dead?*

When Mother came to say goodnight, I asked, "How come Gassam is letting Fatima take care of him now after he wanted to be dead because of her, and why isn't she happy that he might be out of her life for good?" She took a deep breath and sat on the edge of my bed staring down at her hands folded in her lap.

After several nods to herself and another deep breath, she answered, "Well, Honey, it seems people are complicated no matter where in the world they live. Not all love comes galloping up on a white horse like in the movies. Some is quiet and built up over time."

She paused and took another deep breath before going on, "Remember how wrong I was about Emmanuel's wife family? Let's hope Gassam and Fatima find their own happy ending. People usually choose what they know. Change is not easy. It is often extremely difficult and frightening."

Alex left home. Will I have to do that too? Growing up is a scary change.

I fell asleep thinking about what she said and realizing how wise she was and how safe and known her goodnight hug was.

U.S.A
HOME LEAVE
1953

WE ENTERED THE FIRST PHASE OF PREPARING TO LEAVE.
Mother called this "loose packing." It was more like Packing Battlegrounds.
The State Department had strict rules about weight allowance from post to
post, and how much could accompany us personally to and from the States
on our diplomatic passports. We put things that absolutely had to go with us
(like my fishing pole) into one pile. A second pile contained things we wanted
shipped to our next post, like Lady's collar. It smelled of monkey and carried
memories of her on my shoulder, picking at my hair, nuzzling me. And the
image of her screaming after our car when we deserted her.

My rock collection caught Mother's eye. "No Deedee, you cannot take
your rock collection. It is too heavy. We can't waste our weight allowance on
a box of rocks."

"But this one is from The Taj Mahal." I showed her a translucent white
pebble. "It's so small, no one saw me put it in my pocket." I picked out another
small jagged stone that was rust colored. "This one is from where I got
jaundice on our picnic. And the round ones are from the rock garden in our
back yard in Vienna.. And the one that is split into little slices like a loaf of
bread is from the camping trip on Mt. Demavend. And look! This is lava.
Igneous! I have sedimentary too. And marble. I'm going to be a geologist. I
WILL NEED THEM."

Now Mother smiled. "Haven't heard geology mentioned before. I'll see what I can do to have them included." If she noticed Lady's smelly collar, she didn't mention it.

The rock problem soon took second place to our biggest battle for the one thing that had to go with us on the plane, under diplomatic immunity. Mother, Patty, and I formed a coalition held together by the lingering horror of leaving Lady behind.

Father was firm opposition. His neatly crossed arms signaled a tough defense. "No. I am not going to ask for a favor like that. Absolutely not."

Mother murmured in her gentlest purr how devastating it would be for "the girls to go through such a trauma twice." I stomped, slammed doors, and shouted I would always cry, all my life, thinking about Lady. And Patty sobbed, drenching the very object of contention that was clasped in her arms---Lulu.

It was Patty's bargaining between rasping gulps that softened Father's resolve. "You can sell Francis, my donkey, and use the money to buy Lulu's ticket. And all my allowance forever."

A few days before our departure, word came that Lulu's travel request was approved.

We left Iran knowing that Fatima returned to her village to live with her mother and her children. Gassam was hired by the Americans who took our place. He sent Fatima money for living and the children's schooling. Mother knew Fatima was doing even better. When we left Tehran, Mother was wearing only four of the scads of bangles she had collected from the gold merchants in the Bazar. Because of Mother, Fatima had a future. She would outlive Gassam and be a rich widow. Because of Fatima, Mother was proud of, in her words, "the tiny hole I punched in that wall women are forced to live behind."

It was hard walking out of our front door for the last time. I loved our house, and Fatima, and the swimming pool, and would miss everyone that had been part of our household. I stared at the well as we passed it, knowing I would hear the story about Gassam getting stuck many times in our summer ahead. I would miss seeing the mountains in a distance, the street vendor's calls, the donkeys, the busses, even the demonstrations. I loved Iran. For a fleeting second I grimaced at the thought of the rounds of relatives and being a houseguest waiting for us but smiled remembering how good it felt to be a part of a big family in my own country. Then the most important thing of all about home leave flooded my thoughts. Alex was there. Waiting for me.

After a two week debriefing in Washington, we began our second cross country drive. Father planned to stop at various university campuses so I would have an idea of what colleges I would like to apply to. He reminded me, "After all, only one more year and then you'll be a senior and then graduate and go off to the States for school."

Before leaving Washington, we had visited Georgetown University. Mother used the word "surly" when filling Father in on the day's doings. Georgetown's pathways were filled with students striding ahead with purpose and stacks of books. Mother tucked my arm under hers and said, "You will part of this in just two years. Isn't there a nice feeling here?"

My answer may have sounded a bit surly. "It's Okay, I guess, but why can't I go wherever you are? Why can't I just stay with you until you come home for good?"

"Honey, every little bird must learn to fly. Georgetown is a good choice because your father will always be based from Washington so we will always come here first." The busy students passing us became a blur. I glanced at Mother as we stood arm and arm. Her eyes were shiny with imprisoned tears, too.

None of our stops impressed me much because my one objective was to get to California and Alex.

Father purchased a Studebaker for our drive across country. The car astounded me. The front and back looked alike. *How can anyone tell which direction it's headed, silly thing?* The back seat was filled with Patty at one window, me at the other, and Lulu panting between us nudging our hands for constant pets. A swath of crinoline petticoats swayed from the hooks above each back window, curtaining the front from the back. Father insisted on a clear line of vision out the back window which kept Patty and me busy squashing plumes of ruffles to the side. He groused, "I don't see why we have to have those damn things all over the back. Why aren't they in a suitcase?"

Mother soothed, "They would take up the whole suitcase. Come on, Dear, this is what girls are wearing in the States now. Under every teenager's skirt, there is at least one crinoline. It's important to them, and to us, if you think about it. Isn't that the purpose of home leave? To reacquaint ourselves with our culture?"

"Grrhumff."

His bear growl meant reluctant acceptance and for us to stay alert and keep his rear vision path clear if we wanted to have stiff tiers of ruffles beneath our new skirts.

There was no embarrassing pony trot through throngs of sightseers this trip. Mother behaved herself, but Lulu did not. Somewhere in the middle of the country, in a little town on Route 66, at a quick stop for gas and snacks, Lulu slipped out of the car and disappeared.

Patty was beside herself. She sucked in great gulps air between heaving breaths while clasping and unclasping her hands. We were all upset, sputtering, hot, and feeling helpless about how to go about looking for that fluffy little dog in this flat unfamiliar town.

And of course, we were on a schedule. The sooner we got to California, the more time we would have with our family before the next assignment, which was still a mystery. Father growled about wasting time looking for the damn dog. Patty sobbed that she would look for Lulu until she found her no matter what. Mother calmed things down when she said, "Bob, Patty, this is a time for diplomatic compromise. We can all agree on something reasonable, even though no one gets exactly what they want. I insist on a compromise."

It was agreed that we would spend one hour looking for Lulu.

Father had a plan. "If we're going to take this time, which would most likely cause us to have an extra night on the road, we might as well use it wisely. This gas station will be our home base. Meet back here in exactly an hour. Betty, you and I will split up taking the north-south avenues. Girls, stay together. Go down the side streets. Deedee, you are the oldest. Make sure you stay together and keep track how to get back!"

Patty and I searched streets named after the Alphabet. We started down the right side of E Street. We squinted into the front lawns and sides yards of each house.

We called, "Lulu, Lulu. Here Girl. Lulu." Here and there women puttered in their yards or pushed baby strollers. They smiled at us and asked what we were looking for. We explained, jumping over each other's sentences.

"Our dog jumped out of the car."

"She is little."

"And fluffy."

"And we have to find her, or our Father will make us go on to California without her."

Strangers promised if they found her, they would be waiting for us when we retraced our steps back to the car.

Half an hour passed. On I Street I suggested, "What if you take J and I take K and we meet at L?

Patty agreed to the solo searching. She reasoned, "We will hear each other calling Lulu, so we won't really be separated."

After searching K Street, I turned the corner onto L, expecting to see Patty. I walked halfway down to make sure she wasn't in some side yard. My stomach started to churn slowly. Father's words echoed in my ears, "Girls, you stay together. Deedee, you are in charge. Take care of your sister."

It was time to start back. *Think, Deedee!* I gritted my teeth. I knew I absolutely couldn't go back without my sister, but the later we were, the more upset Father would be. *I have to find her! Maybe she went to the next street. She has to be on M Street. She just has to be!* Worry crept up my back and through my stomach.. My skirt was bunchy and the crinoline beneath it scratched my sweaty legs. My blouse was damp and sticky.

I trotted to M Street. *Patty has to be here.*

Thunk! My heart dropped.

The only sign of life was a man in a faded yellow shirt mowing his lawn. I ran to him and asked, "Have you seen my sister? She's eleven, almost as tall as my shoulder, blue skirt, braids, looking for our dog."

He pointed to a house two doors down. "My neighbor took in a little dog she found running down the middle of the street. And a girl looking for a dog came by maybe ten minutes ago. Told her about my neighbor. Sure hope it's your sister and your dog."

I raced toward the house he pointed out. I could see two people through the half opened doorway. *Please be Patty.* I ran toward the door. It opened wider, and Patty stepped out with her arms full of a wiggling, licking, and yipping Lulu!

The next hour of our drive was filled with Patty and me tumbling words over each other's, describing our hunt.

"Everyone was friendly and wanted to help."

"Their gardens were right out to the street where you could see them…"

"And walk to their doors without walls and gates."

When we finally ran out of steam, Mother turned to face us in the back seat, and said, "You have now seen the very heart and backbone of our country. Middle America. Plain, simple. honest people with good hearts."

The rest of our trip gave me plenty of time to think about what Lulu's adventure had taught me. *My country has a big heart in its small towns, and my sister has a lot of determination.*

Two days later. we arrived in California. Aunt Doreen's was our first stop. And there was Alex, taller than before, and still with that glow about him as if the sun had just passed by. He stood apart so he wouldn't intrude on our welcome. I waved at him before being pulled into a whirl of kisses and hugs and questions from Aunt Doreen and Uncle Calvin.

When the greeting frenzy died down, Aunt Doreen suggested Alex show me their garden while she got the family settled in her guest rooms. We walked to the edge of the lawn area that overlooked the city of San Jose and rolling hills beyond. We stood side by side, mute. The air seemed to quiver around us. I took a breath and broke the silence. "I missed you."

Alex answered, "I missed you too." My hand floated on its own accord into his. We walked around the garden, holding hands, asking and answering questions about his family, Francis the donkey, kids at Community school, how high school was in the States, what it was like to live with strangers. Then it was time for him to go. He was not staying for dinner because the bus schedule to Las Gatos was complicated. He would be back tomorrow though. And the day after, he'd join us on the fishing trip.

We spent ten days at Uncle Don's cabin high in the Sierras, not far from Donner Pass. Alex and I fished with Uncle Don and Father. We sat on the stream bank, holding hands. We played monopoly with Patty. We made ourselves useful setting and clearing the two end- to- end wooden picnic tables where all the Carr clan gathered for supper. Night fell. Crickets chirped, and the pine trees rustled with hidden night creatures. After dinner, everyone gathered around a campfire. The grownups nursed another cocktail or two, told stories of their youth, and listened to stories of my family's time away. There was raucous laughter, and sometimes song.

During some of the stories about our time in Iran, Alex would whisper, "That's not exactly the way I remember it happening."

I explained, "I know. Father says because Mother considers herself a poet; she takes poetic license with the truth. That includes inventing words and people like Hanzi Prock." Sitting as close together as the rickety folding chairs allowed, with Alex's arm around my shoulders, I rested my head as near to his as possible. I felt safe, happy, and surrounded by home.

August came and still no word of our next post. We left Father's family and went to Los Angeles for three week stay with Mother's big brother. I was upset at having to leave Alex, but glad we'd be reunited in a few weeks. Father drove, but Mother, Patty, and I flew down in Uncle Hank's tiny airplane. He had me sit in front beside him, with Mother and Patty in the two back seats. Mother was upset and nervous from takeoff to landing., but not because she didn't trust her brother's piloting. He had his own flight school and small airport and flew stunts for the movies. It was his pretending to be asleep and snoring loudly while putting me in charge of keeping us on course. Or his suddenly sitting bolt upright and saying "Uh Oh!" then launching us into several rolls or spirals. He winked at me and said, "Ignore the noise from the back."

Mother sat in front with him on the drive from the airport to his house. I leaned forward to eavesdrop on their hushed conversation. He said, "Sorry, Betsy Boodle, I just wanted to see if she had it in her. She does! Just you watch! We'll have her flying solo before the three weeks are up."

Too excited to hear anything else, I forgot to mope over Alex for a few hours. After all, we were returning to Aunt Doreen's in three weeks, and I would be able to tell him all about flying an airplane.

Four days into our stay, Father received a phone call from Washington. When he hung up, he beckoned to Mother. With his hand in the small of her back, he hurried her into their guest room. Patty and I hurried after them. Before he closed the door on us, I heard, "The Shah fired Mosaddeq, For God's sake, Betty, he was rightfully elected! Goddamn Brits and their oil. Pulled us in with the Tudeh party as bait." Then the door slammed shut.

Father left for Washington and we waited anxiously to find out our next post. I earned my pilot's license with a lot of help from Uncle Hank, and we returned to Aunt Doreen's with plans to stay there as long as it took for Father to find out where we were going next.

Within a week he was able to tell us.

Egypt! Pyramids! Cleopatra! The Nile! Camels! And our own home.

Our enthusiasm dampened when Father explained that it would be several months before we could join him in Cairo. Egypt was in turmoil. Although General Naguib and Colonel Nasser had replaced King Farouk, the army and the Muslim Brotherhood were not getting along. There were riots and demonstrations worse than the Tudeh party staged in Iran. Father promised things would settle soon, and he would have a lovely house and staff in place when we joined him.

Capitola

MEANWHILE, WE HAD A PROBLEM. SEPTEMBER AND THE school year were just around the corner. Where would Patty and I go to school during this waiting period? Aunt Rudy, (Uncle Hank's first wife and one of Mother's very best friends) came to the rescue. She had a small cottage in Capitola which her family used in the summer and sometimes rented out during the year. We were welcome to it for as long as we needed it.

Hurray! Patty and I burst with relief and adoration for Aunt Rudy. Being well behaved house guests in so many different homes all summer had been as much a strain this home leave as it had been three years ago. The endless streams of necessary thank yous, care not to disturb things, people. or routines instigated what Mother called "meechie – meechie" behavior when we pinched each other whenever possible, just to let off steam. And we made faces indicating bad smells when no one else was looking. We slipped unwanted food onto each other's plates.

I was so grateful that sharing a bedroom with Patty in the tiny cottage didn't upset me. We didn't argue over drawer or closet space. We even pooled our bobby pins. Best of all, for once, we would be real American girls going to school "In The States!" Not in the back garden with cobras like New Delhi. Not the Calvert System in the empty ballroom in Paris, or the Army School in Vienna, or singing Holy Holy Holy" on our way to class in Teheran. I was going to be a real American teenager, a Junior at Santa Cruz High.

I was awe struck and out of place my first day. *Wow! What a big school! How will I know where to go?* Most of the students had been together since their Freshman year. I was alone, without Patty, the back-up I could depend on no matter what. She was in a different school. I was stripped of the immediate acceptance that came with being a daughter of the American Embassy. I felt like a pebble watching from the bottom of a stream as students flowed above me. I watched them yelling greetings at each other in the hallways, groups of boys guffawing and pretend punching, groups of girls giggling and fluffing their hair, boy and girl couples attached by the boy's arm drooping over the girl's shoulder, and loners, rushing somewhere they sighted ahead, clutching books to their chests for comfort.

I was invisible until word spread about my being a short timer on my way to Egypt. Then I became an exotic oddity, worth saying "Hi, Cleopatra" to in the hallways.

Mother helped me pick field hockey as my choice of P.E. activity. She said it reminded her of Polo, without horses. It was in this throng of girls in dark blue gym shorts that I found friends and felt at home in Santa Cruz High.

However, Junior Algebra was scary and disagreeable. I went to class with foreboding. In Tehran, I had looked forward to Mr. Pond's 10th Grade algebra classes at Community School. He presented equations as puzzles to be solved or secret messages to be unencrypted. An easy A for me. But at Santa Cruz High, there was no Mr. Pond, only Mr. Ernest Green who paced up and down the tidy aisles between our silent rows of desks. The skin below his nose was thick and in a constant pucker. I wondered if that was because he was super sensitive to the smell of teenagers? The principal had insisted I take a *real* algebra class at a *real* high school if I wanted to go to a *good* university in the States.

From the worried look on my classmates' faces, I knew the Algebra midterm would be as difficult as Mr. Green could make it and vital to my grade. My homework papers had all been correct, and I took careful notes. So far I was doing well. I handed in my exam as instructed: folded neatly in half lengthwise with the problems and answers inside, and my name on the outside in the upper right corner.

Mr. Green personally handed back the test papers with a grade neatly written on the outside directly under the student's name. He did this with a quick glance at the recipient, without comment or facial expression. However, when he came to me, he stopped, stared, coughed loudly, and shook his head before going on to the next name in his pile.

I looked down. There was my name at the top as prescribed. Beneath it the sheet was covered with a big fat black "F." I sat still, stunned in disbelief before embarrassed heat slowly covered my whole body. The classroom clock showed it would be an hour before I could get on the bus and go home. All I wanted in the whole world at that moment was not to cry until I flew into Mother's arms. She would hold my world together.

And she did.

She held me until I finally took a long steady breath. Then she gently lifted my chin up with one hand while smoothing my hair with the other and said, "Are you ready to look at it? Let's see what happened. I can't imagine you were completely unable to pass this test. You understand algebra. Something is out of kilter. Let's go over this together."

She unfolded the test. I had not dared look inside at school. It was worse than I imagined. All I could see was a paper full of red pencil marks and I wanted to collapse against Mother's shoulder again, but it was not available. She was bent over the paper, examining it intently. "Hmm, look at this. What does it mean?" She asked me. She was pointing at small rectangle outlined in red pencil with a red line diagonally struck through it.

I shrugged.

"Look Deedee, these little red boxes are all over the paper. They seem to be placed below each problem. Any idea what that means?"

"No. I don't know what they are. I showed all my work, like Mr. Green said, and I underlined my answers in each problem, like Mr. Pond taught us, see?

Mother found a few sheets of blank white paper. She handed me a sheet. "Here. You work problem number one; I'll do the second. Let's see if our answers match the ones on your test."

They did. We went through the whole test that way. All the answers came out the same, except for the last problem, which I hadn't had time to finish. We both agreed I was on the right track for it though. I had understood everything Mr. Green presented. My homework was always correct. Mother was right. Something was out of kilter. Mother folded the test and tucked it in her purse. She called the school for an appointment with the principal the next day. I was to meet her in his office after my last class. Mr. Green would be there too.

I had told Mother about Mr. Green's upper lip. She was staring at it when I joined them in the principal's office. The two men looked dowdy against Mother's elegant navy linen suit, pearl necklace and earrings. She smoothed my test out on the principal's desk and pointed to each underlined correct answer, explaining patiently that nine out of ten correct answers equals 90%, an A-, not an F.

Mr. Green pointed out the red rectangles, stating that all his students knew their answers were to be placed in a rectangle to the bottom right of each problem. He looked at me, his upper lip curled, and he said, "I didn't have time to decipher how it is done in Egypt."

Mother took a deep breath and replied in honeyed tones, "I am not yet sure how they do it in Egypt myself, especially since their numbers are written in Arabic, from right to left, but I do know we owe much to Egyptian mathematicians. They were building pyramids while savages were busy painting their faces blue in Europe. However, I will be glad to let you know what I find out once we join my husband, a high-ranking officer of the United States Diplomatic Core who has just recently been sent to our embassy in Cairo."

A compromise was reached. My grade was changed to a C. Mr. Green admitted I was a good algebra student, but insisted I learn to follow directions. On our way home, Mother squeezed my hand and giggled. "You were right. Mr. Green looks like he hates the smell of teenagers."

We celebrated our victory by buying the wind-up record player on the way home that Patty and I had our eyes on for several weeks. Patty clinched the deal by reminding mother, "We can play our music quietly in our room while your having your fancy dinner parties."

When Alex came to visit the next Saturday, I played Jo Stafford's *You Belong to Me*. Alex and I felt it was written for us alone, especially because of the line "See the pyramids along the Nile..."

Alex joined us as often as he could that fall in Capitola. Too many times, in my opinion, his weekends were claimed by football. His high school coach considered Alex a treasure trove: a talented athlete steadily increasing in size, who had never been exposed to the game and thus had no bad habits. He was a blank slate upon which to build an impressive player. Alex had grown three inches in the ten months we had been separated. He seemed to be taller and bigger each time he came. I figured Apollo must have looked a lot like Alex: tall, strong, shimmering light brown almost blonde hair, and green eyed.

We spent time at the boardwalk in Santa Cruz, on the roller coaster, ambling through the arcade, and mostly just walking, hand in hand, with the other hand free to hold cotton candy. I loved the pink cloud swirls of sugar and how they melted to just a few granules of gritty sweetness when you chomped into them. We talked about how I was sure to be a hit in Cairo with my collection of hit parade songs, my poodle skirt, and student pilot's license. And about his plans for college, that his coach thought he had a good chance at a football scholarship. And we talked about the coming long separation coming possibly in just a month, then changed the subject quickly.

We also swam and sunbathed at the beach in Capitola if the fall afternoon was warm and sunny. I especially looked forward to the walk home from these outings. Our little cottage was on a cliff above the beach. There were several ways to get back and forth from it to the town, one of which was a long flight of steps going up the cliff from the beach. Alex and I always took the steps.

About halfway up, we left the wooden stairway and looked for a friendly bush or two to shield us from any other stair climbers. We sat on the dusty ground in our hideout watching the ocean froth below us. We reminisced about Tehran, his friends and family there. Sometimes his eyes became full and shiny as he fought against home sickness. However, the real purpose of our stop along the way home was kissing. These were short sessions because Mother had dinner ready and Alex had a bus schedule to meet.

The time galloped by. We whizzed through the holidays, down to the last week, then the last day and finally the last two hours together. On our stop on that hill side, just before Mother, Patty and I were off to Cairo, Alex and I cried together.

I continued crying on the plane all the way to Rome from San Francisco. Even though I was emotionally spent and no tears were left, I pretended to cry more on the last leg of our flight from Rome to Cairo because I believed Alex deserved the whole long journey's cry.

PART VI.
CAIRO
1953

6 Shagret El Dor

FATHER WAS AT THE FRONT OF THE PASSENGER GREETING crowd when we landed. A small wiry man dressed in a black knit vest, tight chocolate brown trousers and jacket, and a dark red fez scrunched on his head stood behind Father. After our tearful greeting (Mother, Patty, and I always cried when overcome with happiness) Father explained, "This is Hassan. He is our driver. Give him your baggage tags. He will take care of everything."

Hassan hurried off in search of our luggage after a curt nod of acknowledgment towards us. The tassel on his fez snapped back and forth with the nod. He did not smile. Patty looked up at Father. "I miss Emmanuel."

Father raised an eyebrow and smiled, "So do I. Things are a little more formal here. You'll see."

I asked Father, "What is our house like? Will I have a room of my own?" I stared at Patty with my eyes squinted to slits to show her that even though we had roomed well together in Capitola, I wanted my own space. She made a face and looked away with her chin up high to let me know she didn't care. I said to her, "You have to get all your things separated from mine,"

Patty glared at me. "You can have your stupid bobby pins back." She turned to Father, "Do we have a big garden? If we have a big garden, maybe the State Department will change their minds and let Lulu come. Aunt Doreen could bring her."

"We're better off without that stupid dog. Poor Aunt Doreen is stuck with her." I muttered.

Mother sighed, "Girls, Girls. No fighting. Even though we are all tired out from our long flight, let's begin this new adventure on a happy note."

Patty latched onto Father's hand as he led us towards our car which turned out to be the black sedan and the only vehicle parked right in front of the exit door. An army guard stood beside it in a light tan uniform with insignias on the sleeve and a rifle over his shoulder. Mother stopped and murmured, "I do have to ask, Bob, how settled are things here?"

"We'll talk about it later. Not in front of the guard, or Hassan," Father answered in the same hushed tone.

Mother nodded. "I see." She followed Patty and me into the back seat and cleared her throat several times until we stopped jostling for the window. I won the window, but Patty evened the score by nestling up against Mother.

Father sat in front with Hassan. The car had barely pulled away from the airport curb when Patty leaned forward and tapped Father's shoulder. She said, "If Lulu can't come, do you think we could get a dog that looks like Lulu?"

I don't think Father heard her because he didn't answer.

I leaned my head against the windowpane. My eye lids drooped. I was almost asleep when Patty poked me. "Move over. I want to see what's under the bridge."

"Bridge?" I sat up.

"Yes." Father turned around from his seat in the front to face us. "Our house is in Zamalek. Zamalek is a small island in the middle of Cairo."

"An island? How can there be an island? I thought Egypt was in a desert, with camels and pyramids." I was blindsided by this island idea.

Father twisted his head around from the front to face me. "Don't forget the mighty Nile, Deedee. Zamalek is an island surrounded by the Nile. "

I looked out the window, down on the river beneath us. In the dusk of evening it was a wide swath of dark ripples. Its sides were lines with small boats, some with sails, some with squat wooden cabins. A giant boat floated down the middle of the river, dwarfing the other boats as if they were ants beside a football. Its white sails almost touched the bridge. "Look at that enormous sailboat!" I said, nudging Patty's ribs.

"That is a felucca," Father said. Some of them are big enough to be restaurants. They have been a part of Egypt from the beginning."

Father pointed ahead of us. "This island is the preferred residential area for most foreign embassy families. As a matter of fact, you remember Hady, from Tehran? His father is the Indonesian ambassador here. He lives just a block away from us."

I smiled. Now I had something important to include in my first letter to Alex besides how much I missed him. I glanced out the window. We were on a busy street lined with two and three-story buildings. Small shops occupied their street level. Hassan began slowing. He rolled down his window and stuck his hand out to signal an upcoming turn just as we passed a tall building. It was maybe fifteen stories high, patterned with rows of balconies, many of which were filled with banks of flowers, small trees and green umbrellas. Vines trailed over railings.

"Gosh! I didn't expect fancy apartment buildings here," I said. My desert and camel stereotype was challenged again. Besides, the January weather didn't match my idea of searing desert heat.

"Oh yes." Father gestured toward the building. "Those are very elegant flats. Zamalek is an expensive place to live. I could have found us a place in

Maadi, much cheaper and full of Americans, but I think Zamalek has a lot more to offer, especially charm." He gave Mother one of their secret language looks. "I know your mother will agree." He turned back to the front and pointing at the tall apartment building added, "Unfortunately, the back of that building looks right into our garden."

Hassan turned down the side street behind the towering apartments. We passed several walled compounds with large houses barely visible beyond their front gates. He came to a stop in front of a house where a guard stood at attention beside its front gate.

Father announced, "And here we are. Number Six, Shagret El Dor.

Patty and I tumbled out of the car after Mother. The guard, stiff in stance and expression, opened the gate. I noticed a polished brass plague centered on the gate. On it Father's name was engraved in crisp no-nonsense capital letters. Below his name, in startling contrast, embossed black Arabic script flowed in graceful curves and loops. We followed Mother and Father for the short distance to the front door.

The door swung open. Inside, three men stood side by side in line. They were dressed in what looked to me like floor length white shirts. The first in line was an older man with a kind round face, and white hair. His dark red fez stood straight, not crunched like Hassan's. Father nodded toward him and announced, "This is Ahmed. He is in charge of everything."

Ahmed smiled. "Welcome Madam. Welcome daughters." The tassel on his fez swung forward and back when he bobbed his head to greet us in turn, first Mother, next me, and then Patty.

The man next to Ahmed was shorter. He wore a vest that looked like it had once belonged to a three-piece pin-striped suit over his long shirt. Father nodded to him. "This is Mohammed. He is our cook. And before you ask, the kitchen is off limits." Mohammed nodded but he said nothing.

Last in line was a tall thin young man. Although he stood still, he seemed to be bouncing. Energy exuded from him. Father gestured toward him. "And this is Mitwali. He is Ahmed's assistant." Mitwali dipped his head and grinned at us showing a mouthful of big teeth. His tassel swung forward past his nose, and back behind his ear with the greeting.

Father cleared his throat. "And now Mohammed, we will have dinner." He turned to Patty and me. "Girls, Mitwali will put your luggage in your rooms. Show him which suitcases are which, and he will show you which rooms are which. Freshen up quickly and then come straight down to the dining room for dinner. No grand adventures tonight." Father pointed to a door opposite the entry. "Meet us there in ten minutes." He knew us well. Our travel fatigue had disappeared. We were itching to run through this big new house, open every door, and fight over whose room was whose. Relief and joy swirled in my head. *I have my own room!*

Ahmed quietly whisked Mother's bags upstairs with Mother preceding him up the steps while Father was speaking to us. I pointed out my suitcases to Mitwali. He gathered all three and headed up the wide winding staircase. I followed two steps behind him until I paused to check on Patty. She stood looking up at me from the bottom of the stairs, alone in front of her luggage. Her face twisted, ready to cry. I realized we had been ranked by our staff. Father was, of course, The General. Then came Mother: Colonel. And I supposed I must be a First Lieutenant and my little sister was a Second Lieutenant. Mitwali was attending to me accordingly.

"Mitwali, wait!" I said. He turned, looking confused. "Stop!" I commanded. He stood still. I ran down the steps and grabbed two of Patty's suitcases. She picked up the third. We started upstairs. Mitwali grinned again and took the heaviest suitcase from me. He struggled ahead of us with four bags, and we struggled behind, with one apiece. At the top of the stairs, Mitwali put Patty's case down and took my three to the front corner room. He returned quickly and carried all three of her cases into Patty's room, between mine and what turned out to be our parent's suite.

A quick survey of my new room almost had me crying with happiness again. A window looked out on Shagret El Dor. I could see the top of our gate guard's head. Directly across the street I noticed a three-story building with a large entrance and a doorman. There were several compounds filling the rest of the block. Because my room was in the front corner of our house, I had a second window on a side wall that overlooked a side yard. That would be a good place to display my rock collection.

I peeked into Patty's room. Her only window looked out onto the side yard. A tangle of vines with white flowers climbed the fence below. Patty was kneeling in the middle of her bed. She waved at me and said between bounces, "Look how big my bed is!" It was a double bed. My bed was only a single. But I liked that because that left me more room for the plans I had for my new space, and it made up for Patty's room having only one window.

The door to our parent's room was ajar. Patty and I knocked. No answer. They were already downstairs. We looked in on a room furnished with a couch, coffee table, several armchairs, and a desk off to one side. One wall had a door at each end. I said outload, "Where is their bed? Certainly, they can't sleep on the couch."

Patty shrugged. "Dunno. We'd better get down there." She pointed to the stairs.

On our way down to dinner I told Patty the things I had learned since our arrival; there were a lot of rich people in Cairo, we weren't in the desert, Mitwali did not understand much English, and the gate guard didn't like us.

Patty squeezed my hand. "But" she said, "We are in our own home."

She was right. I felt relaxed and comfortable already, but it didn't mean I wouldn't miss Alex every second.

At dinner I asked my parents, "Where do you guys sleep? When Patty and I saw into your room on the way down. It looked like a living room. Does the couch pull out at night?"

Mother put her fork down and laughed. "It is the most marvelous arrangement here. There is a sleeping porch just off the sitting room you saw."

Patty looked at me, then Mother, then Father. She asked, "What's a sleeping porch?"

"Well," Father said. He kept us waiting while he finished cutting the piece of lamb on his plate, "It's a little room just big enough for our bed. It has two solid wall and two walls that are screens. No windows, just screen from top to bottom. Screen walls." He smiled at Mother. "All the fresh air we could ever wish for."

Mother smiled back and nodded. She picked up her knife and fork, ready to take another bite, but added first, "We are thrilled with it because way back when you two were little, we slept on the porch in our tiny house in Virginia. There wasn't room for us to sleep inside because we had you two and Grandpa living with us. We grew to love it out there, even in the cold when it was snowy outside. Now we have another one. It's wonderful!"

Cairo was already a big hit with Mother. *I like it here too, but I know enough about new places to know there will be adjustments ahead.*

New Girls

THREE DAYS AFTER OUR ARRIVAL, WE WERE "THE NEW Girls" at school once again. Mother came with us our first day to be sure we were off to the right start; Patty in seventh grade and I in the second half of my Junior year. Cairo American School, grades K through Twelve, all housed in one building, was in Maadi. This suburb of Cairo was about a thirty-minute drive from Zamalek. American businesses, many of which were there as part of President Truman's Point Four Program, established the school for their families. Most of these families lived in Maadi. Kids biked to school. Just like in the states.

Patty and I were driven to school by Hassan. Usually he picked us up after school unless Father's or Mother's schedule took precedence. When that happened, we went home by commuter train with the small group of school-mates who also lived in Zamalek. Our "Zamalek Gang" included students from Egypt and other nationalities because CAS, like Community School in Tehran, provided an opportunity for English immersion.

Within two weeks, I was aware of an undercurrent of tension between the Maadi kids and Zamalek residents. Twice when Hassan stopped the car in front of the school and held the back door opened for me, two fifth grade boys on bikes whizzed past between me and car shouting "Oh, Your Ladyship, your chariot is here." Or I caught the tail ends of giggled conversations about a gathering held at someone's home in Maadi, a gathering that I hadn't been invited to because I lived in "Fancy Downtown Cairo," too far away for an early evening get together on a school night.

Some teachers had been imported from the states by the school board, but many came from within the international community in Cairo. Tuition was expensive. Class sizes were small. The students were well behaved. Alongside the scholastic challenges, the school offered an elected student government, a student court, a student generated yearbook, a drama club, a choir, field trips and dances and an athletic field that accommodated almost any sport. Just like a real American school.

It wasn't long before Mother joined the school faculty. It seemed right to have her there. I was proud of being her daughter. Her eleventh grade social studies was my favorite class. I mulled the lesson she presented on happiness over and over. She said, "People are happiest, most satisfied with life, if they are working successfully towards a desired goal. The attainment of the goal isn't as important as the progress towards it. But," she warned, "You have to have a desired goal for that to work." That haunted me on nights I had trouble falling asleep. I wondered, *What is my desired goal? My big life desired goal?*

My small present time goal was to be near young handsome Mr. Minotti. He taught French and Track. He was a great fan of the recent Olympic Games held in Helsinki. We studied the origin of the Olympics in French class. I took up the fifty-yard dash, the 400 meters, the javelin, the shot put, the high jump, the broad jump, the pole vault and the discus throw. The pole vault and discus were my best events. I loved bursting into a pounding run to build momentum, planting the pole in the earth with a solid stab, then soaring over the bar to land in the waiting sand pit. The fact that the bar usually followed me into the pit didn't matter. As thrilling as the pole vault was, the discus throw offered me more.

My parents chose to name me after a Goddess: The mighty Diana. Huntress and Protector of young maidens. Goddess of the moon, forests, hills, and archery. Apollo's twin. As I twirled for the wind up with the discus cradled in my hand, I left the world around me. When I let the sphere go to sail through the air, I became one with the mighty Goddess Diana. The feeling of tapping a hidden cache of strength washed over me. I missed Alex, but I was happy.

Patty and I hurried Hassan to get us to school early enough to join the clump of Maadi and Zamalek schoolmates usually gathered at the base of the wide front stairway waiting for the doors to open. I relished starting the day nestled within this horde of friends, trading homework answers and gossip before the last-minute scramble up the concrete steps ahead of the late bell. That is where I was when an unfamiliar car pulled up in front of the school. The driver walked around to open the passenger door.

Our huddle turned its collective heads to stare. Two girls climbed out of the back. They wore clothes that signaled "First Day at the New School Outfit." I smiled. They looked about the same ages as Patty and me and certainly lived in Zamalek since they arrived by car and chauffer, not bike or foot. *Hurray! Hurray! We can have best friends almost next door just like the Maadi kids.* A woman followed the girls out of the car. She had to be their mother, here to ensure her daughters were placed correctly.

The younger sister held her mother's hand as they started up the steps. The older girl, the one I dubbed as future best friend, hesitated at the bottom. She glanced towards our swarm. She took a deep breath then followed her family by placing her left foot on the first step, turning her body sideways so her left side faced uphill, then lifting her right foot to join the left. Up went her left foot to the next riser. With her body remaining sideways she completed that step the same way.

"Oooh!" I whispered. "Poor thing. She must have a sore leg."

As I watched her climb the third step, empathy swooshed out of me and disappointment seeped in its place. And scorn. It was her skirt. She wore a tight straight skirt that imprisoned her legs.

Impulse overcame me. I lunged up the stairway in my gathered skirt, two steps at a time. I paused for a second beside the new girl. With my voice reflecting the contempt I felt for self-imposed helplessness and rage for repression of women, I stared in her face and yelled "Freedom!" before continuing my unencumbered race up the steps. I didn't look back and soon forgot about my outburst.

On our ride home from school Patty turned toward her window, staring out, without a glance toward me. My chatter about almost dropping the shotput on my foot in gym class floated unattended in the air. Her silence squished my words.

"What's wrong with you?" I half shouted at her.

No response.

"Oh, for God's sake, if you're mad at me, at least tell me why."

She borrowed one of Mother's long sighs and moved closer to her window.

"Come on. Out with it!" I moved toward the middle and crossed my arms like Father does when he demands an answer.

She turned to stare at me. "Deedee, How could you?"

"How could I what?" I hunched my shoulders to show I had no idea what she was talking about.

"How could you be so mean to Sandy's sister?"

"Sandy? I don't know a Sandy."

"Yes, you do. She just came today. Remember?"

"Oh. The new girls." I moved back to my side.

"Yes. And you embarrassed her sister so much that she went to the bathroom and cried before her first class. You are mean and horrid and stuck up, and Sandy might not be my friend because of you." Patty folded her arms across her chest and wrenched herself back to stare out her window.

"Humph" was my only retort at first. "Humph" again as an unfamiliar and unpleasant feeling crept down my arms. "Well, I didn't mean to hurt anyone's feelings. I just couldn't stand seeing that girl so strapped into a skirt she couldn't even walk up the stairs. She might as well wear a steel pipe. It's almost as bad as being in one of those black bags some women have to wear here."

"Huh. That's how much you know. Sandy told me that full skirts aren't the style anymore. Crinolines are out now. And pencil skirts are in, in, in! So you don't know anything."

"Phew! Glad to hear about crinolines. I hate them. Father does too. Remember how he told Mother not to pack any for our move? Let's stomp on the ones we sneaked in when we get home."

My attempt at humor fell flat. Patty didn't budge from her window.

I couldn't stop myself from adding, "Anyway, I like my skirts. You'll never see me wrapped up like a mummy."

Silence grew heavy again. *Time to be serious. Time for a plan.*

The unpleasant feeling grew stronger. With my hands on my stomach to ensure a calm reasonable voice, I tried again. "Okay, Okay. I'm sorry. I'll do something to make it up to them. I'll ask Mohammed to make cookies and I'll take them over to their house today and tell Sandy's sister I'm sorry. Do you know where they live? It can't be far from us. Maybe we can set up carpooling, maybe even tomorrow."

Patty snorted. "They live in Maadi."

"What? But they came to school in a car. With a driver. Sandy probably mixed Maadi up with Zamalek if she told you they lived there."

Patty whirled to face me. She flung her arms wide and spat out, "See! You are a stuck-up snob, just like the Maadi kids say. A lot of them have cars and drivers. They like coming to school on bikes. I wish I could too. I wish I lived in Maadi. I hate being stuck in Zamalek with you." She turned away from me, arms crossed again, and stared out her window.

The rest of the way home we sat with our backs to each other, arms clenched across our chests, glaring out our windows.

That new nagging feeling had settled in the bottom of my stomach. My mind jumbled up with anger and whatever else that feeling was.

I knew Maadi annoyed me. In my mind it was an affront to the quiet dignity of Ancient Egypt. Its streets reverberated with young Americans calling out to each other. Patty spent more and more time there and less time tagging along after me. She wanted to be a part of the easy access to friends and school, the relaxed neighborliness, and the impromptu parties and secret clubs. I think she saw it as the town that returned Lulu to us. "A small American town with a big heart" in Mothers words. Patty felt at home in Maadi. I did not. It was out of place.

I liked the voices of Zamalek. They were the language that belonged to the land. Vendors and shop keepers shouted melodic enticements, men huddled on the sidewalk, sipping tea throughout heated discussions in Arabic.

Feluccas, those swan like boats I saw the night we arrived, whispered by on the Nile, their tall white sails stretched upward like wings pointing to the sky. Thousands of years ago, boats like these floated down the river transporting great blocks of rock for the pyramids.

Downtown, across the bridge from Zamalek, in the heart of Cairo, minarets echoed calls to prayer that wove in and out and above the bustle of humans, animals, and machines. Hassan drove me across the bridge to The Egyptian Museum on days that his schedule allowed and I was his only after school passenger because Patty was visiting friends in Maadi. He granted me an hour's visit there while he waited with the car to whisk me home before his next assignment. I thought about how I felt protected and welcomed standing before statues of Isis and Bast. After all, it is said that Diana, and Artemis before her, were modeled on Bast, the cat Goddess of Ancient Egypt.

I did a lot of thinking during that silent angry ride home with Patty. By the time we pulled up to the house, I realized I had a big adjustment to make. *Patty is growing up and away from me. She is right. I did a terrible thing hurting that poor new girl.* The unpleasant feeling in my stomach now had a name. Shame.

I apologized to Kathy, Sandy's sister, in front of the gang at the bottom of the steps before school the next day. Although I didn't change my mind about Maadi, I knew I had learned a lesson about judging others too quickly. And that my sister was a person in her own right, not just my shadow. Since she loved Maadi so much, and I loved Zamalek, two questions haunted me when I couldn't sleep. *Where do I belong? Where is home?*

Summer

WHEN SUMMER CAME, MAADI WAS NO LONGER A BONE OF contention. Although Patty spent time there with her friends, a lot of our days were spent at the Gezeira club. This splendid left- over from the British Empire sprawled over half of Zamalek. The club came with its own set of sounds different from those of downtown Cairo. A typical visit to the club began with the sound of Mother's voice reminding me, "Deedee, be sure to take Patty to the club with you. I don't want either of you going there alone." Next our front gate clanged behind us as the guard stood at attention, eyes forward, with no indication that he noticed our existence. But when I sneaked a look back over my shoulder, and listened carefully, I could almost hear him scribbling in the notebook he pulled out of his pocket. *Is our coming and going so important that he has to record it? Why?*

We walked the several blocks from our house to the Cornish, the road- way that bordered the Nile. Above us, persistent flocks of pigeons cooed. Below on the river, boatmen shouted to each other in the guttural staccato of Arabic. Between us were the bickering sounds of sisterhood.

"Patty, hurry up, you are walking too slow. I want to get there in time to get a tennis court."

"Okay. Is this fast enough for you?"

"For Pete's sake, Patty, not that fast. But don't drag behind like a wet rag either."

"You can't do that, Deedee. Mother said it isn't good to eat stuff they sell on the sidewalk."

"Don't be a tattle tale. I love pigeon kabobs. I'll buy you a stick if you want."

"Eww!"

When we entered the club grounds we could hear the whop- splot- whop- splot of tennis games and the rapid smack smack smack echoing from the squash courts. The huge pool sent up delighted shrieks, laughter, and splashes. Neighs from the polo field and stables sometimes floated in the background. Often three loud claps punctured the air. That was how patrons summoned servers for another drink or sandwich. Patty and I joined friends at poolside tables. Supplied with cokes and fries, I waited for my tennis court reservation..

Tennis was not a primary interest of mine, although I did take lessons from club instructors. Some tennis courts (the ones I reserved) were near the basketball court, and that was where the good-looking Russian boys hung out. They reminded me of Alex, I was prone to hitting long lobs that landed near (preferably in) the basketball court.

"So sorry," "Excuse me." "Pardon again," "Could you throw that back?" were met with indifference at best, and most often cold stares straight ahead ignoring my interruption. I complained to one of my Egyptians friends who sometimes played on the court with the Russians. "Why don't they notice me, Emil? At least smile? I'm not going to bite. I just want to make friends with them. They look like nice guys."

Emil had joined me poolside and had just ordered a coke and fries to match mine. He shook his head. "I thought you Americans hated Russians. I thought you hated communists. You think they are all evil and inhuman." He stuffed fries into his mouth, so they hung out, looking like fangs.

That was worth a snort before explaining, "Oh. Of course, I hate communists. But those guys don't look mean, like Stalin. I'm sure they wouldn't send babies to Siberia to die. Or bomb us." I nodded and smiled toward the basketball court during my explanation to show how sure I was that the basketball players were the exception.

Emil banged his coke down with enough force to splash some out of the glass. "Ha! You Americans don't see the big picture. The communists are building something new. A new world of equality. To do that, they have to flay the corpse, the old ways, before they can build it up again."

"Flay? What do you mean, flay?" I waved a French fry back and forth to show how lightly I took his argument.

Emil folded his hands, leaned forward, and looked straight at me. "They have to clean the bones to put new skin on them."

"Yuck! Eewee. That's awful! "I put my French fry down. Emil continued to sit still and stare at me. I looked away and asked, "Anyway, how can I make friends with these guys?"

"You can't. Give it up Deedee. Even if they wanted to pay attention to you, they can't. Some of them are students here but some of them are in the army: guards for the Russian embassy. Talking to you is absolutely against the rules for them. You are not worth that risk. But you're right, they are nice guys. Leave them alone." He got up and dove into the pool without finishing his snack.

It took another month of tennis reservations, but I made contact. One day, several lobs brought me close enough to hear one of the basketball players call another Sasha. Sasha was one of the cutest guys on the court! Sandy brown crewcut, blue shorts, white t shirt, sturdy, not quite as tall as Alex, and often laughing. I aimed a lob intended for his foot. It hit him in the stomach. I sprinted onto their court, full of apologies. "Oh Sasha, I'm so sorry." He smiled and held the tennis ball out to me.

One of the Russians who looked older, and stern, barked something at Sasha in Russian. Sasha dropped the ball at my feet. He picked up his towel at the edge of the court and left without a word or glance in my direction.

For several weeks there were no more Russians on the basketball court. When their game picked up again, Sasha wasn't with them.

"Why isn't he here?" I asked Emil, after telling him what happened.

"He won't be back, Deedee. I guess you didn't know that "Sasha" is usually a special nickname for Alexander, one that only good friends and family use. He probably is still trying to explain why you called him that."

That added another worry that gnawed into me before I fell asleep. *How could I ever make it up to Sasha if I had caused him that kind of trouble. Why was the world so complicated, anyway?*

Summer ended with no conclusion to my Russian problem. With September, twelfth grade and bright shiny American boys at school diverted my attention from Sasha's fate. During the school year the long languid days at the club became luxury occasions for a few of our Family Sundays.

On those special Sundays, Father reserved horses from the club stables. Children could ride only if accompanied by adults. Although thrilled to be riding again with my parents, I chaffed under this rule. When within the sight of the grooms, I did my best to demonstrate I was a competent rider (thanks to Sgt Buckley) and to convince them their rule needed changing. I knew that club rules were changeable because one evening I overheard Mother and Father talking about how "scandalous and unforgivably discriminatory" it was that the club only recently changed their rules to allow Egyptians to become members. Mother said, "Colonialism rot!" That sounded like pretty bad swear words the way she said it.

After the allowed hour and half ride along the club trails, we completed our outings with lunch in the club dining room on starched white linen table-cloths. This elegance was not the norm for our Sundays, although floating down the Nile while being served luncheon on a Felucca came close. There were outings to the Red Sea where we snorkeled. I loved swimming with fish and watching their lives. I lolled in the water, thinking about my life ahead. *I can be a marine biologist! Maybe an Egyptologist geologist with a specialty in ocean stuff.*

We spent a couple of Sundays in Alexandria. I expected to see the library that Mother went on and on about, but there were only replicated scrolls. I did collect a small rock from the shore where our guide, Alim, told us that not too far away Cleopatra's palace lay hidden beneath the sea. And probably the missing library was there too. *Aha! that would work for an Egyptologist marine geologist.* Alim said Cleopatra used to stand where I was standing, looking toward Greece, and thinking of faraway Marc Anthony. I stood there, with my new stone in my hand, and sent thought waves to far far away Alex. *I wonder if he can feel me missing him.*

We still had picnics.

Sometimes they were late afternoon tailgating at Saqqara. The step pyramid was a good drive from Cairo. Mother insisted. "Saqqara is best at sunset." Our trips were planned to give us time to eat by daylight. When the sun beat down on it, and silt whirled in eddies near the ground, the pyramid looked dusty, rocky, and old.

Once I whispered to Patty, "It's gonna crumble away someday."

"You aren't allowed to climb it anyway," she hissed back.

But when the sun began to sink, and the sky turned golden and rose, the pyramid loomed majestically before us. Soon it became velvety soft in the fading light. Mother would hold her hand out toward it and say things like, "Somewhere deep inside there the Pharaoh Djoser is pleased." Patty and I snickered when she mentioned the Pharaoh. We called him "King Joe" in whispers behind her back.

Sometimes she admired the structure over its contents. Then she said things like "Ah! What a wonderous architect Imhotep was." Sometimes she stood before the pyramid watching the sun creep down its steps into darkness and ask, "Isn't it amazing?" Once she snorted and said, "Deedee, perhaps we should send Mr. Green a picture of this with a little excerpt about the great mathematician Imhotep." That was our secret joke. It helped me recover from algebra class at Santa Cruz High.

Once, in the British Tradition, we rode horses from Gisa to Saqqara in an all night ride across the desert with very little trotting allowed by the guides. The desert by moonlight was a study of sharp contrast. Swaths of sandy silt glowed in muted tones of ochre, tan, and gray. Huge black shadows skirted our path and stretched into an endless beyond. I rocked in the saddle wondering why the desert frightened people. The night seemed swollen with ancient history. And that thrilled me. I felt almost swollen too, with loving my family, feeling safe and belonging.

We arrived at Saqqara as the step pyramid unveiled in early morning light, and breakfast and Hassan were waiting for us. I knew I was in love with Egypt forever.

But our favorite family Sundays happened on the nights when we picnicked at Giza beside the smallest of the three pyramids. We tried to make this a monthly ritual, preferrable in full moonlight.

In-between

UNLIKE OTHER POSTS, OUR EGYPTIAN STAFF DID NOT LIVE with us. Ahmed, Mitwali and Mohammed had Sunday off. Hassan did too, except when he returned early in the evening to drive us to this best of all picnic spots. Father gave him a bonus for overtime, so we assumed Hassan didn't mind coming back, but since he never smiled anyway, we couldn't tell for sure.

These outings began with an invasion into Mohammed's kitchen. Mother led us through her family recipes for potato salad, deviled eggs, and southern fried chicken. Platters of cheese and olives and drinks for grownups and kids were part of the menu too. Cobbler was always included. We stacked the used bowls and pans neatly by the sink to greet Mohammed when he returned early Monday morning.

Because we were older and bonded to friends, Mother and Father allowed us to invite one, sometimes two, guests to these outings. This meant a full carload to and from the pyramids. While we positioned ourselves in the crowded car, the gate guard took out his notebook. His head moved up and down as if he was counting and describing each passenger. His record keeping was beginning to annoy me rather than just pique my interest.

The windup record player from Capitola went with us. Hassan helped set up the picnic meal on a blanket spread out on the hard-packed ground beside the Little Pyramid. The four pillows that had been squashed in the trunk with the food and blanket were placed where Mother and Father could plump them up against some of the big rocks strewn around. We chose Menkaure's pyramid, because it was at least three football fields from Cheops and Khafre's larger and more popular pyramids. Our special place seemed private, just for us. Mother, scanning the structure from base to top, would smile and say quiet reverent things like, "Menkaure doesn't mind our being here, I'm sure. He must feel neglected at times. Poor dear." I added to that, but only to myself, not out loud. *Yes, poor old Menkaure. His tomb was raided a bunch of times, a horrid sultan put a gash in it trying to knock it down, and his sarcophagus sank to the bottom of the sea on its way to England. If his Ka is still floating about inside here, it must be livid.* I liked the Egyptian religion's idea of a Ka being person's spirit in and after life.

Hassan kept as far apart from us and our American pop music as possible. His most important job on these trips was to converse with the lone guard who patrolled the three pyramids and the sphinx at night. Money slipped from Father through Hassan to the guard, and we were left alone, in the moonlight, at the base of the Little Pyramid. Father referred to this transaction as a "rental fee."

Father would never do anything illegal, much less subject his family to a questionable act. However, we all sensed instinctively that even though we were the only people visiting the site at night and there was no rule against our picnics, any raucous or irreverent behavior on our part would hasten such laws being made and enforced. It was fall 1954. Freshly awakened Egyptian pride had spread to the feet of the sphinx.

The night Patty brought her two best pals, Sandy and Brian, we were extra careful to keep the record player on low to make up for what Father termed "a herd of youngsters." Rosemary Clooney whispered, "Hey There, you with the stars in your eyes," and "Shh-Boom" sounded more like a just plain "shh" warning.

The music made me miss Alex. *I wish he were here. He would love this, the pyramids by moonlight. We could dance.* I carefully left "our song" out of the stack of 45's we packed for the picnic. It always made me cry. Alex continued to keep up his promise of mailing me 45's of the latest hit tunes, just as he had when I was left behind in Teheran. Our correspondence endured, even though it had waned from twice a week to around once a month. We each lived our immediate lives fully, he in California, me in Cairo, but we were counting down the nine months left to go before I would see him again. Our bond held.

Mother's mantra for providing food for a gathering was "There is never enough unless there is too much," Patty, Brian, Sandy and I stuffed ourselves on fried chicken and potato salad. We ate to the burping point, yet there was plenty left for Hassan and the guard too. After a meal like that, the only way to recover from being over-full was to go for a "walk around the pyramids." At least, that was what Patty and I always said we were planning but our secret ritual on these picnics was to climb Menkuare's pyramid on the side away from our parents' and the guard's wandering eyes.

Patty nudged me. "It's time for our walk around the pyramids," I announced.

Father stood to face us. He looked back and forth between Patty and me to signal the seriousness of his response. "Okay, kids. Be back in half an hour. On the dot. Tomorrow's a school day. We need to get everyone home early tonight. Deedee, you are in charge. Be back at eight thirty. Not a second later."

"Why does she have to always be in charge?" Patty asked. "I'm old enough to be in charge of my own guests."

Uh Oh. She's showing off for her friends. Bet she's planning to ditch me. Well, that's fine with me. I've climbed up enough times.

But Father was firm. He leaned toward Patty. "Yes, you are in charge of your guests. But Deedee is in charge of you as well as your guests. Do what she says and be back on time." Then he turned to me. "Deedee, use your head. Four youngsters are a crowd and crowds draw attention. Don't make a scene."

Darn! I had to ride herd on three eight graders who wanted to lose me as soon as possible. Sure enough, they raced off in a clump around the corner of the pyramid before I even started to follow. *Darn! Darn it! Now I have to catch up and climb with them since Father is so adamant about keeping them in check.* When I rounded the corner, they were not in sight.

I hurried towards the most likely place they would be hiding from me, the mounds of decaying tombs littered behind The Little Pyramid. Keeping my voice quiet enough not to alert the guard but loud enough for anyone hiding in the rubble in front of me to hear, I said "Come on out, you guys, I know you're in there." The silence was empty enough to signal they were not there.

I ran toward the pyramid at my best fifty yard dash speed. I spotted them giggling and climbing up our usual path. They must have been hiding at the base of the pyramid, waiting for me to take the bait and head off on a wild goose chase.

It was difficult to shout orders in a hiss. I held my hands in front of my mouth to make a megaphone. "Wait for me!"

Patty turned to her companions. They huddled together, whispering.

"Okay Miss Bossy Pants. We're coming down now, Your Highness."

The three of them began their descent. I sighed in relief and was feeling good about being a responsible adult, until I noticed they were not heading straight down. No, they scuttled across the face toward the entrance opening that was below them and off to the side. Logic and caution warned me that their target was obviously against the rules. A forbidden entrance to all but those with special permission. Absolutely off limits to American teenagers at night without a guide accompanying them.

A sense of panic lodged in the back of my neck. If I hurried, I could reach the entrance before they did. It was easier to climb upward than sideways like Patty and her friends were doing. Up, up, granite block to granite block, scrambling to the doorway, I made it seconds ahead of them.

"You are not going in there!" I flung my arms across the opening with my back to Patty and her friends who were crowding around my feet. I didn't have time to turn to face her before she shouted at me.

"Yes, we are! I heard that people do it all the time."

Patty's really showing off tonight, and I have to stop her! Without making a scene. Halfway turning to talk under one arm and still block the entrance with my body, I said in a more reasonable voice, "It's not open to the public. I have never seen anyone go in. Anyway, if they do, it's with a guide who knows what he's doing and has lights and things."

"So, the big seventeen-year-old is a scaredy cat." I couldn't see her face, but I could hear the sneer on it.

Still twisting to talk under my arm yet maintain position over the entrance, I answered, "No. Just sensible." I remembered Father's serious gaze before we left but it didn't seem to have made an impression on my sister.

Patty said to my back, "We're going in whether you like it or not."

When I whirled around to face her so I could give her a look to show how determined I was, Patty's hands reached for my shoulders. She gave me a shove so she could slip past me. However, instead of getting me out of her way, the push sent me backwards inside the passage. Brian and Sandy crowded behind Patty. I found myself stumbling backward as they pressed forward, forcing me further into the pyramid.

"Stop pushing me! This is not the place for fooling around!" I turned away from them to face the darkness ahead. At that moment there seemed to be only one option. The three of them were not going to politely turn around and go back and there was not enough room for me to slip past them to make my way out. *Don't make a scene.* I would have to compromise.

"Okay. Okay. We will go just a short way, and I'll lead." *At least I will still have some control.*

Bent slightly over to avoid scraping my head I crept forward step by step. The path sloped downward. I felt my way with my arms out to the side and my hands creeping along the stone walls on each side of me. The passage floor was hard packed, no stones interrupted as I carefully slid one foot at a time out ahead.. After ten steps or so there seemed to be a passageway leading off to the right while ahead the downward slant became steeper. The smell of old rocks clogged the air. My outstretched arms bent closer to my body. The tunnel was narrowing. Dim splotches of light glowed, then faded haphazardly off the surface above our heads. I shuddered. A heavy damp feeling of dread began to ooze into me.

My hands on the wall made tiny scratching sounds as they moved forward across the stone. My feet sliding on the path made scuffling sounds, but I heard something else besides the four of us. I held up an arm to signal "Stop!" I took a deep breath and held it to hear better. Yes. Muffled rustlings echoed ahead like they were trapped inside a deep well. Silently the space in front of me screamed. "Go! Get Out! Leave!" A current of air slid past my left ear. Less than a second later, air moved past my right ear in the opposite direction. A cold metal netting of fear dropped down over my head. Fear more intense than the rattling of our front gate in Tehran when the mourners at Moharram passed by. Fear almost as paralyzing as when I came face to face with a sea snake on one of our snorkeling trips to the Red Sea.

"Well?" Patty asked from behind me. "Why are you just standing there?"

My voice started out low and guttural, then it rose to a high-pitched shout. I had no control over it. "Because the whole pyramid is warning us. We have to go! We have to! We should not be here. Out! Now! I mean it!" I moved close to Patty who was at the front of her pack. When our noses were about to touch, she realized how intensely I felt we had to get out. And that if necessary, I would physically fight her and win right there.

"Okay, okay. I suppose you think some Ka is talking to you. You're a looney bin. You're crazy! You think you're so special, the big boss of us! I hate you!"

But she turned around and we all worked our way out. I brought up the rear of our line. I had no idea what, if anything, was behind me.

We made it back to the picnic site three minutes early.

Hassan had already begun to repack the car. Mother and Father were standing, holding hands, near the base of our pyramid. Father checked his watch and beamed at us.

"Good job!" He nodded approvingly at me, then Patty. Patty tossed her head to look away from me.

Mother motioned to a flat rock nearby. The half-finished pie and four forks on a pile of napkins were on the rock. She said, "I saved the rest of the cobbler for you all. Thought it would taste good after your walk."

I stood apart, alone, I didn't know which group to join. My sister and her friends were devouring what was left of the peach cobbler. They had no intention of making space for me around the rock. My parents were admiring the silhouettes of the pyramids against a pale sky. Out of the corner of my eye, I noticed Mother was watching me.

Soon she walked over to me and put her arm around me. "I know that the others aren't speaking to you. I won't ask, but there were obviously hard decisions you had to make. I'm sure whatever you did to make them angry with you was the right choice. I know it is hard to be an 'in-betweener' Honey. Come join us for a while." She led me to the grownup side where Father was waiting.

For the next few weeks, I went through our daily routines feeling proud of my "almost adult" status. I didn't throw the usual fit when Patty snuck into my private bathroom drawer and raided my bobby pin supply. I refrained from yawning during the chess games Father scheduled for the two of us every Thursday. I didn't complain that I never got to work the mainsail, only the jib, when we tacked back and forth across the Nile every other Wednesday. My room stayed tidy including the rock collection rearranged to show off two new additions from the bottom of the Red Sea. However, my smug self-congratulations on being so grown-up came to an end several weeks after our Little Pyramid picnic.

The Telephone

IT WAS THE TELEPHONE'S FAULT.

I was alone in the house. The servants were taking an afternoon break before dinner. Mother had a faculty meeting. Patty would stay in Maadi and ride back with her, and Father was still at work, but would be heading home soon. Hassan would drop him off before driving to Maadi for the rest of the family. I sat at my desk, looking out the window, relaxed and ready to begin reading the next social studies chapter. Just as I opened the book to Chapter five, the phone rang. All the way downstairs, at the bottom of the steps, it rang.

I stomped down the stairs listing all the reasons I was upset with the phone.

First, it was downstairs and I was usually upstairs.

Second. it perched on a tall spindly stand with no seating or writing space nearby.

Third, it was uncomfortable and frustrating when Jack and I were checking our homework. Jack was my math buddy. He lived in Zamalek, rode the train home after school with me and walked me from my door to the Gezeira Club and back again when Patty wasn't available. Jack was tall, lanky, from Montana, and a fellow senior. When an important assignment was due, I hunched on the bottom step beside the phone stand, notebook balanced across my lap, and the receiver crushed on my shoulder. My neck ached from keeping it in place to prevent the notebook from sliding off my knees while reworking problems. We raced to see how quickly we could get the same, and therefore correct, answers.

Fourth, I heard strange clicks and felt another presence when I was on the line, and that made me question myself. *Was there really someone there? Who would want to listen to my teenage stuff, and why? Were our gate guards really tracking me, or just logging events during their watch? Was there really a sea snake and did the pyramid warn me to leave, or was that nerves? Was I in danger of having a screw loose, like Patty said?* I was fed up with feeling I was either under surveillance by phone spies and gate guards or worrying that I might be a bubble off.

I reached the bottom of the steps by the seventh ring. Yanking the receiver off its cradle, I grumbled "Hello, without the prescribed and practiced, "This is the Carr residence, Deedee speaking."

The caller's voice had a tone of urgency. "Hello. Is this the Carr residence? If so, may I speak with Mr. Carr? I am calling from the embassy."

Uh, oh, time for manners. "He's not home yet but should be soon. This is his daughter speaking. May I take a message?"

"Click swish, click, click," whispered in the background.

"Just tell him Mike called about the upcoming farm prospectus." The voice added another sentence or two, but I was too intent on what was going on inside the phone behind his voice, to get the rest of his message straight. The caller thanked me and hung up.

But the line was still open. I sat on the bottom step. *I'm not hanging up until whoever is there does.*

"Click. Zzzzz. Click"

I held my breath listening to the phone's insides whirring while mentally counting the passing seconds in one thousands. At one-thousand thirteen, there was another click and a barely audible human mumble.

That does it! I shouted into the mouthpiece, "Okay! Whoever you are, get the hell off my damn phone!"

The line went dead.

Immediately remorse replaced anger. I slumped forward, my face in my hands, shaking my head side to side, shocked at how easily those swear words flew out of my mouth. I had never uttered "hell" or "damn" out loud until that moment. Maybe in my brain but never out loud. Mother proclaimed swearing not only un-lady-like, but also a sign of diminished intelligence coupled with a sparse, nearly illiterate, vocabulary.

Father would be home soon. *Before the others. I'll have him to myself. It's time to find out if he knows what's going on.* The phone message would be a perfect opportunity to bring up my suspicions about the gate guards as well as the phone. I went upstairs to watch from my window for Hassan to pull up and drop Father off. The minute I saw our car coming down the street, I ran downstairs and opened the front door.

"Well, well," Father said, "A welcoming committee." He held one arm out for a hug. His briefcase (which was really a big leather envelope with a zipper) was tucked under his other arm.

I hugged him, then blurted out, "Someone from the embassy named Mac called for you. He sounded worried and said something about a farm, maybe about expecting animals soon, maybe call him back, but I'm not sure because of the spies."

"What in the world are you talking about?" Father stared at me with one eyebrow raised like a dark question mark. "Mac? Mac Who? I don't know anyone named Mac and I don't have anything to do with farm animals. That kind of thing is a Point Four concern. President Truman has all kinds of experts here for that." He turned to close the door behind him. He paused with his hand on the doorknob. Still facing the door, with his head slightly cocked, he asked, "And what do you mean by spies?" He turned around to face me.

I took a step back to have room to point dramatically first at the phone, then at the front gate. "I think people are spying on us! The front guards write in a notebook every time we come and go, even just walking. And I'm sure someone is listening to our phone calls. I hear clicks and even voices when no one is there. Anyway, I think I got rid of the phone spies." I jerked my thumb back to indicate the phone behind me.

He shook his head side to side the way parents do when their children bewilder them. "And how do you think you got rid of your phone spies? What did you do?"

I stared at the floor. Embarrassed and dreading his reaction I mumbled, "I shouted in the phone as loud as I could for whoever was there to 'Get the hell off my damn phone.' I know I shouldn't have used bad words but when I heard voices after Mike hung up I was so angry I didn't think. I'm sorry. I'm really sorry."

Father crossed his arms. He frowned and stared straight in my eyes. "You're right. You should not have said anything. Your outburst was childish and embarrassing to our reputation. Shame on you!"

We stood facing each other. Neither of us spoke. The air around soaked up our silence. I lowered my head and stared at the small rug we were standing on. Mother had collected many small, several medium sized, and two large, elegant Persian carpets during her trips to the Teheran Bazar. Under her direction, Mitwali often changed their locations. We never knew which carpet would be where, but we knew there would always be one nearby. The one I was standing on was dark red, with geometric designs woven in black. The downward slant of my face amplified how hot my cheeks felt. I wondered if they were the same color as the rug. Then slowly it dawned on me that Father had not said my suspicions were wrong, or that I had a runaway imagination, or a distorted bent for secret agent work. I looked up at him. "So! We are being spied on! Who is doing it? Why?"

Father sighed. That surprised me because Mother was the sigher. He was the pacer, but he wasn't pacing. He stood still while glancing toward the empty stairwell to make sure we were alone. He shifted his briefcase. He said quietly, "You may be right. That's why we all must be on good behavior. Always. As for who's doing it here, I can't be sure that it isn't more than one source. Maybe the Egyptians, maybe the Russians, maybe any one of the embassies." He shrugged his shoulders. "Who knows?" He walked to the stairs and paused with his foot on the bottom step.

I held my breath hoping he wasn't finished explaining.

He cleared his throat and continued. "And why? Because information gathering is an important component in how countries deal with each other."

He took several steps up. I followed two steps behind him. I didn't want to miss a word in case there was more coming. He was almost at the landing when he put his hand on the railing and half turned to look down at me. I stopped too and stayed very still looking up at him. I knew my face was full of questions, but that being quiet was the best way to keep his explanations coming.

His shoulders looked like they were slumped forward under his suit jacket. He shook his head again, just slightly. He added, "It's a part of our life. It's the underbelly of the wonderful places we've been, and the marvelous things we have experienced. It's all part of the game, my dear. And another part of that game is that it's never discussed or treated as an extraordinary event, as you have done this evening." He turned and continued climbing to the landing.

I followed. A lump began to swell in my throat. Somehow I felt smaller. I said to his back, "I'm so sorry. I didn't know."

Father took a few steps across the landing. He stopped and spun around to face me. "Now you do, and it is not to be mentioned again. Do you understand?"

I nodded "Yes."

Father started up the second part of the stairway. I followed with my army of questions gathering force inside me. I couldn't keep them in. I put my hands on my lower stomach to try for a reasonable more grown-up voice. "If the guards spy on us, do any of the servants?"

Father stopped and turned to look down at me. "Probably, but we're not discussing this anymore. I thought that was clear."

His answer made it impossible not to risk asking more.

"I'll bet Hassan is a spy. He never smiles."

Father turned around and continued up the steps. He didn't answer.

I went on, "But not Ahmed. He is too gentle, and not Mitwali. He's too dopey. Maybe Mohammed?"

"Possibly." Father threw that answer over his shoulder. He was off the stairs and walking alongside the stairwell. Soon he would disappear into his bedroom and I would lose him.

With my hands on my stomach again for voice control, I said, "You said you weren't sure who was doing it here. Here. That means they were doing it in the other places too. right?"

Father stopped at his bedroom door. He turned to face me. One eyebrow was up, both corners of his mouth turned down.

"My God, you are persistent. That was a slip on my part, but since you caught it, probably yes. This is the only time we will talk about it, but go ahead, I can see you are burning up with questions." He stood with his back to his door, arms crossed, braced for my barrage. I stood opposite him, with my hands behind me holding onto the railing. I leaned back against it.

I wanted to be comfortable and still, so I could concentrate on our conversation. Certain this would be a onetime opportunity, my questions erupted without any logical organization. "You mean it happened everywhere? Not India! Not Daniel?" The thought of our wonderful Daniel not being on our side made my stomach sink.

Father chuckled and shook his head "No. Not Daniel." Daniel had always been his favorite. They had even corresponded a few times after we left India.

This rare opportunity could not be wasted! Not a second of it! I barreled on. "Maybe Lawrence? I know Kulwant Singh wouldn't spy. He saved Mother from the police. A spy wouldn't do that. Besides, he's a Sikh." I took a breath, remembering Kulwant Sing and how gentle and peaceful he always seemed. Even if he was the source of Patty's and my battle with lice. "So probably Lawrence, right?"

Father's eyebrow rose just barely while he tilted his head slightly to the side. That was a "could be" response. I hurried on. "Peter, I'll bet, in Vienna. Yeah. Peter for sure!"

This was met with a straight steely stare. I read it as a "No comment." Father probably felt anything he said about Peter, The Nazi, would be too biased and bitter for a man of seasoned skills in diplomacy to utter. But he hadn't budged from the doorway. He was open to more questions.

"And Frau Vundra, the old witch in the basement?"

Father said quietly, "I have to admit, I often wondered if she were a plant. Don't know by whom, though." He uncrossed his arms and started to turn away.

In my desperate rush to get every possible suspicion covered, my opinions and questions garbled together and spilled out in a messy heap. "But not Marta. No. And not Irvin, he was too busy trying to kill himself. So was Gassam. And not Fatima because Mother was her bank."

Father turned back to me with both eyebrows raised and half chuckled at the bank reference. Mother hadn't kept it a secret from him after all.

His reaction gave me a reprieve, a chance to keep going. "It was Jamal in Teheran, right? Cause Emmanuel was Christian, so he wouldn't spy for them. Maybe John in India. Ha! It's always the cook, isn't it? I bet it was the cooks everywhere and that is why we're never allowed in the kitchen because that's where all the spy equipment is installed, and the guards always take their break in the kitchen, so do the gardeners, so they can…

"Whoa. Take a breath and listen to yourself." Father put a hand on my shoulder. "This is getting silly. You might need to think that through. A person skilled enough as a cook to plan, shop for, and prepare formal lunches and dinner and be a trained spy at the same time? He would have to be pretty cleaver."

I crossed my arms. "Well, spies are smart, aren't they?"

Father tilted his head back and laughed. "Good point!"

I leaned back against the stairwell railing and lifted my shoulders with my next big question. "But I don't understand why our lives make any difference to the spy world. What do they need that information for? What do they do with it?"

Father shifted his brief case again, glanced at his door, then me. Now his eyebrows were meeting the wrinkles above his nose. He looked more worried than an upset.

"First, before I answer, get away from the railing. It isn't safe and it is distracting thinking of you doing a back dive down the stairwell."

I took a step toward him, away from the railing, and stood very still hoping he remembered my question. He nodded to show he approved of my safer position, then went back to our discussion.

"Well, keeping tabs of our daily lives tells them about Americans, who is important and not important to us, how we behave, what we do and don't like.

Things that might come in handy if they are trying to pass as an American or want to upset us for some reason. Also, the possibility of blackmail."

I gasped. "For money? From me?"

Father shook his head and smiled. "No, I don't think so. It's more like if they overhear a secret, maybe about an accident, or a big debt, it can be used as leverage for favors, information, or access to people."

"Wow!" I shook my head to clear it. "It's complicated, isn't it?"

"Yes. Very. And that's enough. We're done now." Father turned to open his door.

As he entered his room, what I feared was the most forbidden of questions tumbled out of my mouth. "What about the Russian Colonel you met on our camping trip?"

Father walked into his room and closed the door without a word. I wanted to pound on it. New questions surged. I wanted to know everything, but the door was closed. My time had expired.

I sighed and went back to my room and the social studies homework. My mind wandered. *Well, a least I understand why I have to have good manners and not make scenes. All the time Americans are being judged by what I do. I will try harder.* I turned a page and read a paragraph. Then thoughts intruded again. *Poor Mother and Father. They don't have any private time. Maybe that's why they like our Sundays, we are away from the spies at home. Unless Hassan is with us.*

I started to read another paragraph but was interrupted by Father calling me. Maybe my time wasn't up after all! I hurried to meet him in the upstairs hallway. His brow wrinkled in worry and he pulled at his mustache. Something serious was bothering him.

"Deedee, did you say Mike called? I thought you said it was someone named Mac, but I think maybe you said Mike later."

"Yes, it was Mike, I mixed it up at first."

He took a deep breath and hurried down the steps towards the phone.

I leaned over the top stair railing and called down to him, "Aha! That message was in code, wasn't it?"

He looked up a me. His face was flushed. *Uh Oh!* I had gone too far. All he said was one loud. "Stop!" and I knew our discussion was closed for good.

I wasted more homework time trying to figure out what Mike's code was, if it was a code. *A shipment would mean something they were waiting for came.* That's as far as I got. I wondered if we had ever done or said anything that could be used as leverage against Father? *Mother's time in jail, maybe? Did someone report us sneaking in the pyramid? My swearing on the phone?* I didn't have any answers.

Seating

THESE WERE MY MAIN WORRIES UNTIL SEVERAL SATURDAYS later at the Gezeira club when I had just broken the surface after swimming two lengths of the pool underwater. I threw my head back and a took deep breath before noticing Sharif standing at the edge of the pool, looking down at me. He smiled and said, "You look beautiful right now. For a minute I thought you were Arianne."

Sharif was twenty two, handsome, and the most popular member of the international group of young people who hung out together at the club. Arianne was my age, seventeen, French, and admired by all. I was the lone English only speaker in the group; the others sometimes used three languages in the same sentence. I tried to become better friends with Arianne, once even offered her my tennis reservation. But she was too busy with her French life to have anything to do with me.

I climbed out of the pool and joined Sharif and the group. It was a big group this afternoon and buzzing with excitement. Emil was so busy handing out white envelopes to everyone that he didn't notice me as I sat down. I waited to receive mine until I realized Emil's hands were now empty. My heart sank even lower than after Sharif's recent half compliment. Emil's smiling glance around the group stopped when he came to me. He paused, and then said, "Oh no! Didn't you get one?"

I shook my head "No".

He searched his empty bag. "It must be mixed up with someone else's." Everyone checked, but it was not there. By now all envelopes were opened to reveal, in gold embossed lettering, an invitation to Emil's sixteenth birthday celebration. Emil apologized to the group about the invitations being so late. "There was a delay at the printer's end. Good thing I told you all about it before so you knew it was coming." Then Emil smiled at me and said, "Don't worry. I'll understand if you've already made other plans, but I promise I'll get your invitation to you right away." I nodded and said, "Thank you." *Boy, I must have been at the club all the wrong times because I never heard about the party before.*

The invitation didn't come until Thursday. As soon as possible, I had to get Mother and Father's permission to go and schedule a ride there and back with Hassan. Emil lived in Zamalek, no more than ten minutes away. Surely that little bit of time could be spared. In Tehran, The Big Kid group finally welcomed me. The group at the Gezeira Club were mostly older too. I knew the party would be exciting and fun. It seemed glamourous and grownup to be included.

Fortunately, because my parents had no engagements Thursday evening, we could have our traditional Children's Hour before dinner. Unfortunately, Mother and Father were immersed in their plans for the formal dinner they were hosting Saturday. Seating charts and menus consumed them the week before these parties. Patty and I draped over the living room furniture, impatient for attention.

The coming dinner was scheduled to be held in the garden. The weather was balmy. Jasmine laced the night air. Tall brass Dwali lanterns from India, polished to gleam like golden mirrors, would provide abundant candlelight. The dining room table, extended to its full length, would be placed in the middle of the lawn. Mother had weighed the beauty of the garden against the probability of onlookers in the tall apartment building behind us. The sweet smell of jasmine and the plush green grass won.

The seating chart was causing a problem, as usual. Mother and Father sat side by side on the couch, close together, intent on the diagram spread across the coffee table in front of them. Father tapped the chart with the eraser end of his pencil and said, "I knew we should have kept it at ten, not twelve. Twelve opens up more chances of slighting someone, it's hard to accommodate everyone's rank correctly." He looked up at Mother. "I don't know why you insisted on the Johnstone's visiting nephew coming."

Mother folded her hands and took a deep breath. "It wouldn't be right to leave him out. He's their house guest. He just finished his service in the British army and is having a rough time. A dinner party will do him good."

Father half snorted. "Well, it puts everything off." He bent over the chart again. "David, the new Second Secretary, needs to get to know the Indonesians because he'll be working with them. It's going around the office that his wife's very unhappy here and may return to the States for the rest of his tour. An awful thing to do to her husband." He tapped the middle of the chart, "We'll mix them in here with the Indonesians, the nephew, and Janet. Thank God for your teacher friend Janet."

Mother jerked her head up when Father mentioned the new guy's wife. She stood and took a step away from the couch. She pulled herself up to her full height, faced him, and tilted her chin upward which meant she had something important to say and he'd better listen.

"Yes, it is nice of Janet to agree to balance our table out. This will be Rita and David's first formal dinner here, I believe. I want it to be a good experience for Rita. She's so young and new to all this. You're right, Mr. David Rodgers will certainly need a Rita Rodgers in this job." She paused and put her hands on her hips, then said, "A wife is the **most** valuable asset."

Father nodded and replied on cue. "Yes. I am a lucky man indeed. However, I'm not sure how the conversation will flow around the miserable wife and shell-shocked nephew. Janet will have to take the lead."

Mother glanced over the chart. "Col. Johnstone is our highest rank, so he's at the end next to me, and Mrs. Johnstone is on your left. Then there's our own Col and Mrs. Willis. I'll see if I can get him talking across the table to his British counterpart. She sighed. "This is the best we can do. The Indonesians' English does seem to be improving a bit. It's up to Janet. Fortunately, Egyptology, a nice safe subject, is her passion."

This seating chart business interfered with the little time during Children's Hour that Patty and I had to talk to our parents about important things like the slumber party Patty wanted to have next week, and I needed permission for Emil's party. Their seating chart discussion could go on all evening. I jumped up and shouted, "Time out, Time out! Patty and I have some things to ask you. She wants to have a slumber party. And I want to know if I can go to Emil's birthday party. It's a big deal. He's one of my best friends from the club." I held up the invitation. "He lives in Zamalek. I really really want to go."

Both parents turned to scowl at me. Mother sat back down on the couch. She frowned, "Hmm. I haven't heard you mention his name very often. Is he the one who walks you home from the club but only as far as the corner?"

That made Emil sound shady. I was losing ground already. *Think fast. She likes manners!* I said, "That's probably because he's very polite and doesn't want to intrude without being invited."

Mother sniffed. "Walking you to your door isn't the same as coming inside uninvited."

Uh oh. Not going well. Even getting invited in the first place didn't go well. I've got to go to that party! Take a deep breath. Try again.

Oops! Too late.

Mother had shifted her attention from me to Patty. "Patty dear, when do you plan to have this slumber party? Who are you inviting?"

Before Patty could answer Ahmed appeared in the doorway. Mother stood up and said, "I see Ahmed has come to tell us dinner is ready. We'll discuss all this at the table.

Father grunted, rolled up the seating chart, tucked it under his arm, and we all "adjourned" to the dining room.

After Ahmed had placed bowls of soup in front of each of us and left the room, I tried again. "Emil lives in Zamalek, only about five blocks away. I saw the outside of his house when Hassan picked me up at the club and we gave Emil a lift. It's beautiful, way back behind a gate. I know you haven't met his parents, but they're members of the Gezeira Club, so they must be okay. The party's on the same night as your dinner, so you won't need Hassan. That means he can drive me and wait to bring me home as early as you say. Emil speaks French, German, English, Ara…"

Mitwali came to collect the soup before I could finish. Ahmed followed him in with a platter holding lamb chops, peas, and roasted potatoes. He served Mother first, then Father, then me, and finally Patty. It was taking a long time. I needed to convince Mother and Father to feel comfortable about Emil. They wouldn't let me go if they had doubts.

Mother sensed my frustration. She put her fork down, laced her hands beneath her chin, and rested her chin on them. She had a lot of questions. "I don't know Emil. How long have you known him? Where does he go to school? What is his last name? And isn't this terribly short notice?"

Patty answered for me. "Deedee didn't get a real invitation like his other friends did. That's why it's so short notice. She's been waiting for it all week. She really wants to go."

I tried to kick her under the table to shut her up. My legs didn't reach across even though I had slipped down in my chair with my chin below the tabletop. *I'll never tell her anything again, ever. I'll never speak to her again.* I couldn't even glare at her until I worked my way back up into my chair.

"Deedee, for God's sake, sit up at the table." Now Father was irritated at me as well as the seating chart rolled up like a scroll beside his plate. He drummed his fingers beside it.

Darn it! The short notice is going to be a problem. But neither Father nor Mother said I couldn't go yet. There might still be a chance, if my sister didn't butt in again. The phone rang right in the middle of my warning Patty to shut up with my worst slit eyed glare across the table. Ahmed slipped into the room and said quietly to Mother, "There is a phone call for you, Madam. I told you were at dinner, but she say very important."

We watched Mother hurry out the open door. We heard her say "Hello." Then her voice dropped and only the worried tone, not the words, carried to us.

Mother returned from the call frowning. She wrung her hands as she sat back down. She sighed a long sigh and looked at Father.

"What is it Betty? What's wrong?"

"Janet can't make it to dinner Saturday. She just found out that she has an emergency back home and is leaving tomorrow evening. She wanted to notify us right away. She knows it causes a problem."

Father snapped his head up and clanked his knife and fork down. "That's putting it mildly."

"I'm so sorry, Bob. Whatever came up must be critical for her to fly back to the States so quickly. I'm racking my brain, but can't think of anyone else from school that will fill the bill...Maybe there's a single woman in the embassy staff that can balance the nephew?"

Father was quickly smoothing his mustache, over and over.. "We can't ask any of the clerical staff because that would start a turmoil of who was and wasn't asked to do us such a huge last-minute favor." He looked down at his plate and idly rearranged the silverware into new patterns, ending up with something that resembled a tic tac toe square.

A hush settled over the table during my next four slow and careful bites. Finally, Father continued. "We certainly can't ask Col. Johnstone not to include their nephew. As you pointed out, the young man is having a rough time, on "tender hooks" as the British put it. Kenya! What a nightmare!"

Mother shuddered. "The very words 'Mau Mau' make my skin crawl. And he only just turned twenty-one, according to his aunt. Waiting to recover and return for university in Scotland."

This Mau Mau and Kenya stuff piqued my curiosity. I sensed there was a lot they were saying to each other underneath their words. It was hard not to blurt out questions, but this wasn't the right time to interrupt. As far as I had pieced together the dinner they were planning served many purposes: pay back invitations, set up new pay back obligations, get the Colonels in a discussion during which Mother might be able to pick up a bit of information on the Royal Navy's plans, acquaint David Rodgers with his Indonesian counterpart, perk up the nephew, and save the Rodger's marriage.

Father drummed his fingers over the tic tac toe square. "Well, well, what to do? What to do...".

Mother suddenly leaned forward. She glanced sideways at me, and then clapped her hands together. "Bob! Do you remember how the French solved a similar problem at their dinner a few months ago? With their daughter? Arianne? I think that was her name. She filled in for one of their guests who couldn't make it at the last moment because of illness. It worked smoothly. And I believe she is Deedee's age."

Uh! Oh!

Mother's bright blue eyes and Father's soft brown eyes turned my way.

I gulped, choking on the realization that I was now being pulled into an "almost adult" role I didn't want. When Patty and I lurked upstairs during Mother and Father's dinner parties, they seemed to drone on and on forever. And now I would be trapped at that grown-up table, pinned between two strangers who would resent being seated next to a nobody American teenager. And the dinner was the same night as Emil's party. I was doomed. I was going to miss the best party of the year.

The Dinner

TRAINING BEGAN WHILE MITWALI CLEARED OUR DINNER plates, and Ahmed set a small dish of pale green pudding with mint leaves sprinkled on top in front of us. Mother leaned toward me and smiled as she patted my hand and purred, "Honey, you will be a wonderful replacement for Janet. Fresh as a daisy and as bright as they come. You will enchant our guests."

Father added, "I agree. And you have the poise to pull it off. Let's get down to basics. You know all the etiquette of serving, right?"

I mimed serving myself from a platter on my left and leaning back as an imaginary plate was cleared from the right. Father and Mother took turns informing me not to take large servings, sip very little wine and water as there were no bathroom breaks, how I would be responsible to keep the conversation going as I alternated from one side to side, and suggested topics of interest.

Father tapped his seating chart and nodded and me. "You will have Janet's place, in the middle of the table. Mrs. Rodgers will be on your left and the Johnstone's nephew on your right. You understand your role, right?"

I sank into my chair and nodded "Yes." *I won't even sip any water through the whole thing, and while I'm dying of thirst Emil and all his friends will be dancing.*

"Certainly, you won't be slouching at the table like that." Father scowled at me. Mother leaned over to pat my hand again.

I sat up straight. A rod down my back, just like the mean Russian ballet teacher in Vienna had insisted I visualize.

Father nodded. "That's better. Tomorrow night we've got two cocktail parties, then dinner in Maadi, but Saturday morning I'll work on the conversation possibilities with you." He pulled out his chart again. "Hmmm. Yes. You will be seated between Mrs. Rodgers, and the Johnstones' nephew."

"The miserable and the shell-shocked?" I asked in my most innocent voice.

Father glowered at me, then chuckled and rolled the chart back up. He said, "Just remember to stay away from anything to do with the military!"

After dinner Mother joined me in my room to select my attire for the dinner. She ruffled through my closet. "Hmm, we are going for age appropriate sophistication that is fresh and simple at the same time."

We decided on my favorite dress, a white pique with red flowers hand painted across the bottom of the circular skirt and a ponytail held by a small wreath of jasmine.

The preparations for the night began. However, getting the house ready for a formal dinner a dinner party didn't hold a candle to the frenetic sweep of noise that took place before giving a cocktail party. For a cocktail party, all furniture that provided seating was removed from the living room. The resulting living room without seating served to prod guests to continually circulate, cocktails in hand, while murmuring pleasantries and mining tidbits of information. Father explained that the last thing any host wanted at a cocktail party was guests "roosting." The plus side of cocktail parties was a time limit of exactly two hours. Guests dropped in and out of more than one cocktail party and still arrived for a dinner party in time that same night. No one was expected to arrive on time and stay until the end. That would be considered not only slightly rude, but also suspiciously odd. I overhead one of my parent's debriefings after a guest stayed too long. "What do you think he was waiting for? Was he trying to corner one of us alone for some favor? Who didn't show up that he might be meeting on the sly? What do you think it means?"

Preparations for dinner parties seemed more organized to me. Tonight's began with Mitwali barking orders at the extra server hired for the night. They were moving the dining table to the lawn. I peeked over the banister. Ahmed passed below carrying a pile of white linens. It was like a familiar piece of music to me: the rising crescendo of hustle and bustle before guests arrive, followed by a few minutes of whispers between my parents synchronizing their roles. Then the volume rose again as Ahmed escorted arrivals into the living room where Mother and Father stood, ready to greet and offer cigarettes and cocktails.

Father moved me through introductions according to protocol, therefore the last guest I was presented to was a young man who looked as uncomfortable as I felt. Father said, "And this is Douglas Lochmann. He is visiting Col. and Mrs. Johnstone."

I smiled, said "Hello" and reached out to shake his hand.

"How do you do?" he responded in a crisp Scottish accent with an almost imperceptible click of his heels and a bow. I felt my eyes pop open in surprise. His words seemed to have fuzzy burrs all over them. Before I could respond, Ahmed appeared, ringing a small silver bell.

It was time to file outside. The table was covered with a white linen cloth with hand embroidered white roses that matched the napkins carefully molded into birds at each place. Freshly picked white roses floated in silver bowls lined up down the center of the table, interspersed by the tall Diwali lamps with their sparkling crystal globes. Each place setting had three forks, two knives, a soup spoon, a bread and butter plate with small butter knife, a silver finger bowl with rose petals floating in it, and a collection of glasses. Name tags resting in silver holders assigned places.

Ahmed, Mitwali, and the extra server, Fouad, rushed to hold chairs and help seat the ladies. The gentlemen followed. As Father planned, Mrs. Rodgers was on my right and the red-headed Scotsman on my left.

Dinner began. Ahmed, Mitwali, and Fouad entered the dining room single file with Ahmed in the lead. They looked elegant in their cream and white stripped sateen galabias. The black tassels on their dark red fezzes swished forward as they bent to serve our guests. The first course was a dark green aspic with something trapped inside it. I touched the plate. It jiggled, and the Scot watched me out of the corner of his eye. I thought I saw his mouth twitch, but my view was quickly blocked by Fouad silently pouring the first wine into one of the glasses. When all glasses were filled, the table hushed. The guests were well rehearsed in the dance of formal dining. Father stood, looking impressive in his white tuxedo jacket, holding a glass of wine out in front of him. He welcomed each guests with a specific compliment and ended his speech with how honored he and Mother were to enjoy their company, then raised his glass for a toast. All responded with a sip and some muttered "Hear, Hear."

The toast was way too short because now I was faced with what to do with this aspic and the required polite conversation. I turned to Mrs. Rodgers (ladies first) and asked her if she had been to the Gezeira club yet. She had not.

They were thinking of joining. I was on safe ground here, having practiced this part with Father. The only snag I ran into was a slight shudder from her when I mentioned horses. *I probably imagined it.*

I decided it was time to cut the aspic into little pieces. shove them around my plate so it looked like I had eaten some and talk to the ex-soldier on my left.

Had he seen any of the sights around Cairo? Yes, the pyramids and sphinx. He was interested in my story about a sultan's futile attempt to destroy the pyramids which only resulted in one large gash in the side of one pyramid before he gave up.

Fouad whisked away my plate, a signal that Round One was over and Round Two had begun. I caught Father's eye. He gave me a quick nod of approval and turned back to Mrs. Willis.

A small fish complete with head, tail, lemon wedge and parsley was next. It stared skyward. The lemon wedge offered a challenge. *Squeeze but don't squirt.* As I turned to Mrs. Rodgers, I neatly severed the fish head from its body..

She wasn't interested in riding and did not care for horses at all! She tossed her chin and sniffed, then carefully dipped her fingers into the silver bowl, hardly disturbing the rose petals, and slowly wiped her hands. "Really?" I asked in disbelief. *How could anyone not be enamored with the freedom of galloping or the soft velvet nuzzle of a horse eating a slice of apple out of your hand?* She began her story. A lengthy one about her brother's accident on her grandfather's farm in Iowa where one of those nasty beasts threw her brother who was only eight years old. Then it set about rampaging their corn field for the sheer thrill of destruction. Her brother still limps on damp days. I checked with Father again, He jerked his head slightly in the nephew's direction. I nodded back that I understood it was time to talk to him.

But Mrs. Rodgers wasn't finished with her story. I glanced at the nephew who was hunched silently staring at his dish of bare fish bones. I bent over my plate in intense concentration and slowly picked up the lemon slice, only slightly nodding in acknowledgement as the horse saga on my right continued. Mrs. Rodgers abruptly turned away from me to her right.

Oh dear! I gulped down my forkful of fish, skin, and lemon juice, and turned back to her, hoping my inattention hadn't been a serious offense. I could only see the back of her head which was nodding in agreement with the Indonesian gentleman on her right. I turned to my left.

I wasn't sure how to address this dinner companion. His military title had not been mentioned. Sgt? Lt? Maybe Major? Or Mister? I settled on Mister since anything military wasn't a good idea. Had Mr. Lochmann been to the Gezeira Club? Oh yes, he had indeed. He was particularly interested in squash.

The fish went away. A bowl of soup replaced it. A different white wine was poured into another glass for Round Three but Mitwali skipped my glass. I shrugged. *Wouldn't drink it anyway.* I sipped water while parts of the table murmured about how clean and dry the wine was. Ahmed quietly removed my empty wine glass and replaced it with one filled with a dark liquid. The liquid bubbled. *I love Ahmed. He brought me a coke!* I perked up for Mr. Lochmann's sparse sentences. I informed him how lucky he was to get a squash court because I was always put last on the waiting list, maybe because I didn't play well or maybe because I wasn't important enough. He responded with raised eyebrows (bushy ones, I noticed) and a shrug, and a short lesson on how to flick your wrist when using a squash racket.

The soup gave way to lamb and rice and eggplant. Round Four. I hid the eggplant under some of the rice but enjoyed the lamb and rice left over from the eggplant's grave. I happened to look at Mother just as she was checking on me. She smiled, a big wide smile. I smiled back. I was feeling pleased with myself. I doubted that there were many teenagers who would do it any better, even if they were French.

It turned out that Mr. Lochmann and I had riding in common. He clicked his tongue in sympathy when I explained that I wasn't old enough to reserve horses at the club and could only ride with an adult. He agreed he was lucky to be considered an adult. He looked like he was going to add something to that, but Mrs. Rodgers asked me a question. And it was her turn.

Only salad, dessert, and fruit and cheese to go. I warned myself to go easy on the coke because I already looking forward to the bathroom break scheduled after Round Seven.

During salad I learned Mrs. Rodgers had gone to art school and Douglas Lochmann thought riding horses and camels out by the pyramids would be an interesting thing to do. Ahmed refilled my guzzled coke for the second time.

Dessert had me confessing to Mrs. Rodgers that I wanted to sculpture. I told her about the set of sculpture tools I had ordered from Sears, and that my mother thought having children in the far future rather than sculpting would satisfy my urge to create, and that art would not provide me with a college major I could rely on as a career. She mentioned she majored in art just as I turned to tend to the guest on my left. *Ooops!*

I learned that Mr. Lochmann was adjusting to his stay with his Uncle and Aunt. I noticed he used "adjusting," not "enjoying." He wasn't sure when he would return to Scotland and university.

Now I had to really go to the bathroom. I tapped my heel to get my mind off of that problem. Rapid and steady. Tap, tap, tap. Mother must have noticed because when I caught her looking at me, she flashed me a puppy dog sympathy face. Then she was all gracious smiles as she turned back to her charges. *No more water or coke for me.*

Mr. Lochmann wondered if I thought these dinners were too long. He had noticed my tapping.

Mother rose. She addressed the table. "If you gentlemen will be so kind as to excuse us, the ladies will join me upstairs."

I caught her eye as she ushered her guests towards the stairs and made little body bounces to let her know how badly I needed the restroom.

She rescued me.

"Deedee, will you be so kind as to hurry up ahead of us to make sure your sister left your bathroom in good order? We will use both bathrooms this evening." I raced up the steps and into Patty's and my bathroom.

Mother had promised I could be excused when the gentlemen and ladies went their separate ways. Father was entertaining the men downstairs with brandy and cigars, and maybe some serious and privileged discussions. From Mother's bedroom sitting room, the ladies would rejoin them in about half an hour, after refreshing their lipstick, sipping selected liquors, and obliquely planting tidbits of information in gossip. The evening's last dance was a choreography of the party rejoining to exchange pleasantries, and good night.

As I changed for bed I worried. *What if I had been too inattentive during Mrs. Rodgers long horse story? Was I wrong to ask Mr. Lockman if he planned to study medicine? He made an awful face when he said "No!" and muttered something about blood. Will he go off the deep end? Did I measure up to Arianne?*

I tossed in bed, listening to the hum of the conversations upstairs and downstairs, then heard them mingle. The house became quiet. Unexpectedly, there was a knock on my door. Mother and Father came in and stood by my bed. Mother said, "We just wanted to thank you, Honey."

Father leaned over and kissed my forehead. "You did a wonderful job tonight."

Mother tucked the covers around me before she kissed me on the forehead too. On her way out the door she added, "We 'll talk about it more tomorrow. We have some things to discuss with you."

I did well! A wonderful job! I smiled all over. Something seemed unanswered, but I was too tired to figure out what.

Invitations

BREAKFAST WAS PATCHY THE NEXT MORNING. ALTHOUGH IT was Sunday, our family day, Father had to gone to the embassy to catch up on some work. Mother was tired and just wanted to take a cup of tea up to her room and rest there quietly (which meant without her children). Patty and I picked at the fruit and pastry that she had put out on the dining room table for us. The table and all the chairs had been moved back inside from the party the night before. We had the whole formal dining room to ourselves.

I was barefoot and still in my pajamas—the wonderful luxury of a day without a house full of servants and rules of propriety. I leaned back in my chair, stretched my legs straight out in front of me and wiggled my naked toes. Patty paid no attention to me. She sifted through the fruit and settled on a banana, peeled it quickly, and began nibbling it non-stop, starting at the tip, and working toward the end held in her hand, like a giant annoying rabbit. She didn't even sit down, just stood near the fruit platter, banana in hand. And she was dressed. Nicely dressed. Like she was going somewhere and was not the least bit interested how things had gone the night before. The banana consumed her attention. She didn't interrupt nibbling to swallow. It must have simply slid down her throat into her stomach with no help.

I slammed my legs back in place and sat up. "So!" I accused, "It looks like you're ready to go somewhere. I thought the plans were to have dinner on one of the Feluccas this evening. It was your suggestion to eat a fancy dinner floating down the Nile on one of those boats, but aren't you ready a little early?"

Without taking the banana out of her mouth, she answered, "I'm going to church."

"What? How? Is Hassan here to take you?"

"My friend Sharon's family is picking me up in ten minutes. I'll be back in time for the Felucca ride."

"But… But…Sunday is our special day." I took a deep breath. I was excluded, abandoned. No sister to endure, no parental feedback. "But, why are you going to church?"

"Because I want to." She dropped the banana peel on a dish. "Goodbye." And she left.

Our Sundays had always been saved for family picnics and outings. They gathered our family into the nest that was always with us. They meant we were home together no matter where. Patty seemed to be chugging full steam ahead out of our nest. New worries mixed with last night's. *If she is growing up that fast, I guess I had better grow up even faster. Do I really have to try my wings? Fly away? Isn't this home? Where do I belong?*

We dressed well for dinner on the Felucca. Hassan drove us to the dock on the Nile where our floating restaurant was anchored. Its tall white sails made gentle flapping sounds as we boarded. Lining the center aisle, the rows of crisp white linen clothes, sparkling glassware, gold plated silverware, and tall candles lost their splendor for me the minute we were ushered to our reserved table. A familiar couple seated directly across the aisle scrambled to their feet to greet us.

Mother floated forward, "Why, Col. Johnstone. Pamela! How lovely to see you again." She didn't say "Again *so soon*," but to my ears those extra words hung in the air. Father followed suit with hearty handshakes and musing over the wonder of having dinner reservations at the same place and the same time. Patty and I smiled our best manners.

No! No! No! Not another round of polite conversation and perfect manners! Maybe Hassan is waiting at the dock and I can fake a stomachache and go home.

Mother must have had a sixth sense about my plan to bolt. She placed her hand under my elbow and escorted me to my seat, away from the aisle. Patty was seated opposite me. That way Mother and Father had free access to conversing across the aisle, which is what they did. *No discussion about about last night any time soon.*

Patty kicked me under the table. At least she was also annoyed with this interruption to our family dinner. We resorted to the foot fighting that got us through long family dinners during home leave. We never kicked hard enough to cause serious injury or be noticed but with enough force to make it a contest.

After we returned home, I collapsed on my bed, angry and ashamed at myself for reverting to childish behavior just when I wanted so much to be praised for my grownup behavior the night before.

"Deedee!" Father called loudly enough to hear through the door.

Uh oh. Things were going downhill fast. I opened my door and shouted back, "WHAT?"

"Your mother and I are having a nightcap. We would like you to join us. There are somethings we need to talk about."

Double uh oh. As I entered their sitting room, Mother patted the seat on the sofa next to her. A serious talk was coming up. *Did they notice the foot fight? Maybe it's not about tonight, but last night's dinner. Maybe I dreamed they came in my room and said I did well.*

Mother reached for my hand and cradled it in hers. My hand felt cold and clammy nested inside the soft warmth of hers. Father paced back and forth in front of the couch. He cleared his throat. I took a deep breath to brace myself. *Here it comes.*

Mother squeezed my hand and said, "Honey, we are so proud of you."

Father stopped in the middle of his pacing path and turned to face me. "You were spot on last night. Rita told your mother she had a wonderful time with you and wants to make plans for future meetings. And the nephew was smiling by the end of dinner, something his uncle tells me is rare.

He paused. Mother smiled at me and then chirped up at him, "Go on, Bob, tell her the rest."

Father swished his drink. As I waited leaning back against the cushions my body basked in relief and pride. I watched Father's drink swirl around in his glass. It never spilled over when he did that.

In secret, when Patty wasn't around, I practiced swishing water around in my after-brushing-teeth-rinsing glass. Water always went over the side. I wondered how much Father practiced before he was able to do it so well.

Father smiled, raised the glass to me, gave it another swirl, then sipped. I held my breath and waited. He cleared his throat again and looked at me. "Yes, you pulled it off beautifully. We may have to call on you again. Thank you. We are proud of you. But that is not what we wanted to talk about. You did such a good job that a couple of requests have been put to us. To you, really."

The warm feeling that had flooded me leaked away. "Requests" was a scary word. I sat up straight. "What kind of requests?"

"Invitations, Dear. Your father meant invitations." Mother patted my hand to reassure me that "request" was a mistaken choice of words. I wasn't assured.

I crossed my arms. "What kind of invitations?"

Mother's words bounced out. "Well, for one thing, Col. Johnstone would like to suggest that you be invited to a ball for British Naval officers! In Alexandria! They are looking for suitable young ladies who will be house guests of British families stationed in Alexandria. There will be a Grand Ball with dancing! You love to dance. A glamourous weekend right out of Jane Austin!

At first, I was too surprised to say anything. A ball! Dancing! Just like the Bennets! With British Officers. *Uh oh. Douglas is British, maybe an officer. A room full of Douglasses!*

After a deep breath, I asked, "How old are the officers? Does Col. Johnstone know I am only seventeen and haven't even finished high school yet?"

Mother patted my hand again. She said, "You might be a bit younger than most of the other young ladies that will be going, true. But you have social know how and poise beyond your years. It will be fine. You'll be well cared for and never be out of the sight of Capt. And Mrs. Williams, good friends of Col. Johnstone.

"But everyone will be strangers to me," I pointed out.

Mother leaned forward to soothe my hair and assure eye contact. "Not for long. Dear. You are an expert at making new friends. You've been doing it all your life. Think of all the moving around the world we have done! This is a unique and very special opportunity. The British Navy is leaving Alexandria. I understand this is their last ball. I would hate to have you miss such a wonderful a once in a lifetime experience. Besides, it will give you some practice of being off on your own."

I remembered worrying about having to try my wings because Patty was trying hers. Now, it seemed, it was time for me to try mine. I sighed. *It's a scary and lonely idea.*

"Can't you two come with me? You loved balls in Vienna."

Mother shook her head back and forth and said, "No, Dear, we were not invited. Just you. Col. Johnstone's friends will take every bit as good care of you as we would if we were there."

Father added, "And it would be nice to do a favor for the Johnstones, good relations with the British, you know."

. My parents sat still, silently sipping their drinks. Smiling at me. *Yikes. They're kind of counting on me, like I'm part of their team.*

I shrugged. "OK, I'll think about it. Is that all? It sounded like there was more than one request."

Father finished off his drink, placed the used glass on a small tray near the door where Ahmed would pick it up when he brought them their morning coffee, and then he settled down into a large armchair facing the couch.

"You're right, there was another request. And from Col. Johnstone again. Well, rather through him from his nephew. Douglas Lochmann has asked our permission to ask you to go riding with him."

"Horseback riding?"

Father nodded.

"Great! When?"

"On kind of a regular basis, I gather."

Why in the world am I suspicious of what's coming next? I leaned forward, jiggling my heels. "What does that mean, regular basis?"

Father cleared his throat. "Umm. It seems that Sunday mornings are the only time Douglas has the use of their car. I think he intends to engage horses from the club as well as the stables out by the pyramids. The rides would only be for an hour or so. He'll bring you right home. We've already made sure that he is a good horseman as well as a safe driver. Both families will know exactly where you are."

"But Sunday is our special day. Patty is already changing it with her church."

"True. But she promises to be back by noon, and since Douglas is planning your rides at seven, you'll be back well before your sister."

"Seven!" I gasped. "Seven Sunday morning? Seven A.M? You've got to be kidding! I'd have to get up at six! Six thirty if I hurry."

Mother shifted around on the couch to face me. She folded her hands on her lap and bent toward me. She purred, "Just think, Honey, you will be doing a troubled young man a great favor and have a friend to ride with the same time. I must admit, my heart goes out to him. This might be just the ticket to help him recover. And I think it will be good for you too, to do things away from your crowd at the club and at school. There is a world waiting for you. Try new things." She chuckled and poked her finger at my collar bone. "But only if I know about them and they are safe. And when you've had your ride, and come home to a nice breakfast, you'll have time to yourself to read, or do your art thing."

"Do I get to think about this too?"

Mother stood up. "Sure, Honey. It's too late tonight to make any big decisions right now, and tomorrow's a school day. We'll talk about Mrs. Rodger's offer on our way to school."

What? Mrs. Rodgers too?"

"On the way to school, Dear. Goodnight." She kissed my cheek and ushered me out the door.

I sat next to Mother in the back seat on the way to school so I wouldn't miss a word about Mrs. Rodgers' offer. Mother told me I was invited to spend a few Saturday mornings in her studio, the one she had decided to create after our dinner conversation.

Mother put her arm through mine and squeezed like she did when I was a little girl. It meant she was excited, and she loved me. She said, "Honey, Rita looked so happy. She asked me to be sure to thank you for giving her the idea."

Mrs. Rodger's invitation put me in such a good mood, I accepted the other two on the spot. Besides, I loved dancing and horseback riding. *That dinner wasn't so bad after all, even if I did miss Emil's party.*

But several days before my departure date for the ball, I gave into second thoughts which I aired over dinner. Keeping my voice even and as adult as I could manage, looking from one parent to the other I said, "You know, since I'm going alone to Alexandria, surely no one will notice if I don't go."

"Oh no you don't!" Father stood up, leaned toward me and pointed his finger at me. He punctuated every word with a forward jab of that finger. Both eyebrows lowered. "You made a commitment, and you are going to keep it!"

I got the message. This was one of those Big Rules for Life. Right beside Don't cheat, Tell the truth right away, Don't make scenes in public, Don't judge other cultures, Present ours in its best light. Oh yes, and Life isn't fair.

Mother tried to quell my nervousness by reminding me, "Honey, in just five months you will be off, half a world away, starting a new life in Berkeley. This is peanuts in comparison."

Peanuts or not, her pep talk didn't quell my rising panic. *Why did I decide to go so far away to school anyway? I can go to The American University in Cairo instead of Berkeley.* Then I remembered where Alex was. *Why is everything so complicated and scary?*

Early Friday morning, my parents shoveled me and my two suitcases (one for the ball gown and the other for regular stuff) into the back seat. Hassan waited patiently to close the door before taking his place as driver.

The trip seemed as long and confined as an airplane flight. I felt squished even though I was sitting alone in the back seat. Hassan maintained his usual cold silence during the three plus hours. I had plenty of time to stew. *What if no one wants to dance with me? What if the Williams don't want an American teenager for a house guest? Worse, what if I can't think of what to say to all these strangers. What if I make a mess of everything?*

Hassan delivered me to the home of my host family, jerked his head downward in what I suppose he considered a good-bye nod, and immediately returned to the car to get back in time to drive Mother and Patty home from school, and then Father from work. They would be a family of three this weekend. Without me.

Mrs. Williams was soft spoken and gracious in a polite English way. Saturday came with breakfast, then tea, and then time to get ready for the ball. One last check in the mirror reflected my simple apple green ballgown. It had a full satin skirt that whispered against the floor when I twisted side to side. The bodice was also satin but the sleeves, my favorite part, were chiffon tulips and just a shade lighter than the dress. I loved it. I saluted myself in the mirror before joining my hosts.

Capt. Williams drove up to the entrance of the club where the ball was held. A valet parked the car. Music and voices spilled out of the building and over us. I froze the minute I stepped out of the car. Mrs. Williams waited ahead a few steps. She said, "Come along dear. You look lovely. Shall we?" She took my elbow. I took a deep breath. *You can do this. You can do this. Now go do it!*

My first impression on entering the room was of a tide of voices in a sea of crisp uniforms and shiny metal insignias contrasted against bare shoulders and arms in long clingy dresses. Music rose above the talk. A quick glance at the band suggested they were military also. Still guiding me by the elbow my hostess murmured, "Now come and meet some of the fine young men here." She stopped in front of a group of faces "Diana, may I present some of our finest young officers? Gentlemen, this is Diana. Her father is Economic Councilor to the American Embassy in Cairo." *Oh. I get it. I am not just an American teenager; I am my father's rank. Oh well, that might balance out my age. Everyone here but me is way older than Douglas!*

The crisply uniformed officers were as formal as the ball itself. Held stiffly at arm's length, I found myself talking to a chest of medals and ribbons, or a throat of pale freckled skin, or a freshly shaven chin. When I tilted my head back to look directly at the questioners, they invariably were staring off into space above my head, probably deciding which of the bare shouldered forms across the room to ask to dance next.

And the dancing was not what I had imagined. Not after the sessions of tango, samba, rumba and cha cha cha in the upstairs classroom in Teheran, or the waltzing and foxtrot on the rooftop of the Semiramis Hotel with friends from the club, or the jitterbug, swing, and bunny hop at school parties.

No. Not at all what I had imagined. No twinkled eyed Elizabeth Bennet across the room. No swirling gowns of satin gliding to minuets. The evening went something like this: Step, step forward. Then a voice above my head said, "I gather you live in Egypt. Where may I ask?" Back step. Turn. "What do you do in Cairo? Oh. still in school, eh?" Step, step forward.. "The American University I assume. No?" Back step. "High school? Not familiar with that." Forward step, step. "Oh, it's like sixth form? Thank you for the dance. Lovely meeting you." And repeat with the next polite gentleman.

At midnight, the ball was over. My feet were tired from trying to be light and easy to lead while avoiding being stepped on. My back ached from holding a stiff straight posture while reaching for shoulders. I never sat out a dance. My age wasn't as bad a disease as I feared, but I did notice that my most frequent dance partners were the very youngest officers. It was a pleasant evening but without any hint of Jane Austin intrigue. I was proud of navigating on my own in this foreign world. I had glided through all the right manners since arriving and had kept the conversation going with every partner and I hadn't tripped or missed a step even once. I crawled into bed smiling. I had noticed only two handsome young men among the sea of uniforms, but neither was a Darcy. Or an Alex.

The next morning, it took self-control to overcome the impulse to hug Hassan when I saw him standing by the car. He was quick to relieve me of my suitcases and held the door stoically for me to pile in back while I thanked my hosts. The silent drive home seemed quicker. I felt lighter, and enjoyed having the whole back seat to myself. *I did it! I managed the culture gap and the age gap. On my own! A mature young adult! Mother and Father will be proud of me. I'm proud of me.*

Going home was the best part of the trip.

Early Sunday

Riding with Douglas early Sunday mornings became one of the highlights of my week but there was a downside: Father's proclamation. With arms crossed and eyebrow raised (signals that he was presenting a bottom line), he said, "Deedee, there's no one here to answer the door when Douglas comes for you. The servants are off, and your mother and I relish our only morning to sleep in. It is your responsibility to be up and ready early and waiting. We can't have Douglas banging on the door at that early hour. It could make a scene, especially if the guard gets involved. Be at your window, ready to run out the minute you see Douglas driving up."

The words "Douglas driving up" amazed me. None of my friends drove, even the club kids were transported by drivers. I had never been in a car alone, without a driver or chaperone, with someone near my age. It felt grown up. Thinking it through, I saw Father's point. If I wasn't at the door, Douglas would have to turn the engine off, lock the car, come to the door, and wait for someone inside to wake up and answer it, while hoping the guard didn't become agitated during the wait.

I nodded to Father. "I get it. I'll set my alarm for 6:15 instead of 6:30. "

During my Sunday morning vigils for Douglas, I became a part of Cairo waking to a new day. Through my open window, I heard the calls to prayer floating down into the narrow streets and manicured gardens nearby. I imagined men in galabias kneeling on the sidewalk to bow toward Mecca and murmur their morning prayers. Birds trilled, chirped, and cawed. I could faintly hear the rattle of steel shutters going up as shops in the commercial section of Zamalek prepared for the day. Sometimes donkeys laden with sticks of wood, or jangling pots ambled by, followed by their owners flicking the beasts with a small sticks. Sometimes well-dressed occupants of the apartment across the street emerged to step into a waiting car. *Probably on their way to church. Where else would they go so dressed up early Sunday morning? Friday's the holy day for most people here, so if you dress up Sunday morning, you must be going to Church. Like my sister.* I could hear her stirring in her room, getting ready to leave when Sharon's family came by for her at 7:30.

When Col. Johnstone's car turned onto our street, I ran down the stairs and stood in the front doorway while Douglas parked and got out to walk around the car and hold the passenger door open for me. The guard then jerked to attention and scribbled furiously in his notebook. I couldn't help but smile to myself as I climbed into the front seat instead of my usual back seat position. Douglas closed my door and returned to the driver's seat, soon taking his favorite driving position of one arm resting half in and half out his window and the other hand on the wheel. Off we went, like young adults in a movie scene, leaving the guard behind to wonder where we were going and why.

We settled into a comfortable comradery. To and from our rides, I rattled on about Alex. I explained he was my real boyfriend even though I went out with boys from school and the club, usually to parties or events, sometimes dinner and dancing, but always in a group. I told him how Alex had earned a football scholarship to Stanford and was now 6 ft. 3in. Douglas mentioned a childhood friend named Nell who had already started the same university he would be attending soon. He hoped she would not find him too changed, too dreary, after his time away. I knew not to ask him what he meant by that. Father and Mother continued to remind me not to bring up anything to do with his time in the army.

Once I asked, "How come you don't need two hands to drive? Hassan always uses two hands."

Douglas snorted. "Right! Two hands are safer. But remember, Hassan is on his best behavior as an employee. I, on the other hand, am enjoying a Sunday drive with my riding partner."

I often sneaked glances at Douglas's hand on the steering wheel, sometimes even leaned forward to catch glimpses of his feet on the pedals below. *What wonderful freedom it would be to have a powerful machine under my control and go where and when I wanted to!* Douglas never said anything if he noticed my envious looks.

Douglas relished a canter and gallop when out of the stable's sight as much as I did. Although the horses from the club were far superior to the tourist fare in the Maadi stables, near the pyramids, I looked forward to those rides equally because of the quiet grandeur of the early morning desert and ancient monuments.

One morning in late spring on our way home from a ride in the desert, Douglas turned off the main road onto a strip of packed earth. I thought maybe there was a problem with the car. Douglas got out and leaned in his window towards me. He said, "I've been planning a surprise for you. But you have to keep it absolutely secret or I'll be in a great heap of trouble."

From where I sat about two hundred yards of a dirt stretched ahead to end at the edge of a grove of young trees planted in measured rows. Perhaps one day it would be a roadway into a grand estate or through a future Egyptian agricultural project. I scanned the dry grass area bordering the sides of the lane. *What in the world could he have here? An animal?*

Douglas asked, "Can you keep a secret?"

"Yes! For sure." I got out of the car and crossed my heart. Then asked, "What?"

He said, "I'm going to teach you how to drive. I know how much you want to. But it must be a secret."

I closed my eyes and squealed. I was too happy to talk. I did say 'thank you' many times during the lessons though.

His driving lessons were carefully organized. First, he lined the car up so that it was squarely in the middle of the lane, facing the young grove. Then he turned the car off. We exchanged seats. Next, we had to scuttle the seat up so my feet could firmly reach the brakes, the clutch, and the gas pedal. This reminded me of the time in Vienna when Christoff had me jump start Father's car. And how scared and proud I felt. And how furious Father was with Christoff when he found out. Douglas settled in the passenger seat near enough to me to take over the braking and steering in case of an emergency. I gripped the steering wheel and turned the car on with the gear in neutral. Leaning forward to encourage the car to follow, and tightening my grasp on the steering wheel, gritting my teeth, I pushed the clutch in and jiggled the gear shift into first. With my eyes glued to the target trees, I jabbed the gas pedal while releasing the clutch. A series of abrupt forward jerks followed until we traveled the two hundred yards to the end of the road. I braked, shifted to neutral, and turned the car off. Then Douglas and I changed seats again, he readjusted the driver's seat, turned the car back on, and oh so smoothly, it seemed to me, backed the car up and, in about three moves, turned it toward the main road, drove to the entrance of the lane, turned the car around again to face the line of trees at its end, and turned the engine off. Again, I strangled the steering wheel in a death grip, and jerked down to the end of the lane. By our third week of lessons, I managed to drive my section in a straight line with very few jerks along the way. I would soon be ready to learn how to back up, then turn the car around. By this time, I had memorized every pile of dirt along the side of our unfinished road, every rock littering the three-foot clearing on either side, and the vague impression of weeds and bushes beyond that. It was only a small stretch of an abandoned project that jutted, forgotten, off the main highway but this secret place was magically beautiful to me.

I almost ruined things by forgetting to set my alarm one Sunday morning.

Douglas later told me that he had pulled up in front of the house just before seven that morning and patiently waited in the car for more than five minutes. During that time, the guard had taken out his pad. After several minutes of watching Douglas intently and adding brief entries in his notebook, the guard left his post and edged toward Douglas. Douglas, having already grown impatient with waiting, felt extreme annoyance with the guard's deliberate inch by inch advance. He flung the car door open and marched past the guard to our front door. He rang the doorbell several times.

There was no response.

When Douglas put his ear to the door to hear if there was stirring in the house, he noted that the guard was now directly behind him, notebook in one hand, the other resting on the weapon at his hip.

That did it!

Douglas turned his back to the guard and pounded on the door with both fists. The guard ran back to his station and began shouting Arabic into a radio phone. Douglas had no idea who the guard was calling, only that excited Arabic was on both ends of the call.

At this point Father, in his silk dressing gown, opened the front door.

"Your daughter is late!" Douglas later assured me he regretted that he had not said "Good Morning, Sir, sorry to disturb you" first.

"Good Morning, Douglas." Father motioned Douglas inside. "I'll get her," He turned toward the stairs.

"Thank you, Sir, but allow me!" With that Douglas bounded up the steps and knocked forcefully on my door. I guess he figured out which door was mine because he knew I watched the street from my window.

His knocking would have awakened anyone. Patty opened her door, took one look at the red headed Scotsman pounding on my door, squeaked (according to Douglas), and ran into my parents' bedroom.

I woke up, jumped out of bed, rushed to my door shouting, "What's going on?" I yanked the door open. There stood a face filled with fury staring at me in my pajamas and wild hair. One fist was still in the air, ready to pound on the door again. Douglas's mouth dropped open. He lowered his arm. Both arms now hung stiffly at his sides, each ending in a fist balled up so tightly white edges showed around the knuckles.

"EEK!" I shrieked. I ran to my desk, grabbed the robe hanging over the back of the chair and held it in front of me. Facing Douglas while backing away, I made an eek sound again, but not as loudly as the first time.

Douglas's anger melted to embarrassment as quickly as my face flushed to a bright red that matched his blush. He hung his head with one hand covering his eyes for a fleeting second. Then he looked up at me and gulped, "We will miss our start time if you don't hurry."

He whirled around and retreated down the steps. I could hear him apologizing to Father as I threw on my clothes and grabbed a brush and rubber band to tame my hair in the car. I squirted a bit of toothpaste on my finger and worked it back and forth against my teeth as I hurried downstairs.

Neither my scowling father nor I said a word as I hugged him where he waited at the bottom of the stairs. Then I bolted out the front door and clamored into the car without stopping for any polite assistance with the car door. I slammed it shut.

Douglas started the car without a word. His silence lengthened. I peeked at him through the curtain of hair I was brushing. His lips were tightened into a grim straight line. I took a deep breath knowing there were at least two difficult tasks ahead of me: getting Douglas into a decent mood for our ride and facing Father's reprimand when I returned home.

Lifting my head to sweep my hair back into a ponytail gave me a clear view of the street ahead. I gasped and poked Douglas in the arm. "Look! Look! That's the funniest thing I've ever seen."

"What are you talking about?" Douglas hissed through his clenched teeth.

"There. Coming toward us on the other side of the street."

Douglas slowed down to look. He took a deep breath. then followed it with a snort which evolved into a short series of half snort-half chuckles. "Isn't that your...?"

"Yep! It sure is. Mitwali!"

Mitwali was hurtling down the street towards our house on his bicycle with his galabia flapping above his knees. His skinny legs below the knob- like knees looked like old-fashioned engine pistons pumping furiously up and down. His left arm reached up to hold his fez in place while the single-handed steering at top speed down the street resulted in a less than straight safe path. He was yelling at the top of his voice, probably to clear a path ahead.

We laughed together for a full block. Then I began to wonder out loud. "Boy! I guess the guard called him. Can't imagine why. You'd think if the guard was worried about saving me from a wild red-headed foreigner," I paused and turned sideways to point straight at Douglas, " That's you!" Then I continued before he could say anything, "You'd think he would have called the police, or the army, not Goofy Mitwali."

"For all you know, there could be a full militia at your front door right now. Want to go back and see?" Douglas grinned at me with shoulders raised in question.

"No. On to the ride! I'll face it all later. I still wonder though, why Mitwali?" I pulled a knee up on the seat so I could sit sideways facing Douglas. I took a deep breath and said, "Douglas, I am really sorry for not being ready this morning. Father says no one is interested in excuses, just results. So, no excuse. I'm just plain sorry."

Douglas didn't take his eyes off the road, but he said out of the side of his mouth, like a gangster, "Okay Lady, just don't let it happen again."

I turned back to face the front, and grinned. I felt not only grown-up, but also like a movie star in a detective film.

When I returned. Father was sitting with a cup of coffee at the breakfast table, waiting for me. I tried to hide behind my plate stacked with a banana, mango, and three muffins. He peered over his raised cup at me. "You were irresponsible and caused a ruckus that brought our presence here into sharp focus. The guard was about to call for reinforcements, I understand. Somehow he got ahold of Mitwali." Father took a sip of coffee. He started into the cup, as if it would tell him how that happened. He wasn't finished with me. "This kind of thing can work against us by giving ammunition to factions that want to keep the U.S. out of Egypt." He shook his head and finished off his coffee. "I know Douglas used bad judgement in pounding on the door, but there are circumstances involved with him... I really can't hold him accountable at this time. You, on the other hand, only needed to set an alarm clock and none of this would have happened. Your job was to be up and ready. Early, if I remember correctly."

Peeling the banana slowly, strip by strip, helped keep my voice steady. "I know. I'm sorry. Really sorry." Knowing how Father felt about excuses, I didn't offer any. Besides, I did not have one except that I had been out with a group of friends from the club the night before, dancing on the rooftop of the Semiramis Hotel, which Father, of course, knew. Hassan barely got me home before my 11:00 curfew.

"Grounded for two weeks." Father stood up. "Mitwali's day off was interrupted. I figure that's at least half a day's extra pay. That will come out of your allowance."

That was a blow, but I knew it was fair. I stuffed half a muffin in my mouth. Without butter or jam. Atonement.

Father turned to leave the room. I took and deep breath and asked, "So, I can still go riding with Douglas?"

"Yes." Father nodded with a curt dip of his chin. He raised his head and looked straight into my eyes as he reminded me, "We made a commitment to the Johnstones. We keep our commitments." His voice softened. He almost smiled. "Apparently, the rides are helping Douglas recover from the horror of his army days. They tell me he's begun discussing returning to Scotland."

That horror was still a secret from me. Surely, they would explain after Douglas left for Scotland. I hoped that would not be soon because summer was coming, and days without school often stretched out in itchy hot streams of time. Father turned to leave again. As he reached for the doorknob, I squeezed in one more question. "Why did Mitwali come anyway?"

He looked at the floor, shaking his head back and forth. "Maybe he has a friend in the neighborhood who heard the disturbance and called him. Maybe the guard?" Father looked up, staring across the room at nothing. He rubbed his chin and shrugged, "Maybe he is on the same payroll as the guard. You never know."

He left the room. Alone, I found myself whispering, "Clumsy Mitwali. Skinny dumb Mitwali." *Maybe he's in charge of all the guards. Instead of Mohammed, maybe he's their boss and collects all their information. Yes, he's probably the head spy. If that's true, he's an awfully good actor.*

The Present

HAVING TO BE READY SO FAR AHEAD ON SUNDAY MORNINGS meant more time to watch Shagret el Dor outside my window. Two Sundays later, I noticed a young man standing in the entry way of the apartment building across the street. His white tennis shorts and shirt gleamed through the gray early morning. There was something familiar about him. Wanting a closer look, I leaned out my open window although Father would not approve of that. It might draw attention.

The young man looked up at me, then quickly lowered his head and darted away down the street. I gasped. It was Emil. Emil! My best buddy at the club. Emil who walked me home so often, but never to my door. I hung out the window until he disappeared around the corner, going in the direction of the club. Of course! He must have a tennis game scheduled at seven thirty when the courts open.

What was he doing here? He lived blocks away. *Maybe he quarreled with his parents. He never mentions them so they must be a problem. Of course! He's only sixteen, but maybe they kicked him out. Maybe his family kicks everyone out at sixteen.*

Often well-dressed people exited the building alone and I never saw any children emerging. Yes, it was logical. *Oh! Poor Emil! Living alone in a tiny one room apartment. But a least it's across the street from me. At least now he can walk me all the way home from the club and Mother and Father will welcome him as a neighbor. After my ride with Douglas. I'll go to the club and point out the bright side of his exile,*

As soon as I returned from the ride, I gulped down breakfast and changed into my tennis clothes, wrapped my bathing suit in a towel, tucked it into my new pill box purse that served as a tiny suitcase, and hurried off to the club. Patty was at church, but I was too excited about Emil's banishment to mind walking to the club alone. My new purse would protect me from the possibility of pinchers. Often Egyptian men pinched women walking alone. With a quick shoulder movement toward the offending fingers, the ridged purse knocked them off course. For the lower, more often targeted areas of my body, I swung the purse in front of me just as the attacker closed in. This not only blocked the pinch, but sometimes it even hit the pincher in the groin. If the attacker was coming from the rear, I blocked his target zone by sticking my purse out behind my bottom like a bustle. Walking with a younger sister or friends was less stressful protection, but the purse worked.

Emil was on a court when I arrived. I sat on the bench along its side to wait politely until his game was over. He nodded formally in greeting but did not interrupt the play. I had signed up for the same court when his time was over, figuring we could begin our game immediately after he told me his sad story. The game ended. I smiled, waved, and patted the bench beside me to signal we would talk before playing. Instead of walking toward the bench, Emil walked to the opposite side of the court. He headed toward the clubhouse.

"Emil. Emil. Wait." Certainly, he knew that his appearance so early across the street raised questions, and also that I was ready for a game. He wasn't so much a better player that he could just walk away like a tennis snob. The score had been seven to five, a tie breaker, the last time we played. "Wait!" I was shouting by now. Emil stopped. He hung his head while I trotted up to him.

"What's wrong with you? I have this court next, by the way, so we can talk before our game. You must tell me why you are living across the street and not with your parents. Are they awfully mad at you? Did you do something terrible? What did you do?" Emil stared at me. His eyes were popped open, his eyebrows raised. But he said nothing.

After a few seconds of silence, I filled the space between us with more questions. "Or do they just think at sixteen it is time to live on your own? Tell me what's going on!" Emil's eyes were still wide, his eyebrows still up, but now he was shaking his head. He took a step back. Perhaps he was too embarrassed to talk about his problem. I reached out and patted his arm. "You know I'm your friend. You can trust me. Why are you living across the street?"

Emil hunched his shoulders and shook his head. "You have it all wrong. You are an American. You won't understand."

"What won't I understand? My parents get mad at me too. I get grounded all the time; you know that. Just got through with my latest grounding today, as a matter of fact. What did you do? Why did they kick you out?"

"No, no. I am not kicked out. My parents are not upset with me at all. I really don't think you will understand this."

"Well, I certainly can't understand it if you don't explain it to me. You came out of the apartment building across the street at six forty-five in the morning dressed for tennis. You were obviously coming here from there, not from your parents'. It doesn't make sense to me." Emil remained still, but I was feeling antsy. I began bouncing the tennis balls off my racket, like the hotshot players do before serving.

"You are too American to understand."

"At least give me a chance to try." I missed a bounce and had to retrieve the tennis ball rolling away.

When I faced him again, Emil said, "Okay. You remember I just had a birthday?" He crossed his arms over his chest, imprisoning his tennis racket beneath them.

"Yes. I really wanted to come to your party but couldn't." I rolled the tennis ball back and forth on the ground with my foot. It helped my nervousness and at the same time I could give Emil my full attention.

"Well, for my birthday present, my father gave me a mistress. Just as his father gave him when he turned sixteen."

"A mistress? What on earth do you mean?"

"He gave me his mistress to use as my own. She lives across the street from you, on the second floor. I visit her on Saturday and Tuesday."

I had come across the word mistress in a book, and it didn't seem to be a good thing. I slapped my racket against my leg and tried to stay calm even though I felt like my body had gone into full danger alert. I had to give

Emil a chance to come up with a reasonable explanation, one that was not so disturbing to me.

"I'm not sure what you mean. I'm not really sure what a mistress is."

"Deedee, she is a woman my father has intercourse with and now I do too. She is nineteen and very kind. You would like her. My father pays for her apartment and all her living costs. She makes us both happy. That is why I avoided your gate guards, so they didn't think I was visiting you too."

I was too stunned to do anything but stand frozen in the hot morning sunshine. As Emil's explanation slowly penetrated I felt small rivulets of foul-smelling grease invade my body. I shuddered in revulsion every time a new realization came to me.

Then I shrieked at Emil, "You're horrid! Repulsive!" I threw my tennis racket at him and started running. I ran all the way home, all ten blocks without stopping, with my purse bumping against my legs and hips. I ran past the pigeon kabob vendors calling out their wares, past the feluccas floating on the Nile, past astonished pedestrians and past our gate guard with his mouth agape and hand on his phone. I burst into the house, raced to my room, slammed the front window shut and pulled the curtains to blot out the apartment building across the street.

Mother heard me come in. She sat beside me on my bed and listened to me rant. Then she asked Father to join us. I crossed my arms and sat hunched in a dark pout as she explained to Father why I was so upset.

"Well." he said. "Well, well. That certainly is different."

"Different! It's slimy. Awful! Horrid!" I shouted at him.

Father nodded in agreement. "The sharing part is particularly disturb-ing." He and Mother exchanged one of their secret glances. Somehow, I felt they were finding the whole thing amusing, even while comforting me. Then he turned to me. "But, Deedee, you know cultures are different. Our way is not the only way. It is for us, of course, but we can't make the whole world follow in our image. Americans are often viewed as puritanical, especially by people who consider themselves…" He paused, searching for the right words, then took a deep breath and finished with, "more sophisticated, more worldly."

He went to my window and opened the curtains as he continued, "Some things you have to accept as another way, one you don't have to agree with, or approve of, but one that is none of your business."

"Ha!" I crossed my arms and turned my back to the window. My parents left to give me time to think things over. I kicked my bed. *Jeez. Accept this? Why am I so angry? It's none of my business but it makes me think of Dara saying her life was over because she had to marry that old guy her parents liked. And Fatima couldn't have her own salary. I'll **never** be owned! I'm so glad I'm going to live in the States where there's Liberty for All.*

I still have almost four more months here. How can I ever even look at Emil again?

The Vespa

IT WAS SEVERAL WEEKS BEFORE I FELT COMFORTABLE GOING to the club where I might run into Emil. I accepted that Emil's life was none of my business and I found a new club pal to play tennis with and walk me home. Nadim. Nadim fascinated me because he had the perfect Ancient Egyptian profile. His face looked like it came right off one of the frescos from the tombs of pharaohs. And he had a Vespa. He poked along beside me on the way to my house, his legs dangling over the sides of the scooter as he paddled it along with his feet. I did not dare accept his offer to ride on the back. I worried my parents would view a scooter as a dangerous thing to ride on and I was sure that straddling the rear seat would not be what Mother considered lady-like. I envied Nadim his little machine and his freedom.

Nadim was a far better tennis player than I, but he didn't mind playing with me when he had no other matches scheduled. He drifted in and out of the International Group as they sat circling tables filled with snack orders. He didn't seem to have a lot of spending money or a driver and he seemed to care much more about his life as a student beyond the club than his visits to it. His group of fellow students at the American University in Cairo were on tight budgets, but occasionally, when a good film came to a theater in downtown Cairo, they organized a movie night. Nadim invited me to join them the following weekend. I was honored. Serious university students, most of whom had seldom set foot in Zamalek, were far beyond any Big Kid Group.

I never expected such a solid "No" from my parents when I asked if I could go.

"I don't know this Nadim you are talking about at all." Mother started. "Where does he live? Where does he go to school? What is his last name? What do his parents do? We know nothing about him."

Father said, "Your mother is worried because Patty told her you were friends with a young man who rides a motorcycle, and who is not a member of the club but sneaks in, and who lives outside of Zamalek, in downtown Cairo. Is any of that true?"

I answered that he and his parents belonged to the club, he went to the American University, he spoke English, French, Arabic, and some other languages I couldn't remember, he was a good tennis player, I didn't know where he lived, and yes, he had a motor scooter,- a vespa, not a motorcycle.

"Well," Father said, "You won't be able to go next Saturday anyway because Hassan will be busy with us all evening. He won't be able to squeeze a trip to the downtown Cairo cinema."

"He wouldn't have to. I could ride on the back of the Vespa if I wear the right skirt."

"No, you could not!" Mother snapped.

"Out of the question!" Father's response overlapped Mother's. They agreed that I could not be with Nadim other than at the club in the daytime. The reason they gave was that they knew nothing about him, or his university student friends and for my safety they wanted to know the people I was with. I wondered if in their minds they got motor scooter mixed up with motorcycle and linked motorcycle to danger like in tough guy movies and so Nadim too became dangerous. *Or maybe it's because he has the freedom to come and go as he pleases without asking for adult permission.*

Mother waved conversation about Nadim away with a flick of her hand, and asked me, "How is that nice boy, Jack, your math partner from school, doing? He goes to the club too, doesn't he? Jack is a better escort for you. Stick with Jack."

"Yeah. Jack is great. But he doesn't go to the club that often, and he doesn't play tennis. Only basketball." I was annoyed with myself for feeling annoyed. Jack was a good friend. I liked him best of all the boys at school. His honesty and height reminded me of Alex, and I secretly thought of him as my almost real boyfriend. *So why do I feel boxed in because Mother wants me to trade Nadim's company for Jack's?*

Mother could tell I was gearing up for an argument. She smiled one of her 'I love you anyway smiles,' hugged me, and said, "Never mind. All this will fade away into your childhood, and you'll begin a new life at Berkeley in two months. I am proud of you, Honey. You always do the right thing, and I trust you completely." With that she whisked off to her room and closed the door which meant she declared quiet time for a nap, or to read, but not to discuss my growing frustration.

I was left standing at the top of the stairs with angry questions roiling full steam. *What was this bit about trusting me? What did I need to be trusted for? To spend more time with Jack and less with Nadim? And why is Berkeley going to solve everything?*

And what was Patty doing dropping in my room several times this month? Looking around slowly like she's measuring and mentally placing her things around, getting rid of mine? Of me? I bet she moves in the day I leave.

Maybe I won't go to Berkeley after all! Nadim and his friends like the American University here just fine. I could keep my room, still be a part of the family with all the trappings. I could get a degree in Egyptology and Marine geology, or medicine here.

But then I'd still be tied up with all the rules here and wouldn't it be wonderful to be free to drive anywhere or to have a hamburger whenever I wanted without planning it with the cook days ahead? To be a normal American girl like the ones in 'Seventeen?' To choose my classes and friends and schedule myself? Me as me, me alone. Me. Not someone's daughter? And be with Alex?

Boy did I want to spill all these thoughts out on Mother right now. I crept close to her closed door and let out the loudest sigh I could. And waited. My lower stomach was urging me to burst in the room and have her soothe away troubled thoughts like always. Nothing stirred behind the door. I sighed again, this time to myself. *I guess growing up is learning how to live alone with your own feelings.*

I went to bed wondering why Mother's trust seem so heavy, and why the future was messing up the present.

A phone call to Jack the next day assured me that he was happy to spend time at the club with me. It would be no problem to walk me to there and home again although his house was three blocks away. While I waited for tennis courts, swam, snacked and sunned poolside with whichever friends happened to be present, he spent most of his time playing basketball. I didn't go stand on the sidelines watching his half court games. The Russians had vacated the basketball court long ago. It was no longer an exciting place to be.

The mess of angry questions inside my head had cooled down to a simmer of resentment when Nadim called a week later. It was after ten and

I had just changed into my pajamas. Mother and Father were attending a formal dinner. Patty was already asleep. The servants had gone. I answered the phone with the practiced, "Hello. This is the Carr residence. With whom would you like to speak?"

This was met with laughter, then, "Hey! Nadim here. Sorry to laugh. That is certainly a formal greeting. I'm at a friend's house in the neighborhood. It's a beautiful night. Full moon. Thought maybe you might like a short ride up and down the corniche."

"What?"

"A short ride. Right now. It's too nice a night to miss. Something to remember when you're stuck in traffic in California." Nadim considered California a place stuffed with movie stars and cars.

"On your scooter?"

'Of course, would have to be the Vespa. I can be at your gate in five minutes."

"Oh!" I held the receiver out in front of me at arm's length, staring at it. My first instinct was to shout "Yippee!" and run out of the house and leap on the back of the scooter, pajamas and all. At the same time, my whole being felt cold and prickly. *What would my parents say?* I had been difficult, stubborn, pouty, thrown tantrums, stalked out, slammed doors and bent rules, but I had never blatantly disobeyed except maybe on that fishing trip in Iran.

But now I am not a child, I'm a young lady. How many chances will I have to ride along the banks of the Nile on the back of a vespa in full moon light? Never again! Time is short. Only five weeks left.

Nadim's voice broke my stupor. "Hey, are you there? Did you hang up?"

The receiver seemed to resist being brought back to my face again. It took two deep breaths and a long sigh before answering. "Okay. Give me ten minutes. I'll meet you outside the gate."

In too much of a hurry to think about what was right or wrong or pay attention to how shaky and weak my legs felt, my thoughts swirled around getting ready. *What to wear? A full skirt will be easiest for straddling, A scarf to keep my hair from blowing all over the place. No need. A ponytail would take care of that. A blouse that stays tucked in so it won't billow up my back. Tennis shoes. Ready! Go!*

Nadim was waiting in front of the house. He was seated on the scooter, keeping it balanced with his legs tapping the ground on each side and giving it little spurts of gas now and then. I hesitated a second in the doorway, checking that no one was witnessing my rash decision. No people or cars interrupted the softness of the night. A few scattered windows in the apartments across the street glowed behind drawn curtains. For an instant my mind wandered. *Is this one of Emil's nights? What was that schedule? Tuesdays?*

I shook that thought out of my head and focused on Nadim. He waved to me, leaned to the side to pat the seat behind him, and smiled. The gate guard, notebook in hand, had left his post and was standing close behind Nadim. He snapped his head up when I headed for the back of the scooter. *Uh oh. I forgot the guards the Egyptians assigned to us. I hope he doesn't call for my parents. But why would he?* Throwing all caution to the wind I looked straight at him and said, "Zaida!" I knew that was either hello or goodbye, or maybe both, used by Egyptian Christians. I had never acknowledged any of the guards' presence before. *Might as well go full steam ahead into my daring adventure.* I swung my right leg over the small seat behind Nadim in my best horse mounting style but found it took some time to adjust my skirt to cover the front of my legs.

The guard stepped back a few paces from the scooter, never taking his eyes off Nadim except for a few furtive glances at my preparations.

Nadim turned his head so he faced me. "Ready yet? He gunned the motor.

Satisfied with the modesty of my clothing, I sat up straight with a hand on each of my knees. In my firmest voice, with a matching nod of my head, I answered, "Yes. Ready!"

Nadim looked at my hands and laughed. "You have to actually hold on to me, unless you want to fall off backwards right into the guard."

Oh My God! A sudden realization swept over me of how far the rules of proper behavior for young women in Egypt were being pushed. *Alone with a man on a scooter at night! Plus putting hands on him! It will send the guard into a fit of shock. But I've already gone too far to turn back. Dismounting and retreating into the house won't undo a thing but cause more confusion. Probably another frantic return of Mitwali!*

The moonlit street remained quiet and empty except for the guard, Nadim, the scooter, and me. If I fell off the back of the scooter, I would indeed land upside down at the guard's feet. He was that close behind us, standing rigid with his mouth open and pencil raised. I stared at my hands. *What should I do? It's now or never.* My parents would probably be home in an hour. *What if they left their dinner earlier than usual? What if the scooter and our voices woke Patty?* I took a deep breath of the soft night air. *Stop it Deedee! You are eighteen years old and you already made a choice for a once in a lifetime memory of Egypt.*

I slowly moved my hands to place them lightly on each side of Nadim's waist, and sat up straight, putting as much distance between our bodies as possible.

"OK. I'm ready."

Nadim turned to the guard and spoke to him in Arabic. The guard answered briefly. Then with a new spurt of gas we lunged forward, causing me to lurch backwards and instinctively wrap my arms around Nadim for safety. I gulped in air and shouted over the back of Nadim's shoulder, "What did you say to the guard?"

"I told him not to worry. That I was a friend of the family and came to show you how beautiful our Nile is in Egyptian moonlight and tonight was your only chance to see it. I assured him we will be back in twenty minutes."

"And what did he say?"

"He said the Nile is our treasure, and he will not record our leaving. But—if we aren't back in twenty minutes, he will call the police and report me for kidnapping. I saw him look at his watch. We are being timed!"

Soon we were on the Cornish. It stretched out before us in soft shadows along the bank of the Nile. We had it all to ourselves. Nadim drove slowly so we could look down at the river breathing ripples of moonlight. We passed several feluccas anchored at its side. The evening breeze stirred their tall sails like giant butterflies folding and unfolding shimmering wings. Fresh cool air brushed against my face. My ponytail swished back and forth and sometimes straight out behind like that of a real horse galloping into the wind.

Suddenly the scooter dipped sharply to the left. Nadim called out over his shoulder, "Lean with it. Don't fight it. We're turning around. It's already been ten minutes. Time to start back."

"Oh my gosh! That went so fast." I tightened my grasp around Nadim and kept my body in line with his. The surface of the road seemed way too close. I closed my eyes and frantically wondered how far we could lean before tipping over.

The scooter straightened up and we began our return journey. After a few minutes Nadim asked, "Do you know what slalom skiing is?"

"It's when they swoop down the hill in big curves, back and forth, right?"

"Yes. Hold on," The scooter banked to the left in a wide half turn, then shifted to lean to the right in another. Then left again, Then right. I hung on for dear life and squealed.

"You're getting the hang of it," Nadim shouted backward. I squealed again and hung on tighter.

A car's headlights loomed behind us. Nadim steered close to the road's edge while it passed. It slowed down just ahead of us, then resumed its speed and disappeared. And the corniche was ours again.

We made it back with two minutes to spare. The guard acknowledged our return with an upward thrust of his head. His hands were at his sides. No notebook. *Good.* Maybe my twenty minutes of independence would slip by unnoticed. I waved goodbye to Nadim and sprinted up the steps to bed.

But not to sleep. The ride had been wonderful, but now worry settled in. How far behind me were my parents? I listened by the window for Hassan to deliver them. As soon as the car pulled up, a safe half an hour after my return, I crept to my door to listened behind it to hear what they were saying on their way up the stairs to bed. Their voices were normal. I caught snatches of their debriefing each other on information gathered at dinner. All was well. Relief and sleep.

The only plan for the next day was the weekly chess game with Father before dinner. I was surprised to hear Ahmed greet him earlier than usual. *Odd. Father never gets home early. Oh well, he'll probably rest before our game since he has extra time.*

Within a minute, Mitwali tapped on my opened door. He stood in the threshold. His face above the long flat shaft of his white galabia looked small and scrunched. His fez seemed darker and less jaunty than usual.

"Father say you come down now."

"Now?"

"Yes, Miss." He turned abruptly and strode away without the usual toothy smile. I gulped shafts of panic. *Does Father know about my ride?*

The Reckoning

RUSHING INTO THE LIVING ROOM, I GREETED FATHER WITH, "Are we starting our game early?"

The chess board was not set up as usual. Father was pacing back and forth in front of the couch. He turned to me and indicated one of the armchairs. "No. We will not be playing chess today. Sit down."

The chair was too big for me to be comfortable in without ditching my shoes, curling my legs up under me and leaning back into its cushions. Instinct told me this was a time to sit up straight, ignore the cushions, and keep shoes and feet planted on the floor. My skin felt damp. *Am I in trouble? Does he know about the ride? How could he? Did the guard tell on us through Mitwali? Or maybe someone in that one stupid car...?* I crossed my fingers on both hands, hoping that the summons wasn't about me.

Ahmed hovered nearby. Father nodded to him. "Ahmed, we will have our cocktails here. And please ask Madam to join us."

Father resumed pacing back and forth in front of me. There were deep creases filling the space between his eyebrows. I waited silently while becoming aware of small hot and cold tingles running up and down my back.

Mother entered the room in her blue silk kimono with white irises embroidered on the back. I guessed she was planning a short nap before dressing for the two cocktail parties on their schedule this evening. She glanced at me, then went to Father and put her hand on his arm, and asked, "Is something wrong?"

Father stopped pacing. He touched her elbow with one hand and indicated the couch with the other. "I think we need to sit for this, Betty."

She stepped back to look him squarely in the face, then turned to me, raising her shoulders in question. I shook my head to let her know that I had no idea what it was about either. She sat down. The kimono fell in graceful folds around her.

Father settled beside her. He leaned forward, forearms on his thighs, Mother sat back, waiting. I waited too, sitting straight in the chair. The round table between the couch where my parents sat and me was topped by an intricately designed copper tray, a cherished treasure from the bazaar in Tehran. There was a lot to discover in that tray. By now I was sure something was very wrong. *Whatever is upsetting him must be much bigger than a twenty-minute ride on the corniche.*

Our wait ended when Father cleared his throat and said, "David Rodgers called on me this afternoon." He glanced at Mother, "You are good friends with his wife, right?" She nodded. He looked at me and continued "David had some very disturbing news for me."

I vaguely remembered David Rodgers, but I certainly knew his wife. Not only had I been seated beside her at my parent's dinner party, she had also given me a sculpture lesson. She mentioned that her husband would be out of town for a while working with some of the Point Four people. He must have just returned. That gave me all kinds of ideas of what Father's disturbing news could be. *Maybe there was an outbreak of typhoid and we all needed new shots. Point Four dealt with that kind of thing. Maybe David Rodgers was really one of our spies and knew someone was planning to assassinate Americans.*

Father continued, "David came into my office and closed the doors for a private conversation. At first I couldn't imagine what he would have to say that was so delicate." Father's voice was close to a growl. He looked up from under his eyebrows at me.

Uh oh. I felt pinned, like an insect on the display board in science glass.

I looked at the floor while Father continued. "When he and his wife were returning from a dinner last night, they decided to have their driver take the route along the corniche because it was such a beautiful night."

My heart began thumping with hollow thuds in my ears. I stared at the galloping Persian knights etched on the copper tray.

"That's nice." Mother said. "It truly is a lovely drive."

"No. It was not nice." Father's voice rasped. "They saw a young couple doing daring loops on a motorcycle ahead of them. The young lady was glued around the driver and whooping wildly. David thought she looked familiar, so they asked their driver to slow down to check." Father stopped talking and sat up straight. He looked at me and pointed. "You!"

My head jerked back as if the slap I felt was real, not imagined.

Mother gasped. She blurted out, "Oh, it couldn't have been. Not Deedee! Not on a motorcycle. Not at that hour. Certainly, they were mistaken!"

"Were they?" Father asked me.

Tears had already started blurring my vision, but I knew both parents were staring at me. Every piece of furniture in the room seemed to lean toward me, waiting for my answer. I glanced at the doorway, planning escape. *Dash out of the room, up the stairs, lock my door and not come out until they get so worried that I'm starving to death that they forget about the ride.*

Mother's voice floated over the tray. "Deedee?"

I focused on the tray and discovered rabbits hiding from the galloping knights. If only I could shrink like Alice in Wonderland and join them. I mumbled. "It was only for twenty minutes. To see the Nile in full moonlight. To remember it."

Then anger began to rise inside me, shrinking the sobs gathering in my throat, making me stronger. Anger at myself for sounding so whiney, so babyish. And anger at Mr. Rodger's interpretation of my short adventure. A fiercely squeezed blink cleared my eyes enough to look at my parents, from one to the other, back and forth. "It was a scooter, not motorcycle. A vespa. And we only made four loops. So I could learn what to do during turns. I was holding on so I wouldn't fall off. You have to do that when scooters turn. The gate guard timed us; we made it back before twenty minutes were up."

I couldn't stop. More words rushed out, like prisoners making a break for freedom. "The corniche was completely empty except for that one car. And it was wonderful, even if Mr. Rodgers didn't think so. I'm sorry that things looked so bad to him. But once, just once, I didn't feel like I was laced in a corset, doing everything not to offend anyone. It was the only chance I would ever have to be so free and part of the night. And the Nile was beautiful!"

The living room filled with stillness. Neither parent said a word. Mother looked away from me.

Remorse drowned out my anger. I squeezed my throat tight, but a sob escaped. After a deep breath, I said, "I'm sorry, very sorry. I am sorry for letting you down."

I hung my head. Neither parent spoke.

Mother sighed. She touched Father's arm. He looked down at her hand, then at me. "Go to your room. Do not leave it tonight. Mitwali will bring your supper to you. We'll finish this discussion tomorrow."

Usually my room was my kingdom, my special sanctuary. It housed my treasures; the rock collection that followed me from country to country, the ebony heads and hippos from the Muskie, woodcarving tools, and my Jane Austin books. Running my hands over the carefully arranged line-up of rocks on top of my bookcase didn't offer the familiar sense of pride and comfort. Even my favorite rock, the one Alex and I found in a cave near Tehran, the one that had been meticulously sliced by trapped water that froze and split it into separate pieces, so it looked like a small loaf of American bread—even that rock didn't make me smile. It just looked like an old grey rock falling apart.

When Mitwali knocked on my door with dinner, I took the tray without looking at him. Hunger surprised me. Eating soothed the ache. When finished, I put the empty tray outside my closed door, like a prisoner might do. It was a long time before I fell asleep.

The next day Mother was busy and remote. I slunk through the day, dreading my sentencing. Evening came. I waited in my room until Mitwali appeared on my doorsill again.

This time the summons was to my parent's room where we usually met for Children's Hour. Both parents were seated on their couch and already sipping martinis. Mother pointed to the coke waiting for me on the small table beside one of the chairs. I sat, noting on a deep breath that Patty was not there. She usually arrived first to "dibbie" her favorite chair. They must have asked her not to come this evening. That was not a hopeful sign.

Wham! There was no wait. Father began the moment I was seated. "You did let us down by choosing to take that ride after we told you not to see this Nadim person at night. It was against all better judgment. And we had to hear about it from someone from my staff, like office gossip."

Again, I felt as if I had been slapped. "I know. It was wrong and ..."

Father interrupted me before I could finish with "stupid." He said, "But your mother and I had a long chat last night about all times you have done the right thing. About the many times you have represented our family and our country well."

Mother added, "And all you have gone through; jaundice, scarlet fever, and lice. And the schools you have had to adjust to: the army school in Vienna, the missionary school in Teheran, the big high school in Santa Cruz to the little one here. Sometimes just a hint of a school in our garden in New Delhi and the Calvert System we tried in Paris. Yet you have kept up and done it well. In each place you fit in. There have been thousands of times when you have done the right thing and made us immensely proud."

It was Father's turn again. "You have chaffed in your "corset," as you call it, true, and sometimes pushed the limits. But, when all is said and done, despite the restraints and rules and dangers you've lived with, I must say, you turned out well. You've done an amazing job."

He raised his glass. Mother joined him. She said, "A toast to our wonderful daughter."

Father added, "Hear. Hear."

Surprise stunned me. I sat frozen and gaping. Then I shook my head to clear it and spread my arms out wide, to hold the big question, "But, but, am I grounded, or do I lose my allowance forever, or both, what…?"

Mother purred, "Honey, it is time for you to make your own decisions. That is why we are so pleased you are going to Berkeley. It is a time for you to try those wonderful wings of yours. You need freedom to grow without protocol and the constant worry of stepping on a foreign culture's toes."

Completely unmoored in unfamiliar space, I had no response, only a glimpse of unknown adulthood terrain ahead of me. I missed the familiar boundaries to bump against, and to feel safe within. Tears slipped down my face.

Mother came to me and kissed me on the forehead on her way to the door carrying the little bell she used to summon Ahmed. She smiled. "Now, Dear, pull yourself together. Take some deep breaths. Go wash your face. It wouldn't hurt to comb your hair a bit either. Everything's good and will be even better. You'll see. Right now, we'll send for Patty, finish our drinks, and then go down to dinner."

I basked in the glow of their praise, too happy to worry about the future. Only one little question nagged me, nibbling its way from the edges of my consciousness until it finally demanded my attention. Why had my parents been so against Nadim? It didn't make sense. On one hand they spoke glowingly of me trying my wings, facing the big world. Mother urged me to go to the ball, ride with Douglas, expand my experience beyond school and the club. Yet, on the other, when I had a chance to get to know Nadim's group of university friends, they both slammed the door on it as fast as they could. Why? What reason did they have that I could not see? I decided to ask Father about this during our next chess game. He was more likely than Mother to offer the basic reason for their aversion to Nadim and his friends. I had assured them he was a friend, not a boyfriend. It had to be more than the vespa. The next Thursday, as soon as our game started, I asked Father about it before we completed our opening moves.

It turned out the vespa had a lot to do with it.

Father thought about his response through four moves before he said, "The image you riding off on the back of a motorcycle with some young man we have no connection to, into the possibility of a dark future, is frightening to us." He leaned back in his chair, waiting for me to take my turn.

"Dark future? What are you talking about?" I forgot to make the move I had been planning while waiting for his answer. I sat up straight, staring at him.

"The heart of Cairo, where Nadim and his friends are, is a place where we make brief sightseeing visits, or shop, but do not know well. We have no influence, or control, or even presence there. You may not have noticed, but up until this moment, your Mother and I have known exactly where you were, who you were with, and that you were safe. We would be powerless if you became immersed with Nadim and his friends."

He bent his head down over our game, concentrating on moving his bishop across the board.

Father's moves and his answers seemed equally slow in coming. By this time, I had lost track of my game plan, and was ready to move anything anywhere. My question still had not been answered. I said, "I still don't get it. Why are you worried about a dark future because of Nadim?"

Father leaned back in his chair again. He crossed his arms and looked straight at me. "We worry that if you connect to this crowd, they might pull you away to stay here for university, even settle here. The prejudice against women would certainly limit, if not annihilate, your future. You must be able provide for yourself. You must have a career in place. Knights on white horses aren't real."

My game was in shambles, there was no saving it. "But you won't be around when I'm immersed at Berkeley. Why aren't you worried about that?"

"Ah!" Father cleared his throat. He sat up and reached over the board, ready for his next move. He paused, looked up at me, smiled, and added, "We both know that terrain well. Your future is open and bright there. And you forget, we have family and friends close by to help if you need it. Check."

I lost that game, as I did most of our chess games, but I didn't mind. I realized my parents' love and concern would stay with me all my life.

The Soldier's Story

THE NEXT WEEK DOUGLAS LEFT FOR SCOTLAND. HE CHOSE for our final ride "one last go on the good horses." We cantered and galloped covering as many of the club's trails as possible in our allotted time which led to not having taken the time to cool them down with a leisurely end-of-the-ride walk. We returned the horses in a lather. The grooms scowled and muttered among themselves. Tilting my head toward the grooms, I whispered to Douglas, "They're making sure we will get the worst they have to offer next time."

Douglas nodded. "True. The joke's on them. But sad too. I'll miss our rides."

We promised to write to let each other know how our new lives were doing.

The first Children's Hour after he left while Patty and my parents settled calmly into their usual places, I bounced into mine. The question that had been burning in my mind since I met Douglas could be answered at last. As soon as Ahmed deposited our drinks and left the room, I blurted out, "What's the story about Douglas and the army that you wouldn't tell me until he left? He's gone now. Tell me!"

Mother quickly looked at Patty, then turned to Father. He shrugged one shoulder slightly, grimaced and nodded toward the door. Mother stood up and held her hand out to Patty. "Come, Dear. You and I are going to leave these two. Let's take the Sears Catalogue with us. We can start your order."

As much as I wanted to hear Douglas's story, I couldn't help the wave of jealousy washing over me as they left. No Sears for me this time. Instead, Mother and Father were discussing "some essential little dressy dresses" that our seamstress would create for me. It would be wise, they assured me, to shop for the rest of my wardrobe in California, in stores popular with my future schoolmates. And according to Father, that would also launch me into one more life lesson. He was quite serious when he told me, "How to shop within a budget is one of the first things you need to learn now that you are starting off on your own."

This reminded me of many other lessons underlined in my growing up. Like Not everybody thinks the same way we do, but that doesn't make them wrong. This came up a lot of times, first in India when Patty and I played with Sonja, the sweeper's son, and just recently here in Cairo when Emil told me about his birthday present. Or "Sometimes you just plain have to do things you don't want to" when we raced away from Lady, my monkey, while she screamed with outstretched arms chasing after our car. And how I owe the universe not to cheat ever again after my Honesty Award in Teheran. And how someone can love you enough to let you go as Alex's parents did.

Like my parents were doing.

A hush swept over the room. Father leaned back into the couch and took a sip of his drink. "Well," he began, "It's a gruesome story. But I guess you should know this reality too. Along with the wonders and beauty, you certainly have witnessed what your mother calls "the underbelly of life" everywhere we have lived. You know Douglas was in Kenya, fighting the Mau Mau?

"Yes. But you said never to mention it, so that is all I know. And I don't really know what Mau Mau are."

Father put his drink down on the nearby table and clasped his hands in his lap. I held my breath. It seemed to me that important things always hung in the air, making me wait.

"The Mau Mau are a secret army of native tribesmen who are fighting to free Kenya from British Colonial rule. And they are brutal." He shuddered and silently stared at the floor. I counted twenty slow breaths as time ticked by.

"Well," Father began again, "Soldiers makes strong bonds with their fellow soldiers. Battle and danger cement friendships. Douglas was particularly close to two other young men in his platoon, also from Scotland, I believe."

He paused to stare across the room at nothing. I waited, as still as the room, not wanting to slow him down in any way.

He cleared his throat and began again. "This is how Col. Johnstone has put together what happened there. As you know, Douglas does not talk about it. It seems one day the two friends were assigned to a patrol, but Douglas was not. He was worried and disturbed not to be with them because the Mau Mau had been particularly active in the area that week. The patrol was late in returning to camp. Douglas and others at the camp waited and watched for it.

After two hours, they feared maybe the missing patrol was pinned down and needed help. A few of them, including Douglas, volunteered to go look for their friends. The transport was not hard to find. It was parked in the middle of the road, not too far from camp. The search group approached it slowly, making sure there was not an ambush waiting for them. All seemed clear, the missing soldiers were not visible in the truck, nor lying wounded or worse nearby. Douglas went around to the back to check the bed of the truck. That is when he found out what happened to his friends. The bed was completely covered with small pieces of their bodies. A gift from the Mau Mau.

I gasped, "What? I don't understand."

Father finished off his drink. "The Mau Mau chopped them up with machetes. I understand in pieces the size of tennis balls."

Suddenly I understood anguish. It swept over me, chilling, gritty, and revolting. I sank back into my chair, weak and nauseous. "Oh. I wish I didn't know. I'm glad I didn't know. Poor Douglas. How can he ever forget? I don't think I will, ever."

Father rose and crossed the room to stand beside my chair. He patted my shoulder. "You probably won't. Human cruelty goes beyond imagination. But so does goodness. Remember that too."

Falling asleep was difficult for quite a few nights after hearing Douglas's story. Father's words about human cruelty and kindness haunted me until the night I realized that Douglas himself was an example of human goodness. Despite the horror he experienced, he was able to notice what would make someone else happy. He planned my driving lessons.

Goodbye

MY FINAL WEEKS AT HOME WERE A WHIRL OF PLANNING, packing, and goodbye visits. I pleaded with Hassan to squeeze some extra side-trips to the museum and the Muskie shops for me in his schedule.

"Very busy Missy. Very busy."

"But I promise not to take long. And soon, I'll be gone, and you will only have three people to drive around." He smiled!

At the museum, my farewell to the boy king was circling his sarcophagus seven times for luck and finding faces that looked like my friends in the frescos nearby. Standing in front of giant sandstone gods I whispered, "I will never forget you." And another whispered promise to a small glass-cased statues of Isis and my favorite, Bast. "You are part of me forever."

Hassan grumbled when he drove me to the Muskie, "You not go alone. I come in with you." He dragged along with downturned mouth just behind my left elbow. He glared sharply at any young men heading my way. The path to my favorite stall was clear and quick and pinch-less. Voices called from all sides of the street to 'Come look, Missy, Come look!" I bought one last ebony head, a parting gift from Present Me to Future Me.

I called Mother in my room to see my new purchase. I found just the right placement for it on top of my bookcase among other heads, the small herd of hippos, and my rock collection. I pointed it out to her. She ran her fingers over its smooth surface. She stroked one of the hippos. She barely glanced at the rocks. None of these things were going with me.

This was the right time to ask, "Do you promise to save them all, rocks, heads, hippos, and Jane Austin, and send them to me when I have room?"

"Yes Darling, I will send them. All of them." "Mother promised.

"You promise? Including the rocks? They're from all over, you know. There is even one, a tiny blue one, from our garden in India. And some from here, too. Patty said you were going to throw them away as soon as I leave."

"No, Honey, we won't throw the rocks away when you leave. I will keep them with the rest of your things. Don't worry." Her sigh at the end of the promise was a concession to the rocks.

A palpable mixture of dread, fear, and excitement began stalking me. Sometimes it tickled up my back and whispered in my ear, "This will all end far too soon." I reacted to the whispers with unexpected bursts of giggles or tears, slamming doors, and surprising my parents with unexpected hugs.

Late at night, I snuck up the stairs leading to our roof top. Like our house in Tehran, the roof was flat with a low wall providing safety and privacy for sleeping there during the hot weather. We didn't sleep on the roof in Cairo, but I liked to spend time there in the quiet darkness, breathing deeply to inhale the scent of jasmine from our garden below while wondering what would become of me when I left my home to go "half a world away?" That was the phrase Mother had murmured the day we stood on the tarmac in Tehran to say goodbye to Alex. He had survived it well. I gulped in resolute breaths, "I will too." *I can do it. It's not like I'm moving to a foreign country, knowing no one or the language.*

The suitcases were packed, the goodbyes to friends and places completed.

It was time to go.

The route to San Francisco involved a change of plane in Rome. Because the flight schedules necessitated an overnight stay, Father was going to Rome with me to help with handling the complications of international travel. He planned a four day stay for us before my flight to California. While Hassan loaded my two big suitcases and Father's smaller bag and brief case into the car, our family huddled just inside the front door. Mother and Patty were not going to the airport with us. Patty handed me a small package and envelope to open on the plane. She wrapped her arms around my waist and squeezed.

Then it was Mother's turn. She gathered me in a long hug. Her tears wet both our cheeks. She said, "I can't bear to see you get on the plane. I would make such a scene at the airport, standing in a puddle of tears. Know you always always have a home, no matter what. You are the other side of my heart."

I never wanted that hug to end, but Father took my elbow and led me out the door and to the car as I cried, walking backwards, never taking my eyes off my mother and sister. Fifteen minutes into our drive to the airport, my tears ebbed to sniffles and I started frantically checking my purse to be sure everything was there: tickets, passport, wallet, dollars in wallet, American quarters and dimes in coin purse, comb, tickets, passport, handkerchief, lipstick, passport, Kleenex in case of a bathroom with no toilet paper, passport. Father interrupted saying softly, "I think the hardest part is behind you now, and I'm sure you have everything you need in your purse. But it's better safe than sorry." He looked at my denim purse from Sears, now clutched tightly under my arm, and smiled while nodding his head. "I think we can shop for a smart handbag for you in Rome."

"Really? We're going shopping in Rome? For a fancy purse?"

"Oh yes. And for a coat too. A Luisa Spagnola. Your mother planned our shopping trip. You will need a nice coat for evenings in California."

Unwrapping Patty's present helped make the flight to Rome pass by quickly. A paper- back *Wuthering Heights* that fit in my purse.

Father and I had adjoining rooms in the little hotel recommended by friends of my parents. I whirled around my space, touching the bed, the dresser, the plain wood chair beside the bed, thrilled to be a grown-up with a hotel room of my own, and relieved that Father's room was on the other side of a connecting door. The bathroom was three doors down the hall.

Knowing how Father loved organization it was no surprise when he presented me with a detailed agenda of our time in Rome.

"Starting tonight we will begin our evenings a little after seven thirty with a stroll around a different part of the city each night. We may stop at a café or two for a glass of wine. Around nine we will select a restaurant along the way and eat a long leisurely dinner. In the mornings, we will leave the hotel by seven thirty for a continental breakfast at one of the little open- air cafes along the sidewalks. Then we will sightsee and work in a little shopping too. And a nap before our evenings." He had a long list places we would visit, including the Colosseum and Sistine Chapel. And a small temple dedicated to Diana. On our last night, we went to the opera for Pagliacci. I sat beside Father, arm to arm, and we cried together through the soaring aria of Pagliacci's grief.

And then it was time. The final goodbye. Father stood at the head of the ramp as I walked down to offer myself to Pan Am's rigid grey belly. My legs moved forward while my heart clung behind. I looked back up the ramp and Father still stood there, He waved and pointed toward the plane. I held my head high so my tears wouldn't drip and straightened my back so Father could see me being brave. I thought of the time before the Foreign Service in Washington D.C. when he used to give me "airplane rides" by swinging me around in a circle by one arm and a leg. I was only seven or eight. Each time, just before he lifted me off the ground, fear almost made me cry, "No. I don't want to." But once in the air, the thrill of circling above ground like a bird, had me squealing in delight and begging for another turn. Maybe this flight would turn out like that.

EPILOGUE

MY MOTHER DID SEND MY COLLECTIONS WHEN I HAD ROOM, but the rocks were missing.

My parents were posted a total of five years in Cairo, during which time Mother and Patty were evacuated to Rome during the Suez Canal Crisis. Father remained in Cairo as essential Embassy personnel. Their next post was Washington D.C. followed by Father's assignment to Bombay as Consul General. It was there that Mother was diagnosed with cancer. She died in 1962. She was 54 years old; I was 25, my sister was 21. Father retired and bought an Airstream travel trailer, joined caravans, resided in Florida for a while, and then moved to Treasure Island in Laguna Beach to be near me and his grandchildren and finally he moved to our vineyard in Cloverdale, California where he died in 1981 at the age of 75.

Patty graduated from the University of Maryland on the Dean's list and pursued French studies for a master's degree from Berkeley where she met her husband, a young Englishman and Rhodes scholar studying for his doctorate in British Colonial History. Patterson (my sister prefers her given name now) taught in private schools for a while in England but chaffed under the condescension toward her American education. She entered law school at the University of Birmingham where her husband was a Professor. She graduated third in her class, then continued the study of law in London to become a barrister, one of the few women to do so, and certainly one of the very few American women to complete this degree at that time. After working as a lawyer in a large business firm, which included attending cricket matches on Sunday as a job expectation, she decided to teach law in London instead. She and her husband have retired to France

My sister is the other side of my heart. We visit each other as much as possible. Sitting by the fire in her and Richard's stone farmhouse in a tiny hamlet in southern Burgundy is my favorite destination.

I didn't marry Alex but remain good friends with him to this day. I earned a B.A in Cultural Anthropology from Berkeley and later received a teaching credential and Masters in Developmental Psychology from Chapman University. I married an All-American Boy. We had two children and were married for twenty five years before divorcing. I began teaching as a help to my husband so he could leave the army and look for a job after he returned from Viet Nam with a chest full of medals. I discovered teaching was the best, most exciting, fulfilling, creative job in the world, and that every day I was surrounded with children and solid, good, kind people who became lifetime friends. I continued my education by becoming an UCI Writing fellow and a GLAD Key Trainer. I have taught at every level, kindergarten through graduate school and adult ESL, but mostly at Estock Elementary School in Tustin, California for thirty three years.

My son and daughter have each had a son and daughter of their own and I am now a great grandmother. I am nested in Southern California near my son's family and a covey of dear friends with whom I travel, take art classes, and diligently attend writing groups. I lived in Colorado for several years to be with my daughter's family. We arrange visits as often as possible. During this Covid siege, she and I play online scrabble several nights a week and cook together via phone every Friday night.

The life lessons and wonder of my childhood, pride in my parents' work, and their love still wrap around me, to be shared with family, friends, students, and readers of this book.